Praise for

HOW CIVIL WARS START

"When one of the world's leading scholars of civil war tells us that the United States stands at the brink of violent conflict, we should pay attention. Drawing on her deep understanding of the causes of intrastate violence in places like Myanmar, Northern Ireland, Syria, and Yugoslavia, Barbara F. Walter argues, chillingly, that many of the conditions that commonly precede civil wars are present today in the United States. This is an important book for all Americans to read."
—STEVEN LEVITSKY AND DANIEL ZIBLATT, authors of *How Democracies Die*

"I wish all the [Jan. 6] committee members would read it if only to expand their imaginations. [Walter] demonstrates that the conditions for political violence are already all around us."
—DAVID BROOKS, *The New York Times*

"*How Civil Wars Start* is a stop sign for us—and an imperative book for our time. The evidence-based preventative measures could not be more urgent. Read and act."
—IBRAM X. KENDI, author of *How to Be an Antiracist*

"For the first time in two hundred years, we are suspended between democracy and autocracy. And that sense of uncertainty radically heightens the likelihood of episodic bloodletting in America, and even the risk of civil war. This is the compelling argument of *How Civil Wars Start*. . . . [Walter] is wary of coming off as sensationalist. In fact, she takes pains to avoid overheated speculation and relays her warning about the potential for civil war in clinical terms. Yet, like those who spoke up clearly about the dangers of global warming decades ago, Walter delivers a grave message that we ignore at our peril."
—DAVID REMNICK, *The New Yorker*

"*How Civil Wars Start* is a sobering but engrossing book. It is so tempting to ignore or deny Walter's carefully researched and reasoned conclusions, which is precisely the response she is warning us against. . . . Highly recommended for anyone interested in preserving American democracy."
—ANNE-MARIE SLAUGHTER, president and CEO, New America

"Walter's *How Civil Wars Start* is the civil-conflict equivalent of *How Democracies Die* by Steven Levitsky and Daniel Ziblatt—a much-needed warning that uses cross-national research to examine the United States. Given how prescient Levitsky and Ziblatt were, and how expert Walter is (she is a leading scholar of civil wars), it is a warning to heed. I've been skeptical of the notion that the United States is on the verge of another civil war. Walter has made me reconsider."

 —JACOB HACKER, *The Washington Post*

"As a political scientist who has spent her career studying conflicts in other countries, [Walter] approaches her work methodically, patiently gathering her evidence before laying out her case."

 —JENNIFER SZALAI, *The New York Times*

"This engaging book from one of the country's most authoritative scholars of civil wars is a dire warning. Governing amid diversity is an incredible challenge, and this book is an important guide to preserving our democracy."

 —KORI SCHAKE, Director of Foreign and Defense Policy Studies,
  American Enterprise Institute

"*How Civil Wars Start* is a convincing, carefully reasoned, and therefore all the more urgent and alarming look at the state of American democracy. A great challenge for Americans is understanding that the forces that have torn apart other societies might do the same to this 'exceptional' nation. Barbara F. Walter has done a great service in demonstrating the risks the United States is now courting—and how they might be offset."

 —JAMES FALLOWS, co-author of *Our Towns*

"[A] bracing manual . . . Walter's book lays out America's possible roads to dystopia with impressive concision. Her synthesis of the various barometers of a country heading to civil war is hard to refute when applied to the U.S. . . . Indispensable."

 —*Financial Times*

"Barbara F. Walter has drawn on decades of experience and unparalleled expertise to write a powerful and indispensable book. *How Civil Wars Start* brilliantly illuminates the history of civil wars and the profound dangers to our union today, serving as both a warning about the stakes in our politics and a call to action for those who want to preserve multiethnic democracy and the values that America is supposed to stand for."

—BEN RHODES, author of *After the Fall*

"Barbara F. Walter, a political scientist at the University of California, San Diego, has interviewed many people who've lived through civil wars, and she told me they all say they didn't see it coming. . . . This is worth keeping in mind if your impulse is to dismiss the idea that America could fall into civil war again."

—MICHELLE GOLDBERG, *The New York Times*

"One of the most-discussed titles of the moment."

—CARLOS LOZADA, *The Washington Post*

"We have all now witnessed the death of the idea of American Exceptionalism. We are in the same boat as everyone else. What do we do? Barbara F. Walter shows the way. . . . Essential."

—JAMES A. ROBINSON, co-author of *Why Nations Fail*

"A vivid, compelling book on a globally vital issue. Timely, important, and original."

—RICHARD ENGLISH, author of *Does Terrorism Work?*

"It turns out that there is a discipline that you might call 'civilwarology'— the study of the factors that lead to civil war. . . . Barbara F. Walter became a civilwarologist nearly a quarter of a century ago and her entry is evidently well-thumbed in the Rolodexes of the CIA and the U.S. State Department. In other words, she knows what she's talking about—which makes this book rather scary."

—*The Times* (U.K.)

"Rigorously researched and lucidly argued, *How Civil Wars Start* is an arresting wake-up call."

—*Esquire*

"This compelling history delineates the path from democracy to autocracy—and warns that the U.S. is heading the wrong way. . . . Barbara Walter does not expect to see a civil war in the U.S. of the order of the conflict that tore the nation apart in the 1860s, but that's chiefly because civil wars are fought differently these days. And it's

about the only comfort a concerned reader can take from this sobering account of how civil wars start and are conducted in our time."
—H. W. Brands, *The Guardian*

"When an academic book on the origins of civil wars hits the bestseller lists in the U.S., it is probably time to start worrying. . . . Disturbing . . . well-documented."
—*Financial Times*

"Although Walter is very clear about the clear and present danger posed by a right-wing insurgency, she does not engage in the sectarian scaremongering sometimes indulged by the American left. . . . *How Civil Wars Start* could be remembered as eerily prescient. The best that Walter and the rest of us can hope for is that her book helped make its message ultimately irrelevant."
—*PopMatters*

"The idea that a second American civil war is brewing is not alarmist hyperbole. . . . The image that should be brought to mind is not of columns of blue- and gray-clad soldiers meeting on battlefields; instead, it lies in the scattered rubble of the federal building in Oklahoma City and the insurrection at the Capitol on Jan. 6, 2021. . . . Arresting reading that identifies obstacles and dangers to democracy, many at the highest levels of government."
—*Kirkus Reviews*

"Walter issues a stark and deeply informed warning that the U.S. may be headed for another civil war. . . . Incisive . . . Distinguished by its lucid analysis and global perspective, this wake-up call rings clear."
—*Publishers Weekly*

BY BARBARA F. WALTER

How Civil Wars Start: And How to Stop Them

Committing to Peace: The Successful Settlement of Civil Wars

*Reputation and Civil War: Why Separatist Conflicts
Are So Violent*

Territoriality and Conflict in an Era of Globalization
(co-edited with Miles Kahler)

Civil Wars, Insecurity, and Intervention
(co-edited with Jack Snyder)

HOW CIVIL WARS START

AND HOW TO STOP THEM

BARBARA F. WALTER

CROWN
NEW YORK

2023 Crown Trade Paperback Edition

Published in the United States by Crown, an imprint of Random House,
a division of Penguin Random House LLC, New York.

CROWN and the Crown colophon are registered trademarks of
Penguin Random House LLC.

Originally published in hardcover in the United States
by Crown, an imprint of Random House, a division of
Penguin Random House LLC, in 2022.

Library of Congress Cataloging-in-Publication Data
Names: Walter, Barbara F., author.
Title: How civil wars start / Barbara F. Walter.
Description: First Edition. | New York: Crown, [2022] | Includes
bibliographical references and index.
Identifiers: LCCN 2021040090 (print) | LCCN 2021040091 (ebook) |
ISBN 9780593137802 (paperback) | ISBN 9780593443378 (export) |
ISBN 9780593137796 (eBook)
Subjects: LCSH: Civil war. | Democratization. | Domestic terrorism.
Classification: LCC JC328.5 .W35 2022 (print) | LCC JC328.5 (ebook) |
DDC 303.6/4—dc23/eng/20211012
LC record available at https://lccn.loc.gov/2021040090
LC ebook record available at https://lccn.loc.gov/2021040091

PRINTED IN THE UNITED STATES OF AMERICA ON ACID-FREE PAPER

crownpublishing.com

2 4 6 8 9 7 5 3 1

To Zoli and Lina

CONTENTS

INTRODUCTION

Adam Fox flipped over the carpet and opened the trapdoor that led to the basement of the Vac Shack Vacuums shop, in Grand Rapids, Michigan. The thirty-seven-year-old had been living underneath the shop with his two dogs after his girlfriend had kicked him out. The owner of the store, a friend, had offered him the space until he could get back on his feet.

The room was a jumble of filing cabinets, dog crates, and vacuum parts. Fox was a frustrated man—and not just because he was practically homeless. This wasn't the first time he had been down on his luck. After graduating from high school, he'd struggled to find a path, working as a contractor for Vac Shack and barely able to pay his bills. He was angry at the Democratic leaders who had let this happen; he often tweeted about Barack Obama and Nancy Pelosi to let off steam. He'd recently found some camaraderie when he'd joined a local militia, but then he'd been kicked out for his anti-government rants and altercations with other members.

Now COVID-19 was spreading. It had hit Detroit and Grand Rapids so hard that on March 23, 2020, Michigan's governor, Gretchen Whitmer, had called for a state lockdown. Her stay-at-home orders extended even to rural areas with few cases. In late April—after yet another round of restrictions—Fox had donned a baseball cap and tactical vest to join hundreds of protesters, many of them armed, to march on the capitol in Lansing. He'd listened outside as Mike Detmer, a Republican congressional candidate, railed against the restrictions as un-American. "We are in a war for the hearts, the soul, the traditions, and the freedom of our state and country," Detmer had declared. "It is up to us to end the shutdown." Afterward, when protesters forced themselves into the capitol to occupy the House floor, Fox had joined them.

But none of this had really changed things, and as more weeks went by, Fox grew restless. That June, he livestreamed a video on Facebook, complaining about recent gym closures and calling Whitmer a "tyrant bitch" who loved power. "I don't know, boys. We gotta do something," he said into the camera. Soon afterward, he reached out over Facebook to Joseph Morrison, the leader of a local militia, the Wolverine Watchmen. Morrison allegedly agreed to help Fox recruit, train, and arm a new paramilitary group. Soon Fox was gathering other men to his cause. One who joined was a retired rifleman in the Marine Corps who had won the Humanitarian Service Medal, the Global War on Terrorism Service Medal, and the Marine Corps Good Conduct Medal. Another had previously started basic training with the Michigan National Guard but had not completed it. One was affiliated with the Three Percenters militia group; another supported QAnon; another followed the social media accounts of the Proud Boys.

There were fourteen of them. Many of the men, like Fox, had attended anti-lockdown rallies. They began meeting in the basement of Vac Shack, where Fox would confiscate cellphones so no one could record the conversations. They also met on Morrison's one-acre rural property for tactical and firearms training. Every Sunday afternoon they would fire hundreds of rounds and practice building explosives.

They considered storming the state capitol—they could take lawmakers hostage, then execute them over the course of a few days. They also considered locking the doors of the capitol and setting the building on fire with everyone inside. Eventually, because the capitol was so well protected, they settled on a different plan: kidnap Whitmer at her vacation home in northern Michigan sometime before the November 2020 election. They would take her to a hidden place in Wisconsin, put her on trial for treason, and kill her.

That August and September, the men spied on Whitmer's home, looking for a nearby bridge to detonate as a way to distract law enforcement agents when they launched their plan. But the FBI was on to them. After discovering the group's activity on social media in early 2020, agents had infiltrated the group online and recruited informants who agreed to wear a wire or gather information. By September, despite Fox's precautions, the FBI had gathered more than thirteen thousand pages of encrypted text messages, as well as photographs, videos, and more than one hundred hours of audio evidence of the kidnapping plot. On the night of October 7, 2020, the feds closed in with a sting: When a handful of the plotters met for what they thought was a weapons buy, they were arrested instead. The FBI raided the Vac Shack basement and executed search warrants in more than a dozen locations. The fourteen men, including Fox, were slapped with terrorism, conspiracy, and weapons charges.

The owner of Vac Shack, meanwhile, grappled with his disbelief. "I knew he was in a militia," he told reporters, "but there's a lot of people in a militia that don't plan to kidnap the governor. I mean, give me a break."

In the wake of the arrests, news reports focused on the true aims of the would-be kidnappers. Even though Michigan leaders, both Democrat and Republican, condemned the plot, President Donald Trump criticized Whitmer, tweeting that she had "done a terrible job" as governor. Fox himself, however, left no doubt about the group's motives. The trial and execution of Whitmer, he'd explained in FBI recordings, were designed to inspire others to carry out similar attacks. The time had come for a revolution, and he and his men would provoke a societal collapse. "I just wanna make the world glow, dude," he told an informant. "That's what it's gonna take for us to take it back."

WHEN I FIRST read about the plot to kidnap Whitmer in the fall of 2020, I was alarmed but not altogether surprised. It fit into a pattern I had been writing and thinking about for decades. There have been hundreds of civil wars over the past seventy-five years, and many of them started in an eerily similar way. As a scholar and an expert on civil wars, I have interviewed members of Hamas in the West Bank, ex–Sinn Féin members in Northern Ireland, and former members of FARC in Colombia. I have stood on top of the Golan Heights and stared into Syria during the height of the Syria civil war. I have driven across Zimbabwe as the military was planning its coup against Robert Mugabe. I have been followed and interrogated by members of Myanmar's junta. I've been at the wrong end of an Israeli soldier's machine gun.

I first started studying civil wars in 1990, and at the time, there was very little data to work with. You could read a lot of books by scholars on civil wars in Spain, Greece, Nigeria, and even America in the nineteenth century, but there were almost no studies that looked at common elements that repeated themselves across countries and over time. Everyone thought their civil war was unique, and so no one saw the risk factors that emerged again and again no matter where war broke out.

But within a few years, our knowledge had expanded. The Cold War was over, and all over the globe, civil wars were erupting. Scholars around the world began collecting data—lots of data—on various aspects of these conflicts. The biggest data collection project is now housed at Uppsala University, in Sweden. It was built in collaboration with the Peace Research Institute in Oslo, Norway (PRIO), and has been funded over the years by the Swedish Research Council, the Bank of Sweden Tercentenary Foundation, the Swedish International Development Cooperation Agency, the Norwegian government, and the World Bank. Carefully trained researchers work together with a network of experts on different countries to collect the data. Today, anyone can access dozens of high-quality datasets (the results are triple-checked) related to how civil wars start, how long they last, how many people die, and why they fight. Scholars have used this data to uncover patterns and risk factors that help us predict where and when civil wars are likely to break out. What can we expect to see in the future, given the patterns we have seen in the past? It's a whole new world of understanding.

In 2010, an article published in the *American Journal of Political Science* caught my attention. Written by a team of academics, it featured the work of researchers who belonged to something called the Political Instability Task Force (PITF), a group of academics and data analysts who were asked to convene at the behest of the U.S. government in 1994. These experts at the PITF had taken civil war data from around the world and built a model that could predict where instability was most likely to occur.

The idea that researchers could predict civil conflict was revolutionary. And so in 2017, when I was asked to join the PITF myself, I did not hesitate. For almost five years, I attended meetings and conferences with other scholars and analysts, in which we studied political volatility around the world—the potential collapse of Syria, the future of African dictators—and came up with ways to further refine the predictive possibilities of the data at our fingertips. Our goal was to try to anticipate violence and instability in other countries, so that the United States was better prepared to respond.

But as I did this work, I realized something unnerving: The warning signs of instability that we have identified in other places are the same signs that, over the past decade, I've begun to see on our own soil. This is why I witnessed the events in Lansing—as well as the assault on the U.S. Capitol in January 2021—with such trepidation. I've seen how civil wars start, and I know the signs that people miss. And I can see those signs emerging here at a surprisingly fast rate.

The plot in 2020 by a group of white nationalist, anti-government militias in Michigan is one of those signs. Civil war in the twenty-first century is distinctly different from civil wars of the past. Gone are the large battlefields, the armies, and the conventional tactics. Today, civil wars are waged primarily by different ethnic and religious groups, by guerrilla soldiers and militias, who often target civilians. The unrest in Michigan, if you look closely, features these very elements. The state is deeply divided along racial and geographic lines: Two of its major cities, Detroit and Flint, are predominantly African American, while its rural areas are 95 percent white. Economic decline in the state has created deep personal discontent, especially among its rural residents, which has led to anger, resentment, and radicalization. Michigan also has a strong anti-government culture and one of the highest numbers of militias of any state, creating ready-made units for violence. It is no surprise that one of the first attempts to instigate a civil war happened here.

That a kidnapping attempt by a group of far-right extremists is a sign of impending civil war may strike you as preposterous. But modern civil wars start with vigilantes just like these—armed militants who take violence directly to the people. Militias are now a defining feature of conflicts around the world. In Syria, anti-government rebels were a hodgepodge of insurgents and freed prisoners, fighting alongside the violent extremist group ISIS. Even Syria's largest early rebel faction—the Free Syrian Army—was a mix of hundreds of small loose-knit groups, rather than a centrally led organization. Ukraine's current civil war is being fought by bandits, warlords, private military companies, foreign mercenaries, and regular insurgents. The same is true in Afghanistan and Yemen. The era of a single, regimented, and hierarchical fighting force in official military uniform using conventional weapons is over.

Today's rebel groups rely on guerrilla warfare and organized terror: a sniper firing from a rooftop; a homemade bomb delivered in a package, detonated in a truck, or concealed on the side of a road. Groups are more likely to try to assassinate opposition leaders, journalists, or police recruits than government soldiers. Abu Musab al-Zarqawi, the leader of al-Qaeda in Iraq, masterminded the use of suicide bombings to kill anyone cooperating with the Shia-controlled government during Iraq's civil war. Abu Bakr al-Baghdadi, the leader of ISIS, perfected the use of massive car bombs to attack the same government. Hamas's main tactic against Israel has been to target average Israeli citizens going about their daily business.

Most Americans cannot imagine another civil war in their country. They assume our democracy is too resilient, too robust to devolve into conflict. Or they assume that our country is too wealthy and advanced to turn on itself. Or they assume that any rebellion would quickly be stamped out by our powerful government, giving the rebels no chance. They see the Whitmer kidnapping plot, or even the storming of the U.S. Capitol, as isolated incidents: the frustrated acts of a small group of violent extremists. But this is because they don't know how civil wars start.

TO UNDERSTAND HOW close modern America is to erupting into conflict, we must acquaint ourselves with the conditions that give rise to, and define, modern civil war. That is the purpose of this book. Civil wars ignite and escalate in ways that are predictable; they follow a script. The same patterns emerge whether you look at Bosnia, Ukraine, Iraq, Syria, Northern Ireland, or Israel. The pages that follow will explore these patterns: We'll examine where civil wars tend to start, who tends to start them, and what tend to be the triggers.

We'll also look at how to *stop* them. An eruption of conflict requires a set of variables to build on one another, like winds in a gathering storm. As I've become increasingly alarmed by the potential of a second civil war in America, I've grown personally invested in what we, as citizens, can learn from experts about defusing these gales and squalls. These incidents have offered us a lesson: We have trusted, for too long perhaps, that peace will always prevail. That our institutions are unshakable, that our nation is exceptional. We've learned that we cannot take our democracy for granted, that we must understand our power as citizens.

Some of the risks have felt immediate, such as the January 6 assault on the Capitol by far-right extremists who hoped to stop Joe Biden's presidency, or the politicization of face masks in the middle of a global pandemic. But there are deeper forces at play, and we must also be willing to acknowledge them. In the past decade, our country has undergone a seismic change in economic and cultural power. Our demographics have shifted. Inequality has grown. Our institutions have been weakened, manipulated to serve the interests of some over others. America's citizens are increasingly held captive by demagogues, on their screens or in their government. We are seeing similar developments in democracies all over the world.

And while we have been busy fighting battles over immigrant caravans and "cancel culture," violent extremist groups, especially on the radical right, have grown stronger. Since 2008, over 70 percent of extremist-related deaths in the United States have been at the hands of people connected to far-right or white-supremacist movements. Their growth may have felt imperceptible; extremists typically organize slowly and clandestinely. It took three years for Mexico's Zapatista to grow to twelve members, and over six years for a group of thirty Tamil teenagers to form the Tamil Tigers of Sri Lanka. Al-Qaeda leaders sheltered with tribes in the desert of Mali for years before they joined the rebellion there. But now, it seems, the evidence is everywhere. Americans are no longer surprised to see armed men at rallies and paramilitary groups converging at protests. It has become commonplace to see Confederate flags for sale in Pennsylvania convenience stores, or American flags with a thin blue line and insignias of all kinds. We are now beginning to understand that bumper stickers like the circle of stars around the Roman numeral III, the Valknot, and the Celtic Cross are not innocent. Instead, they are symbols of America's far-right militant groups, which are becoming increasingly visible, vocal, and dangerous.

America is a special country, but when you study the hundreds of civil wars that have broken out since the end of World War II, as I have, you come to understand that we are not immune to conflict. Here, too, there is anger and resentment and the desire to dominate rivals. Here, too, we fight for political power to protect a way of life. Here, too, we buy guns when we feel threatened. So in those moments when I would prefer to look away or take comfort in the voice that says, *No, that could never happen here,* I think of all that political science has taught me. I think about the facts before us.

And I think about the time I met Berina Kovac and we shared stories about political violence, and how it tends to sneak up on people. Berina had grown up in Sarajevo. As militias began to organize in the hills and suburbs, as former colleagues increasingly targeted her with ethnic slurs, she continued to go to work, attend weddings, take weekend holidays, and try to convince herself that everything would be fine. But late one evening in March 1992, she was at home with her son, just a few weeks old, when the power went out. "And then suddenly," Kovac told me, "you started to hear machine guns."

HOW CIVIL WARS START

CHAPTER 1

THE DANGER OF ANOCRACY

Noor was a high school sophomore in Baghdad when U.S. forces first attacked Iraq on March 19, 2003. At age thirteen, she had seen her country's leader, Saddam Hussein, condemn U.S. president George W. Bush on TV for threatening war and had heard her family talking around the dinner table about a possible American invasion. Noor was a typical teenager. She loved Britney Spears and the Backstreet Boys and Christina Aguilera. She would watch Oprah and Dr. Phil in her free time, and one of her favorite films was *The Matrix*. She couldn't imagine U.S. soldiers in Baghdad—where life, though sometimes hard, had mainly been about hanging out with friends, walking to the park, and visiting her favorite animals at the zoo. To her, it just felt unreal.

But two weeks later, American soldiers arrived in her part of the city. The first sounds she heard were airplanes and then explosions late in the afternoon. She rushed up to the roof of their house, following her mother and sisters, not knowing what they would find. When she looked up at the sky, she saw armored vehicles floating under parachutes. "It was like a movie," she said. A few days later, American soldiers walked down the street in front of her house, and Noor ran to the front door to watch them. She saw her neighbors also standing in their doorways, smiles on their faces. The soldiers smiled back, eager to talk to anyone who was willing. "Everybody was so happy," Noor recalled. "There was suddenly freedom." Less than a week later, on April 9, her fellow Iraqis descended on Firdos Square in central Baghdad, where they threw a rope over the enormous statue of Saddam Hussein, and, with the help of American soldiers, tore it down. Noor thought to herself, *You know, we can have a new life. A better life.*

Life under Saddam had been challenging. Noor's father had been a government employee, yet like many other Iraqis, the family had little money. Saddam's failed war against Iran in the 1980s had left Iraq poor and in debt, and things had gotten only worse in 1990 after he invaded Kuwait and economic sanctions were imposed. Noor's family, like most Iraqi families, struggled with rampant inflation, a crumbling healthcare system, and shortages of food and medicine. They also lived in fear. Iraqis were forbidden to talk politics or to criticize their government. They came to believe that the walls had ears, and that Saddam's security services were constantly watching. Saddam had been brutal to his enemies and rivals during his twenty-four-year reign. Iraqis who criticized the president, his entourage, or his Baath Party could be put to death. Journalists were executed or forced into exile. Some dissidents were imprisoned; others simply disappeared. People heard stories of how prisoners were tortured— their eyes gouged out, their genitals electrocuted—then killed via hanging, decapitation, or by firing squad.

But now the Americans had come, and eight months after Iraqi citizens dragged Saddam's statue to the ground,

U.S. soldiers found the fearsome dictator hiding in an eight-foot-deep hole near his hometown of Tikrit. He looked dirty and dazed. With Americans in charge, most Iraqis believed that their country would be reborn and that they would experience the freedom and opportunities available in Western countries. Families dreamed of experiencing true democracy. The military, and perhaps the judiciary, would be reformed. Corruption would end. Wealth, including oil profits, would be distributed more equally. Noor and her family were excited for independent newspapers and satellite TV. "We thought we would breathe freedom, we would become like Europe," said Najm al-Jabouri, a former general in Saddam's army. They were wrong.

When Saddam Hussein was captured, researchers who study democratization didn't celebrate. We knew that democratization, especially rapid democratization in a deeply divided country, could be highly destabilizing. In fact, the more radical and rapid the change, the more destabilizing it was likely to be. The United States and the United Kingdom thought they were delivering freedom to a welcoming population. Instead, they were about to deliver the perfect conditions for civil war.

Iraq was a country plagued by political rivalries, both ethnic and religious. The Kurds, a large ethnic minority in the north, had long fought Saddam for autonomy; they wanted to be left alone to rule themselves. The Shia, who made up more than 60 percent of Iraq's population, resented being ruled by Saddam Hussein, a Sunni, and his mostly Sunni Baath Party. Over decades, Saddam had been able to consolidate power for his minority group by stacking government positions with Sunnis, requiring everyone to join the Baath Party to qualify for jobs regardless of religion or sect, and by unleashing his murderous security forces on everyone else.

A mere two and a half months after the invasion, Iraqis coalesced into competing sectarian factions, dictated in part by two fateful decisions by the U.S. government. In an effort to bring rapid democracy to the country, Paul Bremer, the head of the United States' transitional government in Iraq, outlawed the Baath Party and ordered that all members of Saddam Hussein's government, almost all of whom were Sunni, be permanently removed from power. He then disbanded the Iraqi military, sending hundreds of thousands of Sunni soldiers home.

Suddenly, before a new government could be formed, tens of thousands of Baath bureaucrats were thrown out of power. More than 350,000 officers and soldiers in the Iraqi military no longer had an income. More than 85,000 regular Iraqis, including schoolteachers who had joined the Baath Party as a condition of their employment, lost their jobs. Noor, who is Sunni, remembers the feeling of shock around the country.

Those who had been locked out of power under Saddam, however, saw their opportunity. Political jostling broke out almost immediately among figures such as Nouri al-Maliki, a Shia dissident who had returned from exile, and Muqtada al-Sadr, a radical Shia cleric who wanted Iraq to become an Islamic regime. Though the Americans had hoped to broker a power-sharing agreement among Sunnis, Shiites, and Kurds, they soon acquiesced to the demands of Maliki, who wanted a government that, like the population, was majority Shia. For Noor, what resulted wasn't democracy. It was chaos followed by a power grab.

Regular Iraqis, especially Sunnis, began to worry. If the more numerous Shia were in control of the government, what would prevent them from turning on the minority Sunnis? What incentives would they have to give them jobs, or share critical oil revenues? What would keep them from exacting revenge for Saddam's past crimes? Former Baathist party leaders, intelligence officials, and Iraqi army officers, along with Sunni tribal chiefs, soon realized that if they wanted to retain any power in the new democracy, they had to act fast. Nascent insurgent organizations began to form as early as the summer of 2003. They found easy recruits in Sunni cities and Iraq's Sunni-dominated countryside where citizens increasingly felt politically and economically aggrieved. As one Sunni citizen noted, "We were on top of the system. We had dreams. Now we are the losers. We lost our positions, our status, the security of our families, stability."

Sunni insurgents didn't go after American troops at first (the Americans were too well armed). Instead, the insurgents focused on easier targets: those individuals and groups who were helping the Americans. This included the Shia who enlisted in the new Iraqi security forces, Shia politicians, and international organizations, including the United Nations. The insurgents' goal was to reduce or eliminate support for the U.S. occupation and isolate the American military. It was only afterward that the insurgents began to target American troops, planting inexpensive but highly effective roadside bombs along important supply routes. By the time Saddam Hussein was captured in December 2003, guerrilla war had broken out.

The fighting escalated in April 2004 when Shia factions began to compete for power. The most notorious was a Shia militia led by Muqtada al-Sadr, who played on Shia nationalists' anger at U.S. occupation to gain support. He, too, targeted American allies and troops in order to convince the Americans to leave. By the time Iraq's first parliamentary elections were held, in January 2005, it was clear that Sunnis would play, at best, only a secondary role in government. Some hoped the Americans would step in to strengthen the constitution, or rein in Maliki. But the Americans had become worried about their long-term entanglement in Iraq and did little to intervene. As acts of violence toward coalition forces continued to escalate, so did fighting among Iraqis, who fractured into dozens of regional and religious militias to try to gain control of the country. Many had the support of the local population and received money and weapons from foreign rivals. "Saudi Arabia supported the Sunni militias, and Iran supported the Shia militias, and then you had Muqtada al-Sadr, who promoted himself," recalled Noor. "People everywhere started taking sides."

Soon it was too dangerous for Noor to leave the house or even to walk to the grocery store. Rival militias were fighting for territory, and snipers waited to pick off anyone in the street; roadside bombs and military checkpoints became a fact of life. At the zoo, where Noor had spent so many weekends with her friends, the animals were either starving to death or eaten by people increasingly desperate for food. Noor and her family didn't know what to do. First, they fled to a relative's safer neighborhood, and then in 2007, they left Baghdad altogether because they no longer felt safe anywhere in the city. They traveled by bus to Damascus, where they were content, at least for a time. They did not know that the blood and chaos of civil war would eventually fill the streets of Syria, too.

It had taken American forces only a few months to re-move Saddam Hussein from power and set Iraq on the path to a democracy. But almost as swiftly, the country descended into a civil war so brutal that it would last for more than a decade. Like the dictator's fallen statue, all of Noor's hopes—for a new voice, for new rights, for new dreams—had been smashed to pieces.

OVER THE PAST one hundred years, the world has experienced the greatest expansion of freedom and political rights in the history of mankind. In 1900, democracies barely existed. But by 1948, world leaders had embraced the Universal Declaration of Human Rights, which was signed by almost all of the UN member states. It asserted that every person had the right to participate in his or her government, the right to freedom of speech, religion, and peaceful assembly, and that they had these rights no matter their sex, language, race, color, religion, birth status, or political views. Today, almost 60 percent of the world's countries are democratic.

Citizens of liberal democracies have more political and civil rights than those who live in non-democracies. They participate more in the political life of their nations, have greater protections from discrimination and repression, and receive a greater percentage of state resources. They are also happier, wealthier, better educated, and generally have a higher life expectancy than people who live in dictatorships. It's the reason refugees risk their lives to reach Europe, fleeing more repressive countries in the Middle East, Central Asia, and Africa. And it's why President Bush, after invading Iraq, felt confident that the United States would establish "a free Iraq at the heart of the Middle East" and inspire a "global democratic revolution."

There's another big benefit of democratic governance. Full democracies are less likely to go to war against their fellow citizens and against citizens in other democracies. People may disagree about what form democracy takes. They may be frustrated with democracy's need for consensus and compromise. But given a choice between democracy and dictatorship, most will gladly take democracy.

But the *road* to democracy is a dangerous one. When scholars around the world first began collecting data on civil wars, in the early nineties, they noticed an interesting correlation: Since 1946, right after World War II ended, the number of democracies in the world had surged—but so had the number of civil wars. They seemed to be rising in tandem. The first wave of democratization began in 1870, when citizens in the United States and many Central and South American countries began to demand political reform. (Black people were not full participants in American democracy until the 1960s, though they temporarily gained more rights during Reconstruction.) The second wave emerged immediately after World War II, when newly defeated countries and postcolonial states tried to build their own democratic governments. The third wave moved through East Asia, Latin America, and southern and Eastern Europe in the 1970s, '80s, and '90s, when more than thirty countries transitioned to democracy. The latest wave began to develop with the U.S. invasion of Iraq in 2003 and seemed to gain strength as Arab Spring protests spread across the Middle East and North Africa.

Civil wars rose alongside democracies. In 1870, almost no countries were experiencing civil war, but by 1992, there were over fifty. Serbs, Croats, and Bosniaks (Bosnian Muslims) were fighting one another in a fracturing Yugoslavia. Islamist rebel groups were turning on their government in Algeria. Leaders in Somalia and the Congo suddenly faced multiple armed groups challenging their rule, as did the governments in Georgia and Tajikistan. Soon the Hutus and the Tutsis would be slaughtering each other in Rwanda and Burundi. By the early nineties, the number of civil wars around the world had reached its highest point in modern history.

That is, at least until now. In 2019, we reached a new peak.

It turns out that one of the best predictors of whether a country will experience a civil war is whether it is moving toward or away from democracy. Yes, democracy. Countries almost never go from full autocracy to full democracy without a rocky transition in between. Attempts by leaders to democratize frequently include significant backsliding or stagnation in a pseudo-autocratic middle zone. And even if citizens succeed in gaining full democracy, their governments don't always stay there. Would-be despots can whittle away rights and freedoms, and concentrate power, causing democracies to decline. Hungary became a full democracy in 1990 before Prime Minister Viktor Orbán slowly and methodically nudged it back toward dictatorship. It is in this middle zone that most civil wars occur.

Experts call countries in this middle zone "anocracies"—they are neither full autocracies nor democracies but something in between. Ted Robert Gurr, a professor at Northwestern, coined the term in 1974 after collecting data on the democratic and autocratic traits of governments around the world. Prior to that, he and his team had debated what to call these hybrid regimes, sometimes using the term "transitional" before settling on "anocracy." Citizens receive some elements of democratic rule—perhaps full voting rights—but they also live under leaders with extensive authoritarian powers and few checks and balances.

Civil war experts have known about the relationship between anocracy and civil war for a long time. It's why we were so critical of President Bush's decision to try to catapult Iraq from autocracy to democracy in 2003. We understood that a major political transition in Iraq was likely to trigger civil war instead. Experts have seen this pattern repeated around the world over the last century. Serbs went to war against Croats almost immediately after Yugoslavia began to democratize in 1991. The same was true of Spain in the 1930s: Spanish citizens got their first taste of democracy in June 1931 after holding their first democratic elections; five years later, Spanish citizens rose up when the military launched a coup to try to take control of the country. And Rwanda's plan to democratize was the catalyst for the Hutu genocide against the Tutsis. It's no coincidence that the biggest civil wars raging today—in Iraq, Libya, Syria, and Yemen—were born from attempts to democratize.

Categorizing countries as democracies, autocracies, or anocracies is painstaking work. Researchers have spent decades collecting detailed information about the types of governments that exist around the world and how they have changed over time. There are several large datasets, each measuring different variables, but most conflict researchers tend to rely on the one that has been compiled by the Polity Project at the Center for Systemic Peace—a nonprofit that supports research and quantitative analysis on democracy and political violence. Ted Gurr started this project, which is now led by his former associate Monty Marshall. The dataset is useful because of its long historical time frame, the large number of countries it includes, and because it was one of the first to attempt to quantify a country's system of governance for statistical analyses. One of the most influential measures in the dataset is called the Polity Score, which captures just how democratic or autocratic a country is in any given year. It is a 21-point scale that ranges from −10 (most autocratic) to +10 (most democratic). Countries are considered to be full democracies if they receive a score of between +6 and +10. If a country receives a score of +10, for example, its national elections have been certified as "free and fair," no important social groups are systematically left out of the political process, and major political parties are stable and based on mass national constituencies. Norway, New Zealand, Denmark, Canada—and, until recently, the United States—all have a +10 rating.

On the other end of the polity index score are the autocracies. Countries are considered autocracies if they receive a score of between −6 and −10. Countries that receive a score of −10, such as North Korea, Saudi Arabia, or Bahrain, offer citizens no role in choosing their leaders, and allow their leaders to rule much as they like.

Anocracies are in the middle, receiving a score of between −5 and +5. In anocracies, citizens get some elements of democratic rule—perhaps elections—but they also get presidents with lots of authoritarian powers. Fareed Zakaria calls these types of governments "illiberal democracies." But you can also think of them as partial democracies, faux democracies, or hybrid regimes. Turkey became an anocracy in 2014 when President Recep Tayyip Erdoğan tightened the government's hold over the courts, the media, and elections. Zimbabwe appeared to be on a path toward greater democracy after President Robert Mugabe resigned in 2017, but has since returned to old patterns of political repression, especially with regard to violence around elections. Iraq never made it to full democracy. It, too, is an anocracy.

The CIA first discovered the relationship between anocracy and violence in 1994. The U.S. government had asked the agency to develop a model to predict—two years in advance—where political instability and armed conflict was likely to break out around the world. What were the warning signs that a country was heading toward violence? The government would then put the countries that had the most warning signs on a watch list.

The Political Instability Task Force (the one I later joined) came up with dozens of social, economic, and political variables—thirty-eight, to be precise, including poverty, ethnic diversity, population size, inequality, and corruption—and put them into a predictive model. To everyone's surprise, they found that the best predictor of instability was not, as they might have guessed, income inequality or poverty. It was a nation's polity index score, with the anocracy zone being the place of greatest danger. Anocracies, particularly those with more democratic than autocratic features—what the task force called "partial democracies"—were twice as likely as autocracies to experience political instability or civil war, and three times as likely as democracies.

All the things that experts thought should matter in the outbreak of civil war somehow didn't. It wasn't the poorest countries that were at the highest risk of conflict, or the most unequal, or the most ethnically or religiously heterogeneous, or even the most repressive. It was living in a partial democracy that made citizens more likely to pick up a gun and begin to fight. Saddam Hussein never faced a major civil war during his twenty-four years in power. It was only after his government was dismantled and power was up for grabs—when it went from −9 to the middle zone—that Iraq erupted in war.

WHY DOES ANOCRACY put a country in such danger of civil war? A closer look at the governments and citizens who are weathering this middle zone offers some insight. Anocracies tend to share certain characteristics that can work together to exacerbate the potential for conflict.

A government that is democratizing is weak compared to the regime before it—politically, institutionally, and militarily. Unlike autocrats, leaders in an anocracy are often not powerful enough or ruthless enough to quell dissent and ensure loyalty. The government is also frequently disorganized and riddled with internal divisions, struggling to deliver basic services or even security. Opposition leaders, or even those within a president's own party, may challenge or resist the pace of reform, while new leaders must quickly earn the trust of citizens, fellow politicians, or army generals. In the chaos of transition, these leaders often fail.

When I asked Noor about the transition in Iraq, she recalled the unease many Iraqis felt about their new government. "Maliki got into power, and what did he do?" she said. "Nothing. Everybody started complaining about him. People were unemployed and they didn't have the money or the food to feed their families. What were they going to do?"

These weaknesses set the stage for civil war because impatient citizens, disgruntled military officers, or anyone with political ambitions can find both a reason and an opportunity to organize a rebellion against the new government. Former rebel leaders in Uganda, for example, admitted that they were much more eager to organize violence after they discovered that their government's intelligence services were ineffective; they could rebel knowing that their plan was unlikely to be discovered. This is also what happened in Georgia when it held its first democratic elections as an independent country in 1991, after the Soviet Union dissolved. Though a reformist named Zviad Gamsakhurdia won the presidency, he faced challenges almost immediately, both from opponents, who accused him of being too authoritarian, and from ethnic minorities—the Ossetians and the Abkhazians—who were unhappy about their representation in government. The following year, armed supporters of the opposition staged a coup, overthrowing Gamsakhurdia; within six months, violent conflict had broken out between ethnic Georgians and Abkhazians. By 1993, the young country was engulfed in civil war.

A primary reason for revolt is that democratic transitions create new winners and losers: In the shift away from autocracy, formerly disenfranchised citizens come into new power, while those who once held privileges find themselves losing influence. Because the new government in an anocracy is often fragile, and the rule of law is still developing, the losers—former elites, opposition leaders, citizens who once enjoyed advantages—are not sure the administration will be fair, or that they will be protected. This can create genuine anxieties about the future: The losers may not be convinced of a leader's commitment to democracy; they may feel their own needs and rights are at stake. This is the situation the Sunnis found themselves in when the United States transferred power to Maliki. They rightly understood that they were powerless to force the majority Shia to do anything. From their perspective, they were better off fighting while they were still relatively strong, rather than wait for their rivals to consolidate power.

And because the government is weak, events can easily spiral out of control. This happened in Indonesia after President Suharto, an authoritarian, was forced to step down after the 1997 Asian financial crisis. Within weeks of entering office, Suharto's successor, Vice President B. J. Habibie, enacted rapid reforms: He allowed political parties to organize, removed press censorship, freed political prisoners, and made plans to hold free and fair elections for both the parliament and the presidency. He also finally announced on January 27, 1999, a willingness to give the small island of East Timor independence, dramatically reversing the government's previous refusal.

But this opening started a chain reaction, as other discontented groups in Indonesia seized the opportunity to claim power for themselves, too. Shortly thereafter, the Christian Ambonese, an ethnic group in the province of Maluku who were displeased with the increasing Islamization of Indonesia, declared an independent republic. West Papuans, who had long chafed under Indonesian rule, voiced their own desire for independence. Meanwhile, in the province of Aceh, activists argued that if East Timor had been granted freedom, "then there is no reason Aceh should not be next." Habibie's government could not keep up. Struggling to maintain control, he shut down independence negotiations in some provinces and allowed government crackdowns in others. Soon, Indonesia was caught up in civil war on multiple fronts: among Muslims and Christians in Maluku, among Timorese and Indonesian paramilitary groups, and among Aceh separatists and the Indonesian government.

A painful reality of democratization is that the faster and bolder the reform efforts, the greater the chance of civil war. Rapid regime change—a six-point or more fluctuation in a country's polity index score—almost always precedes instability, and civil wars are more likely to break out in the first two years after reform is attempted. Ethiopia's recent political violence and escalating civil war, for example, is a consequence of its attempts to quickly democratize. In 2018, the Oromos—Ethiopia's largest ethnic group—got their long-awaited wish when, after two years of protests, the country's prime minister, Hailemariam Desalegn, agreed to transfer power to Abiy Ahmed Ali, an ethnic Oromo. Abiy seemed to be a democrat's dream. He promised free and fair elections, instituted a more legitimate and inclusive political system, and invited long-exiled Oromos to return home. His reforms were, according to an American foreign service officer in Addis Ababa, "beyond our wildest dreams."

But returning Oromo leaders constituted a new elite that was ready to exact revenge. A weaker military made it easier for former soldiers to begin to agitate. By redistributing power to Ethiopia's administrative regions, Abiy created strong incentives for rival ethnic groups to compete for regional influence. A mere five months later, violence broke out. Mobs of roaming Oromo youth celebrating the exiles' return sparked ethnic violence that eventually led to dozens of deaths and thousands fleeing to Kenya. Many observers found the conflict particularly astonishing because there was, in the words of one Ethiopian analyst, "such a remarkable level of democratic opening in the country." The opening had simply happened too fast. Today, a full-scale civil war has broken out in the Tigray region of Ethiopia, where former government officials—purged by Abiy—have rebelled, vowing to regain their recently lost power and influence.

But democratization is possible. Though the path to democracy is treacherous, the risk of civil war fades when a country takes its time, evolving its political system gradually. Mexico weathered democratization relatively peacefully. Its transition lasted nearly twenty years, from 1982 until 2000, when the National Action Party (PAN) became the first opposition party to win a presidential election since 1929. The state remained strong and continued to function while democratic institutions matured. Slow reform reduces uncertainty for a country's citizens and is less threatening to incumbent elites, setting a conciliatory tone and providing them with opportunities to gracefully relinquish power. The result is often less violence.

UNTIL RECENTLY, the way most countries ended up in the dangerous anocracy zone was when dictatorships were overthrown, as happened in Iraq, or autocrats were forced to embrace democratic reform as a result of mass protests. But after almost half a century of increasing democratization, countries, especially newer democracies, began to move in the opposite direction. Even once-safe liberal democracies, such as Belgium and the United Kingdom, saw their polity index scores lowered. Since 2000, democratic leaders who came to power via elections have begun to consolidate authoritarian rule. Civil war experts are once again worried. We understand that backsliding almost certainly means that the middle zone is likely to expand.

We've seen this in Poland, where the Law and Justice

Party won elections in 2015; the president, prime minister, and deputy prime minister have since systematically taken control of the courts, restricted free speech, targeted political opponents, and weakened the electoral commission. In Hungary, Prime Minister Orbán has steadily transformed the country into the European Union's first non-democratic member. The government controls the media, imposes Kafkaesque regulations on pro-democracy parties, and moves forcefully to silence voices of dissent. Orbán and his party may have won the national vote in 2018, but international monitors reported that the opposition was fighting on an unequal playing field. According to the V-Dem Institute, another research institute dedicated to tracking global democracy,* twenty-five countries are now severely affected by a wave of international autocratization, including Brazil, India, and the United States.

Democratic countries that veer into anocracy do so not because their leaders are untested and weak, like those who are scrambling to organize in the wake of a dictator, but

---

* There are three widely used datasets that measure a country's system of governance: Polity V, Freedom House, and V-Dem. Each relies on its own definition of democracy, and therefore measures democracy in different ways. Polity V, for example, is particularly interested in the durability of different types of governments and their political institutions, focusing heavily on the democratic and autocratic features of a country. V-Dem (which was introduced in 2014) is keen to uncover the many varieties of democracy around the world and includes five detailed dimensions of democracy (electoral, participatory, egalitarian, deliberative, and liberal dimensions). Freedom House focuses heavily on individual freedoms and includes detailed measures on citizens' political rights and civil liberties. Despite these differences, scholars have found a high level of agreement in terms of how countries are coded in each dataset, and high intercorrelations between the democracy measures included in each.

rather because elected leaders—many of whom are quite popular—start to ignore the guardrails that protect their democracies. These include constraints on a president, checks and balances among government branches, a free press that demands accountability, and fair and open political competition. Would-be autocrats such as Orbán, Erdoğan, Vladimir Putin, or Brazilian president Jair Bolsonaro put their political goals ahead of the needs of a healthy democracy, gaining support by exploiting citizen fears—over jobs, over immigration, over security.

They persuade citizens that democracy as it has existed will lead to more corruption, more lies, and greater bungling of economic and social policy. They decry political leaders' compromises as ineffective, and the government as a failure. They understand that if they can persuade citizens that "strong leadership" and "law and order" are necessary, citizens will voluntarily vote them into office. People will often sacrifice freedom if they believe it will make them more secure. Then, once in power, these leaders plunge their countries into anocracy by exploiting weaknesses in the constitution, electoral system, and judiciary. Because they typically use legal methods—partisan appointments, executive orders, parliamentary votes—they are able to consolidate power in ways that other politicians are unable, or unwilling, to stop. This increasing autocratization puts countries at higher risk of civil war.

The moment of peak risk occurs smack in the middle of the zone—between -1 and $+1$. This is when the government is likely at its weakest in terms of both institutional strength and legitimacy. The risk of civil war remains relatively low for autocracies in the initial stages of democratization; the risk of civil war does not surge until they are almost

at −1. A country may start out with a polity index score of
−6, say, move up the scale as it implements reforms, and
then, just at the moment it is halfway to democracy, experience a civil war. If the country can survive this treacherous
period and implement even greater democratic reforms,
then the risk of conflict sharply reverses.

For a decaying democracy, the risk of civil war increases
almost the moment it becomes less democratic. As a democracy drops down the polity index scale—a result of fewer
executive restraints, weaker rule of law, diminished voting
rights—its risk for armed conflict steadily increases. This risk
peaks when it hits a score of between +1 to −1—the point
when citizens face the prospect of real autocracy. The chance
of civil war then sharply drops if the country weathers this
moment by becoming even more authoritarian, or changes
course and begins to rebuild its democracy.

The decline of liberal democracies is a new phenome-

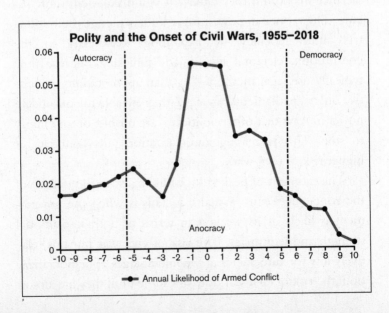

non, and none have fallen into all-out civil war—yet. One cautionary tale is Ukraine, whose citizens took to the streets in 2013 to protest the increasingly autocratic rule of Viktor Yanukovych. Yanukovych, the leader of the country's pro-Russia party, had won the presidency in 2010, in a runoff election rife with accusations of fraud and voter intimidation. His predecessor, a pro-European, anti-corruption moderate, had been in office for more than five years, during which Ukraine's polity index score had risen to a +7. But almost as soon as Yanukovych took office, he set about cementing his own power. Yanukovych ran against "the West"—the idea of increasing ties with the European Union—and instead championed Russian-speaking voters across Ukraine, especially those in the eastern part of the country, who wanted stronger ties to Russia. To many Russian-speaking Ukrainians, his autocratic tendencies were the lesser of two evils; they would rather have an authoritarian who was on their side than a democrat who was not. Yanukovych investigated political opponents and threw rivals into prison. He cracked down on journalists critical of his administration. He filled ministry spots with party members and gave loyalists from his eastern Ukrainian home region of Donbas jobs on the police force, in tax services, and in the courts.

When Yanukovych announced his intention to strengthen economic ties with Russia, rather than the European Union, citizens—many of them young people from European-leaning western Ukraine—decided they'd had enough. Demonstrations, known as the Euromaidan protests ("Euro" for the desire for ties with Europe, "maidan" for the main public square in Kyiv) began in the capital city and spread across the country. Protesters toppled the statue of Lenin in

Kyiv, clashed with police, and demanded new elections, freedom of speech, and closer ties to the EU. At first, it seemed that democracy had been saved: After months of unrest, including a violent confrontation between government paramilitary forces and citizens, the Ukrainian parliament voted to oust Yanukovych, who fled the country. New elections were held in May 2014, ushering in President Petro Poroshenko, an ethnic Ukrainian businessman intent on integrating with Europe. "We had dreams of a new life and an amazing sense of solidarity," recalled pro-West Ukrainian professor Anton Melnyk.

But just as anocracy creates losers in places that are stumbling toward democracy, like the Sunnis in Iraq, there are also losers in places struggling to retain democracy. In Ukraine, these were the pensioners, villagers, and unskilled workers in the eastern part of the country who had benefited from Yanukovych's Russian connections. Many of them had emigrated from Russia in the early 1950s to work in the region's coal mines. They were ethnically Russian, spoke Russian, and their jobs were almost entirely dependent on trade with Russia. Now, with the pro-European Poroshenko in charge, this enclave feared their voice and priorities would be ignored. Like the Sunnis, these eastern Ukrainians decided they had to secure their own interests before it was too late. Within weeks of Yanukovych's ouster, separatist militias declared their own autonomous states—the Luhansk and Donetsk people's republics—and quickly captured stocks of weapons to defend their territory. By this time, Ukraine's polity score had slid to a +4. The country was nearing the danger zone for civil war.

The decline of democracy in Ukraine had created a weak and fractured government. Protesters had rejected an anti-democratic leader, but the acting president was weak and parliament was still filled with Yanukovych loyalists. By July the ruling coalition had collapsed, leaving the prime minister with too few votes to continue to govern. In addition, the parliament was so divided between the eastern and western parts of the country that it failed to come to agreement, leaving civil servants—policemen, doctors, teachers—with no wages. Fistfights started breaking out between legislators from rival parties.

Mikhail Minakov, a Ukrainian philosopher, political scholar, and historian, knew the moment his country's democracy was beyond repair. Though he lived in Germany, he had been watching with alarm as militias began to form, and he'd decided to fly to Ukraine to enroll in the Ukrainian army. He would fight on Poroshenko's behalf and for a democratic Ukraine. When he showed up in Kyiv on March 3 and headed to the army recruitment headquarters, he found five hundred men already waiting, standing outside closed gates. They'd been there for hours. They pounded on the door, waiting for someone to come. Finally, at 10:00 A.M., a junior officer walked out. He was drunk. "Your motherland is not fucking in need of you," he declared to them all. He told them to go home. At first, Minakov was shocked, until the meaning of the officer's words sunk in: He was telling them not to be naïve. "There was no government. There was no state. . . . The constitution didn't work, there was no party, there was no police," said Minakov. "There was an implosion of local authority." It was then that Minakov realized that the government was too weak to function.

By April 6, after weeks of protests in eastern Ukraine against Yanukovych's forced resignation, pro-Russian activists took control of the region's security services and began to arm themselves with automatic weapons. They were going to defend their claim of independence, using force if necessary. At first, the government could do nothing to counter the separatists in the east; after two decades of corruption and neglect, the Ukrainian army was in shambles. But soon Ukrainian volunteers, like the ones who had shown up at the recruitment headquarters, formed a sort of paramilitary force. By June, clashes turned into conventional battles, as Russia quickly supplied the separatists with heavy weapons and tanks. "It went very, very fast," said Minakov.

THE LOVE AFFAIR with democratization that marked the twentieth century and the very beginning of the twenty-first century is over. It ended in 2006, when the number of democracies around the world reached its peak. Even democracies once considered secure, such as France and Costa Rica, have experienced erosion, as have places like Iceland, which has not protected rights and freedoms equally across all social groups.

And yet not every country that becomes an anocracy experiences civil war. Some places, such as Singapore, remain anocracies for years and never descend into violence; they find peace and stability in the middle zone. Others, such as the Czech Republic and Lithuania, move rapidly through the middle zone, from autocracy to democracy with few consequences. Some democracies that have crossed into anocracy have resisted civil war by resorting to straight-up repression, as Nicolás Maduro has done in Venezuela: unleashing security forces, postponing regional elections, replacing parliament, and rewriting the constitution to expand his executive power. Others have evaded civil war by using a gradual, sneakier hand, like Putin in Russia or Orbán in Hungary. These leaders maintain the guise of democracy—elections and limited individual freedoms—and cement their popularity with effective propaganda, control of the media, and sometimes xenophobia. Citizens, rather than revolt, have acquiesced to their rule.

Why do some countries safely navigate the road through the anocracy zone, while others become engulfed in cycles of chaos and violence? The story of Iraq again offers a clue. When I asked Noor to describe what changed before civil war erupted in her homeland, she looked at me for a moment. Soft-spoken and reserved, she radiated the quiet confidence of someone who doesn't break easily. Her face, however, was heavy with sadness. "People began asking whether you were Shia or Sunni," she said.

People had never asked her this before, she explained. In Baghdad, there were no Shia or Sunni neighborhoods; she had never been told she couldn't marry someone from a different ethnic or religious group. She had no sense that she was a minority or that religion mattered; she didn't even know which of her friends were Shia or Sunni. "But then people started asking about it publicly. What are you? Where are you from? What is your religion?"

Noor shook her head. "I would say, 'I am Iraqi. Why are you asking me this'?"

CHAPTER 2

THE RISE OF FACTIONS

The men in military uniform inched the casket out of the blue train as if it contained the most precious cargo. The inhabitant was Josip Tito, former president of Yugoslavia, who had died the day before. This train trip was important. It was designed to help Yugoslavian citizens mourn their beloved leader; the three-hundred-mile route meandered across the small country over the course of eight hours so that everyone could pay their respects. In the hilly Zagorje region on the border of Croatia and Slovenia, where Tito was born, people lined the tracks four deep. Along the route, people stood, waiting in the rain, to watch the train go by. A group of widows in heavy black clothes stood in a field and bowed their heads.

Tito was known for his love of cigars, his crisp white military uniform, and his determination to unite Yugoslavia under his complete control. He was adored for being a World War II hero who had fought against the Germans and Italians, and the first communist to successfully challenge Stalin. He had improved life for many Yugoslavs, elevating them from poverty to the middle class in a generation. As the blue train made its way to Belgrade, in Serbia, people repeated a famous poem: "Comrade Tito, from your path we will not stray!"

When the train arrived in Belgrade on May 5, 1980, hundreds of thousands of people were waiting. They stood umbrella to umbrella in every street. The pallbearers carried the casket, gingerly, up the steps to the ornate parliamentary building where it would lie in state. Yugoslavians would have several days to mourn before one of the largest state funerals in history would be held. Margaret Thatcher would attend. So would Leonid Brezhnev, Yasser Arafat, and Vice President Walter Mondale. For now, there was a pervasive quiet. The shock and sadness on people's faces said it all. This man had single-handedly—albeit ruthlessly—held together one of the most ethnically diverse countries on the planet.

When Tito came to power in 1953, Yugoslavia was a daunting cultural landscape, an amalgam of eight peoples, five languages, and three religions. Serbs and Croats speak the same language but use a different alphabet, while the Slovenes speak a different Slavic language altogether. Serbs, Croats, and Slovenes are all Christian, but the Serbs are mainly Eastern Orthodox, while the Slovenes and Croats are mainly Roman Catholic; they take their guidance from different religious leaders. Bosnian Muslims are ethnically the same as Serbs and Croats, but they converted to Islam, many under the threat of death, during the Turkish occupation. Kosovo, an autonomous province within Serbia, was almost entirely Albanian, while Vojvodina, another autonomous province, was a mish-mash of Hungarians, Romanians, Slovaks, and Ruthenians. John Reed, author of *The War in Eastern Europe,* described Macedonia, a former Yugoslav republic, as "the most frightful mix-up of races ever imagined [where]

Turks, Albanians, Serbs, Rumanians, Greeks and Bulgarians lived . . . side by side without mingling."

Yugoslavia's peoples had not always been peaceful. During World War II, a Croatian ultranationalist, fascist, terrorist organization—the Ustashe—sided with the Germans and were allowed to rule Croatia as a result. The leader of the Croat Ustashe state was Ante Pavelić, a rabid nationalist with a brutal formula for ridding Croatia of non-Croatians: "One-third we will kill, one-third will be driven out of Croatia, and one-third we will convert to Catholicism." By the end of the war, the Ustashe had killed between 500,000 and 700,000 Serbs, as well as tens of thousands of Jews and Gypsies.

Tito was born to a Croat father and a Slovene mother, and he was determined to unite Yugoslavia's disparate people—it was the only way to maintain Communist party control and solidify his own rule. He knew he needed to weaken the political power of the Serbs, the largest of the groups. (Serbia had been an independent state before the war.) His solution was to divide Yugoslavia into six republics: Bosnia and Herzegovina, Croatia, Macedonia, Montenegro, Serbia, and Slovenia. Each ethnic group would have a geographic home base, but the borders were drawn so that the more populous Serbs were dispersed throughout each of the other republics except Slovenia. As compensation, Serbs were given the most political power at the national level relative to the other groups. Any displays of ethnic identity Tito ruthlessly squashed, preaching "brotherhood and unity" instead. It was a brilliant divide-and-rule strategy. But with Tito now dead, the future of Yugoslavia was unclear.

Tensions broke out almost immediately. In 1981 Albanian students in Kosovo protested, demanding that Kosovo become a republic in its own right rather than part of the Serb republic. Serbian historical sites in the region were desecrated, violence erupted, and hundreds of ethnic Albanians died. Meanwhile, the entire Yugoslavian economy began to collapse; the country's currency, the dinar, plunged in value, the unemployment rate grew to almost 20 percent, and another 20 percent of the population was underemployed. Deteriorating living conditions and increasingly obvious signs of government corruption corroded the legitimacy of the ruling League of Communists. This exacerbated ethnic resentment from non-Serbs against the Serbian "ruling class" and from the "have not" Serbian republic against the more well-off republics of Slovenia and Croatia.

In Serbia, a Communist party leader named Slobodan Milošević decided to make a name for himself by capitalizing on these ethnic divisions: After being sent by party leaders to Kosovo to help promote peace, he instead—to everyone's shock—promised the Serbs living in the region that he would help them resist Albanian dominance. Kosovo had been the center of the Serbian kingdom during the Middle Ages. It contained the most important Serbian Christian monuments, monasteries, and churches. Serbs viewed Kosovo as their cherished homeland. By emphasizing ethnic identity rather than political ideology, Milošević quickly gained the support of these Serbian citizens, even those who were anti-Communist. Such an overt show of nationalism was scandalous—Tito would never have allowed it—but Milošević continued undeterred. Over the next several years, he set about reasserting Serbian rights: He rewrote Serbia's constitution to undermine Kosovo's autonomy, replaced leaders in the Serbian province with his own supporters, and took control of the police and the courts, as well as the media, which he used to spread a message of Serbian aggrievement and empowerment.

Milošević envisioned a Yugoslavia in which Serbs—who were a majority, after all—would finally have the representation and influence they deserved. With Serb loyalists in government in the provinces, he now had a greater voice at the federal level—four out of eight representative votes for Serbs. He held "rallies for truth"—over one hundred in a year, reaching five million people—to spread ideas of nationalism and inspire Serbs in other regions of Yugoslavia to seek power. In March 1989, when Albanians demonstrated in Kosovo to reclaim some of their political rights, Milošević ordered the fifteen thousand Serbian troops and tanks stationed in the region to crush the protests. Twenty-two people were killed, whom Milosevic decried as "separatists and nationalists." Around Yugoslavia, other ethnic groups watched in horror as the Serbs seized control over Kosovo's police, judiciary, and security forces.

That same month, a revolutionary wave to end communism was spreading throughout Central and Eastern Europe. In Yugoslavia, leaders in other regions—Croatia, Slovenia—began proposing that the country switch to a multiparty system and hold elections. Milošević resisted the idea. Instead, that June, on the six hundredth anniversary of a historic battle between the Serbs and the Ottomans—a key event in Serbian history—he delivered a speech in Kosovo to a crowd of roughly one million Serbs from all over Yugoslavia. It was the obligation of Serbs, he asserted, to "remove disunity, so that they may protect themselves from defeats, failures, and stagnation in the future." He vowed that Serbs would no longer compromise or suffer defeat. Reminding his listeners of the conflict with the Ottomans, he said, "Six centuries later, now, we are being again engaged in battles and are facing battles. They are not armed battles, although such things cannot be excluded yet."

To the rest of the people in Yugoslavia, the message was loud and clear. Tito's brotherhood and unity were officially over. Serb nationalist leaders were determined to regain what they believed was rightfully theirs—control over the whole country—at whatever cost. And Milošević's speech made clear that they were not taking armed force off the table. Within two years, a once-united Yugoslavia would violently disintegrate, and the world would come to know the term "ethnic cleansing."

IN THE EARLY twentieth century, when civil wars first emerged as an increasingly persistent problem, most were provoked by ideology or class. The Mexican Revolution, which began in 1910, centered on a series of armed struggles between wealthy landowners fighting to maintain power and a coalition of middle-class workers, peasants, and organized laborers calling for reform. Similarly, the Russian Revolution was driven by jarring political and economic inequalities as working-class Russians, serfs, and soldiers rose up against the monarchy to create the world's first socialist state. This pattern was repeated in China in 1927 when the Chinese Communist Party under Mao Tse-tung rebelled against the corrupt and authoritarian Nationalist government under Chiang Kai-shek. During the Greek Civil War in the late 1940s, families turned on each other in a clash that divided generations and pitted fathers against sons—one loyal to the monarchy, the other fighting to dismantle it and install a communist government. Like those before it, it was a classic battle over ideology, the dividing lines drawn down the middle between the left and right.

But starting in the mid-twentieth century, more and more civil wars were fought by different ethnic and religious groups, rather than political groups, each looking to gain dominance over the other. In the first five years after World War II, 53 percent of civil wars were fought between ethnic factions, according to a dataset compiled by James Fearon and David Laitin, two civil war experts at Stanford University. Since the end of the Cold War, as many as 75 percent of civil wars have been fought by these types of factions. Think of the many wars that have made headlines in the past several decades: Syria, Iraq, Yemen, Afghanistan, Ukraine, Sudan, Ethiopia, Rwanda, Myanmar, Lebanon, Sri Lanka. All were fought between groups divided along ethnic or religious lines, and oftentimes both.

So when researchers started studying civil wars more systematically, they focused on ethnicity as a potential cause, or at least an underlying source, of violence. Donald Horowitz, a professor at Duke University, published the first big study on the topic, which he called *Ethnic Groups in Conflict*. The book presented case after case of different ethnic and religious groups fighting one another throughout the twentieth century. All you had to do was look around the world and it appeared as if ethnic diversity within a country was a key factor in the outbreak of war. Yugoslavia was a prime example.

But the dawn of datasets cast doubt on this theory. While civil wars were increasingly being fought by ethnic factions, researchers such as Paul Collier and Anke Hoeffler at Oxford, and Fearon and Laitin at Stanford, found that ethnically diverse countries were not necessarily more prone to war than ethnically homogeneous ones. This was a puzzling finding: If diversity didn't matter, then why did so many civil wars break down along ethnic or religious lines?

This prompted the Political Instability Task Force to include more nuanced measures of ethnicity in their model. Instead of looking at the *number* of ethnic or religious groups in a country or the different types of groups, they looked at how ethnicity was connected to power: Did political parties in a country break down along ethnic, religious, or racial lines, and did they try to exclude one another from power?

The PITF had been collecting and analyzing data for years when they discovered a striking pattern. One particular feature of countries turned out to be strongly related to political instability and violence. It was an acute form of political polarization that they called "factionalism." Countries that factionalize have political parties based on ethnic, religious, or racial identity rather than ideology, and these parties then seek to rule at the exclusion and expense of others. The citizens of the former Yugoslavia could have organized themselves around their political beliefs—they could have coalesced around communism, as Tito had encouraged, or liberalism, or corporatism. Instead, leaders chose to activate ethnic and religious identities and then sought total domination.

For the next five years, the Political Instability Task Force evaluated and reevaluated the variable to make sure it was valid. Monty Marshall, one of the leaders of the PITF, together with Benjamin Cole, studied hundreds of countries and their level of factionalism over seventy years. They found that the biggest warning sign of civil war, once a country is in the anocracy zone, is the appearance of a faction. According to Marshall, "We studied every situation of factionalism and I'm completely convinced that [this is] the strongest variable outside of anocracy." Two variables—anocracy and factionalism—predicted better than anything else where civil wars were likely to break out.

Countries that are considered "factionalized" have identity-based political parties that are often intransigent and inflexible. Boundaries between them are rigid, leading to intense competition and even combat. The groups that are competing are often about the same size. In fact, it's this balance of power between the two groups that creates such fierce rivalry; the stakes of winning or losing are high. These parties can also be personalistic in nature, revolving around a dominant figure who often appeals to ethnic or religious nationalism to gain and then maintain power. A coherent policy platform is often absent.

Experts assess the level of factionalism in a country based on a five-point scale that goes from a fully competitive political system (5) to a fully repressed system (1). Factional systems receive a rating of 3. (A country's factionalism score tracks with its polity index score; as a nation becomes less politically competitive, it also becomes less democratic.) Fully competitive systems are countries with stable, non-ethnic political parties that regularly compete in elections and voluntarily transfer power when they lose (Germany, Switzerland, Denmark, Australia, Canada, and France are all classified as "competitive" political systems). On the other extreme, fully repressed systems tend to be highly authoritarian: Competition isn't possible and citizens have no ability to form factions even if they wanted to. If Milošević had tried to build a nationalist Serb party under Tito he would have been crushed. Political systems that are factionalized fall in the middle. In these countries, citizens are able to form political parties, but at least one party is based exclusively on ethnicity or religion, and when it gains power it favors its own constituents at the expense of everyone else. Factionalism is unyielding, grasping, identity-based politics, and it's often a precursor to war.

Think of the hundreds of armed groups in Syria, for example, that have waged war against one another largely along religious lines—Shia, Sunni, Alawite, Salafist—as well as the factions that fought one another in Lebanon's multifaceted civil war, whose members also self-segregated by religion (Sunni, Shia, Maronite Christian, Druze). All were seeking political power at the expense of the others. Other countries have been driven into armed conflict by competing ethnic groups, including Georgia—where Georgian, Ossetian, and Abkhazian populations fought for political power—and Rhodesia, where the Shona and Ndebele populations fought to depose the country's white-minority government.

Factionalism, experts have found, tends to emerge in a predictable way. Elites and supporters of a particular group sense an opportunity—perhaps a moment of weakness in the regime, or a demographic change that heightens their sense of grievance or vulnerability. They then encourage loyalty, not by rallying people around policy issues but by using words and symbols related to identity—religious phrases, historical rallying cries, visual images. (This is what Milošević did in Kosovo when he invoked the memory of the Ottoman battle.) The rhetoric gradually reinforces the group's separateness, creating tension in society, and if the faction is in power, it will often use its position to suppress rival factions: eroding due process and encouraging open militancy. This increases fear and distrust among rival groups, which further escalates tensions, leading groups to consider force to resolve differences.

This division then expresses itself in the political arena. Political parties begin to coalesce around ethnic, racial, or religious identity, rather than a particular set of policies—as Hutus and Tutsis did in Rwanda, for example, or as many political parties did in Ethiopia. It is a crafty way for leaders to cement both their following and their future. Identity-based parties make it impossible for voters to switch sides; there is nowhere for them to go if their political identity is tied to their ethnic or religious identity.

Politicians who have the support of a hardened faction, meanwhile, have the leeway to pursue a narrow tribal agenda that benefits them and their followers. Political parties and their leaders become predatory, seeking to rule at the exclusion and expense of other groups. They eschew compromise and structure institutions, such as the courts, to incentivize citizens to continue to act or vote based on their identity rather than their beliefs. Yugoslavia didn't erupt into civil war because Croats and Serbs and Bosniaks had an innate, primordial hatred for one another. It erupted because opportunistic leaders tapped into fears and resentments and then released small groups of well-armed thugs on the population in order to gain power.

Such political exploitation only compounds divisions across society. Citizens, feeling insecure about the future and losing confidence in their government to resolve conflict or serve the population as a whole, end up rallying around the most partisan parties—the ones who promise to protect their very lives, as well as their interests, way of life, and conception of what society should be. Politics goes from being a system in which citizens care about the good of the country as a whole, to one in which they care only about members of their group. Andreas Wimmer, a sociologist from Columbia University, analyzed data from almost five hundred civil wars (484) over the past two hundred years and found that once these types of political parties emerged in a country, the likelihood of civil war almost doubled. And if a country was an anocracy at the time, it was as much as thirty times more likely to become unstable.

WAR IS EVEN more likely, the experts found, if at least one faction in a country becomes a *superfaction*: a group whose members share not only the same ethnic or racial identity but also the same religion, class, and geographic location. In fact, war was almost twelve times more likely than if a group was more heterogeneous. Superfactions tend to form because ethnic groups often move together and settle in concentrated geographic regions where people interact exclusively with their own kind. (During World War II, many of the Serbs who survived the Ustashe attacks fled to the predominantly Serb Krajina region of eastern Croatia along the border with Serbia.) But they also tend to form because economic resources are distributed unevenly and often in favor of the group in power. This creates class differences that then merge with ethnic and religious differences.

This is what happened in Sri Lanka, where the Tamils and Sinhalese first divided themselves along ethnic lines and then found additional insurmountable differences in their religions—Hinduism versus Buddhism—and geographic locations, with the minority Tamils living in concentrated regions in the north and east. Tamil insurgents initiated war in 1983 in the hopes of establishing a separate state for themselves. Experts have found that the most volatile countries are the ones whose societies are divided into *two* dominant groups. Often, at least one of these groups is large enough to represent between 40 and 60 percent of the population. This kind of ratio is more likely to lead to armed conflict.

Serbs made up about 36 percent of Yugoslavia's population. They were Eastern Orthodox, used a Cyrillic script, were geographically concentrated in rural areas, and were generally poorer than the Croats and Slovenes. Croats, meanwhile, who made up about 20 percent of the population, were Roman Catholic, used a Latin script, and were more concentrated in cities along the coast. Tito had prevented such superfactions from forming in Yugoslavia when he restructured the government, remade geographic boundaries, and suppressed the political activity of religious institutions. His death, however, created both uncertainty and competition, not only over communism's future, but over who would control the instruments of state. Citizens, faced with a declining economy, sought security in the very layers of identity—ethnicity, language, alphabet, religion, class, geography—that Tito had sought to subvert. In the decade after his death, Serbs and Croats increasingly began seizing upon them in a way that snowballed, differentiating themselves not just by ethnicity and geography but also by religion, language, and economic standing.

This became especially obvious in the political sphere. Five months after Milošević's speech in Kosovo, the Berlin Wall fell, and soon afterward, the League of Communists of Yugoslavia dissolved as the ruling party. The Serbian and Croatian superfactions that had slowly been coalescing suddenly became potent. While Milošević had been busy rallying Serbs around history, class, and religion, Croatians, too, had been actively exploring nationalism. They had formed political parties around ethnic identity, most notably the ethno-nationalist Croatian Democratic Union (HDZ), whose leader, Franjo Tudjman, rejected a communist platform in favor of one espousing Croat values. Calling for a "Greater Croatia," Tudjman promised to end Serbian political dominance by declaring independence for Croats. In 1990, when free multiparty elections were held for the first time in each of the republics, citizens across Yugoslavia rejected communist politicians and instead voted heavily in favor of ethnic nationalist candidates. In Serbia, Milošević—who had changed his mind about elections—won the presidency handily. In Croatia, so did Tudjman.

Tudjman and his HDZ party immediately went to work securing power for their superfaction. They wrote a new constitution that deemed only ethnic Croats as "constituent people," effectively demoting all other minorities in Croatia to second-class citizens—including the sizable Serb population in the region of Krajina. Tudjman and HDZ leaders reinstated the traditional Croatian flag and coat of arms, which included symbols used during the Ustashe era, then began firing Serbs from public administration jobs and the police force, arguing that Serbs had held the jobs because of preferential treatment under Tito.

This unambiguous appeal to identity, and the predatory policies that followed, provoked fear among Serbs who lived in Croatia. Not only did symbols like the Croatian coat of arms spark memories of the murderous Ustashe, but Tudjman's prejudice seemed to provide hard evidence that what Milošević had been claiming all along was true: Serbs were under threat, and compromise with other groups was dangerous. The Croat and Serbian identities—no longer Yugoslavian but separate in lineage, language, and beliefs—were now irreconcilable. Violent clashes erupted in Krajina, as

Serb rebels armed themselves and, with the support of Milošević, began targeting Croatian police units. When Croatia declared independence a year later, in June 1991, Serbs in Krajina announced their intent to secede, so they could remain part of Yugoslavia. The national military, the Yugoslav People's Army (JNA), whose ranks were majority Serbian, immediately supported Croatia's Serb population and rolled in with tanks to occupy different regions of Croatia, expelling non-Serbs. Two superfactions were entrenched, each feeding on the other. It was war.

Perhaps there is no greater picture of the deep divide among superfactions than the attack on the Croatian city of Vukovar. A wealthy, mixed community of Croats, Serbs, and other groups—Hungarians, Slovaks, Ruthenians—Vukovar sat near the Danube, along the border with Serbia. Its people had lived in harmony since World War II, but as gun battles between rival militias broke out, Croatians and Serbians turned on each other. Armed civilians set fire to farms and homes in the region. Croatian police commandeered the Vukovar radio station; Serb militias blocked transport routes throughout the countryside, isolating the town. In the summer of 1991, the Serb-dominated JNA ramped up its offensive, laying siege to the city for eighty-seven days. Up to twelve thousand rockets and shells were fired into Vukovar each day in the most ferocious battle Europe had seen since the end of World War II.

What was remarkable about the attack was not just the fierceness of the ethnic rivalry between Croats and Serbs. It was that the battle, in many ways, embodied one of the greatest fault lines that tend to emerge among superfactions: the urban-rural divide, a divide that has become only deeper in an age of globalization and technological innovation. Cities are increasingly places of diversity, while rural areas are not. Urban areas are also increasingly younger, more liberal, more educated, and less religious. This divide is likely to only get worse, as more lucrative and dynamic industries—from finance and tech to entertainment—become more concentrated in cities. As younger people abandon rural communities, these communities will increasingly become dominated by less-educated manual laborers who often compete with new immigrants and who feel looked down upon by the urban elite. As Sarajevan Zlatko Dizdarević wrote in his journal about the war in his city, "We kept telling jokes at [the Serbs'] expense, while they came down from the hills, dragging one after another, hating us because we knew about soap and water, about washing our feet and wearing clean socks."

Urban citizens, therefore, tend to embrace change and multiculturalism, while rural citizens value stability and tradition. Perceptions of identity further differ because media outlets in the countryside are often fewer than in cities; in Yugoslavia, Serb-controlled radio was the primary means by which rural citizens received their news, and citizens exposed to its broadcast were significantly more likely to favor extremist nationalist parties.

By the time Vukovar finally fell, in November 1991, Serb paramilitaries had expelled at least twenty thousand non-Serbs from their homes. These Serb militias were composed of Serbs who lived outside the major cities. It was, in effect, a battle between rural citizens and the cosmopolitan elite—an assault on urban multiculturalism, according to Belgrade's former mayor. And the assault was particularly vicious: Serbian paramilitaries raped Croatian women and tortured and killed more than two hundred Croat civilians, burying them in mass graves.

Croatia would experience four more years of war, during which both Serbs and Croats sought to cleanse Krajina of members of the other faction through mass deportations and murder. Though the term "ethnic cleansing" would not become widely used until the Bosnian civil war several months later, it had already become a means to control and change the demographics and identity of an entire region. By the time Croatia won, some 220,000 Croats and 300,000 Serbs had been displaced, and approximately 20,000 people had died. The pattern would soon repeat itself, although with even more deaths, throughout the rest of Yugoslavia.

ETHNIC NATIONALISM, and its expression through factions, doesn't take hold in a country on its own. For a society to fracture along identity lines, you need mouthpieces—people who are willing to make discriminatory appeals and pursue discriminatory policies in the name of a particular group. They are usually people who are seeking political office or trying to stay in office. They provoke and harness feelings of fear as a way to lock in the constituencies that will support their scramble for power.

Experts have a term for these individuals: ethnic entrepreneurs. The term was first used in the 1990s to explain figures such as Milošević and Tudjman, but it's a phenomenon that has since occurred many times over, in all parts of the world. These instigators of war are often at high risk of losing power or have recently lost it. Seeing no other routes to securing their futures—because, perhaps, they are ex-

Communists—they cynically exploit divisions to try to reassert control. They foster identity-based nationalism to sow violence and chaos, using a strategy scholars call "gambling for resurrection"—an aggressive effort to provoke massive change, even against the odds.

Though the catalyst for conflict is often ostensibly something else—the economy, immigration, freedom of religion—ethnic entrepreneurs make the fight expressly about their group's position and status in society. Harnessing the power of the media, which they often control, they work to convince citizens that they are under threat from an out-group and must band together under the entrepreneur to counter the threat. They also work to persuade those in their group that they are superior and "deserve" to dominate, often with incendiary language. This is how, at a 1992 rally in the Rwandan city of Kabaya—two years before that country's civil war—Hutu politician Léon Mugesera came to tell supporters that Tutsis were "cockroaches," adding that "anyone whose neck you do not cut is the one who will cut your neck." In 2012, Sudanese president Omar al-Bashir exploited the distrust between Arabs and Africans in his country by describing his political rivals in similar terms: "The main goal should be liberation from these insects and to get rid of them once and for all, God willing."

In an unstable political climate—such as you would find during a political transition toward or away from democracy—multiple ethnic entrepreneurs often rise up at the same time, provoking and begetting others. They can work together, as when politicians and media pundits espouse the same extremism, or in opposition, using each other's actions and views as leverage to exacerbate division. The more layers of identity there are to exploit, as in the case of superfactions, the more fraught this division becomes. What often starts as a fringe movement takes on greater and greater momentum as entrepreneurs publicly question a rival faction's language, history, geography, and religion: A radio interview will lead to speeches that lead to viral social media posts that lead to rallies that lead to clashes on the streets. The fear-mongering rhetoric becomes self-sustaining and circular, as entrepreneurs use the words and actions of their rivals to confirm and inflame the beliefs of their own supporters.

Interestingly, average citizens are often clear-eyed about ethnic entrepreneurs: They know these individuals have their own agenda and are not telling the whole truth. Many Serbs in Krajina did not love Milošević—they didn't trust him, since they knew he had been a dedicated Communist just a few years earlier. It was clear to them that he was more power-hungry than purist; he had pursued pro-Serbian speeches only after realizing that nationalism was an easy way to secure a political base. But citizens become willing to show support if they feel a mounting threat—to their lives, livelihoods, families, or futures—and Milošević's rhetoric steadily sowed doubts. After purging disloyal journalists, Milošević and his government controlled the Politika publishing house, which owned over a dozen newspapers, radio stations, and TV stations—and this allowed him to ply his audiences with unrelenting messages of fear and suspicion. He appealed to Serbia's historic greatness and reminded listeners of past atrocities perpetrated against Serbs. When Croatia declared independence, the main TV station in Belgrade focused its coverage on the Serbs in Krajina who were now defenseless against the "dark, genocidal urges of the Croats."

And yet Milošević would not have succeeded in convincing the Serbs living in Krajina—particularly in peaceful, multiethnic cities like Vukovar—to fight for him had Tudjman not helped confirm their worst fears. Unlike Milošević, Tudjman was a true believer: He'd become a Croatian nationalist a decade earlier, before it was popular or practical to be one. As a history professor at the University of Zagreb, he had glorified the medieval roots of the Croatian nation, denied the severity of the Holocaust, and talked about the "positive achievements" of the Ustashe regime. In the 1980s, after Tito's death, he had traveled to the United States and Canada to raise money from exiles and émigrés with Ustashe sympathies so that he could build a nationalist political party back home. When he finally founded the HDZ, he embraced slogans such as "God and Croats." He started the Croatian News Agency to rival Milošević's growing media empire, arguing over the airwaves that his people needed to free themselves from Serbs and the dirty, dark Muslims of Yugoslavia and join their real home, which was Europe.

If citizens come to believe there is a chance, no matter how small, that the opposition could destroy them, they will turn to a leader who offers them protection, no matter how unscrupulous. Thus, when Tudjman adopted the Croatian coat of arms and purged Serbs from his government, Serb residents of Krajina interpreted their sudden loss as confirmation that Milošević's warnings were true. Likewise, by the time Milošević ordered the Serb-dominated Yugoslav army to move into Croatia, Croatians had begun to believe that their way of life, championed by Tudjman, was under attack. Both factions eventually became convinced that violence was the only way to save themselves and their culture.

·   ·   ·

POLITICIANS ARE NOT the only ones who stoke division over identity. There are also lesser ethnic entrepreneurs: business elites (perhaps seeking brand loyalty), religious leaders (seeking to expand their congregation), and media figures (seeking to grow *their* audience and revenue). These elites also stand to lose in a changing society. And in the former Yugoslavia, it was this secondary network that helped expand the war beyond Croatia.

As violence overtook places like Vukovar, citizens watching in neighboring Bosnia and Herzegovina were confident they would be spared such conflict. The republic had the highest percentage of people who claimed that they were "Yugoslavs" on the national census. Bosnia's capital, Sarajevo, was a modern, diverse city where Croats, Serbs, and Bosniaks had lived together peacefully for decades. Education levels were high, as were intermarriage rates. Six years earlier, in 1984, Sarajevo had hosted the Winter Olympics.

"I was sure that what happened in Croatia wouldn't happen to us," recalled Berina Kovac, who lived in Sarajevo. She had just finished business school at the time, and her husband, Daris, practiced law. Though Serbs, Croats, and Bosniaks had different religious heritages, just about everyone in Sarajevo was secular. Berina and Daris had a wide circle of friends and interesting jobs, and they had never given much thought to anyone's ethnic identity. They were Muslim, but everyone in Bosnia spoke Bosnian, and they all basically looked the same. "We are culturally very, very close," explained Daris. "Looking for differences is almost ridiculous. We are ethnically the same. There is no family in Bosnia without a mixed marriage."

The idea of separate and hostile ethnic identities, therefore, needed crafting—and a host of ethnic entrepreneurs, both inside and outside Bosnia, now rose up to do their part, dominating the airwaves, headlines, and public debates. In Sarajevo, Daris and Berina started to hear Milošević's message—that Serbs needed to live together in one Yugoslavia—echoed by Radovan Karadžić, a former psychiatrist who had founded the Serb Democratic Party in Bosnia and was eager to become Milošević's bullhorn in that region. When elections were held, in November 1990, the citizens of Bosnia and Herzegovina coalesced around three ethnonationalist parties—Muslim, Croat, and Serb—none of which were willing to compromise. "The facts started to get twisted and rearranged," recalled Daris. "There was so much misinformation." In 1991, the Serbian Pale TV company took over Sarajevo's transmitters to broadcast nationalist news to the Serbian areas of Bosnia and Herzegovina. Newscasters mocked Muslim prayers, went on in blackface, made fun of rape victims, held up knives, and spread false news that Serbian children were being fed to the lions at the Sarajevo Zoo.

Before long, the citizens of Bosnia and Herzegovina had stopped calling themselves Bosnians. Instead, they were Bosnian Serbs, Bosnian Croats, or Bosnian Muslims (Bosniaks). Berina recalled the moment she became aware of the shift: at a friend's wedding. The ceremony took place in the town of Višegrad, and many of hers and Daris's school friends had gathered to celebrate. "At weddings in Bosnia, we often sing traditional songs called Sevdalinka, which are old love stories from Ottoman times," she said. "They're usually sad, with a lot of emotion." But when Berina and most of the others began to sing, another friend—a Serb—interrupted. "Enough of these!" he said. "Enough of these Turk songs!"

Berina choked up at the memory. "You see, we are Muslims," she said. "But we are also the same ethnicity as Serbs and Croats. When somebody really wants to insult us deeply, they tell us we are Turkish. It eliminates our Bosnian identity and our roots." In the rhetoric of Milošević and Karadžić, Muslims were a remnant of Ottoman rule, under which Serbs were considered lower status and were rarely permitted to own land. After the outburst at the wedding, the whole room went quiet, and the singing stopped. Driving home that night, Berina and Daris were deeply unsettled. "We knew," Berina said, "that people were changing."

Five months after the wedding, in March 1992, the president, a Bosniak, organized a referendum on Bosnia's independence. Serbian politicians in both Serbia and Bosnia vehemently opposed the vote; they wanted Bosnia to remain part of a Serb-dominated Yugoslavia. When the result came back overwhelmingly in favor of independence, bombings and shootings broke out between Bosnian Serb armed units in the region and the majority-Bosniak government forces. Within a few weeks, Bosnian Serbs—supported by the Yugoslav People's Army (JNA)—held almost 70 percent of the region's territory. Hoping to seize the capital, too, Serbian militias stationed themselves in the hills around Sarajevo and, under the leadership of politician turned military leader Karadžić, initiated a siege that would last four years.

Even then, the work of Yugoslavia's ethnic entrepreneurs was not yet done. In May 1992, Bosnian-Croat politician Mate Boban and Karadžić—with the backing of Tudjman and Milošević—agreed to divide Bosnia into two parts, one Croat and one Serb, excluding the Bosniaks entirely. ("We are bound to the Serbs by brotherhood in Christ," Boban was heard to say in justification, "but nothing at all binds us to the Muslims except the fact that for five centuries they violated our mothers and sisters.") This predatory differentiation would prove brutal: Over the next three years, Serbs and Croats raped, massacred, and exiled thousands of Bosniaks. In Višegrad, where Daris and Berina had attended the wedding, more than 1,500 Muslim men, women, and children were rounded up and killed, then thrown off its famous bridge over the Drina River. Others were burned alive in their homes. (At the start of the war, 63 percent of Višegrad was Bosniak. Today it is almost entirely Serb.)

Berina remembers the moment she realized Bosnia had descended into civil war. She was home on maternity leave with her second son, and had just hired a nanny. One day, the nanny, a young woman from a suburb in the hills, announced matter-of-factly that she had noticed paramilitary groups outside Sarajevo. "We see their fires when they cook their meals," she said. But they were just vigilantes, she continued, not the military, so she wasn't afraid.

Berina, however, had heard the rhetoric of Karadžić. She knew what the militias were after. A few weeks earlier, at a party for her new baby, a work colleague named Sasha had pulled her aside and told her that he had been recruited by members of the Serb Democratic Party. They were going to give him weapons. "I didn't believe him," recalled Berina. "His best friend was Muslim. He'd married a very nice girl and they had just had a baby around the same time as us." Berina shook her head. "He was trying to tell me that something was coming."

A month after the party, Sasha was killed. Berina got the news one day while sitting with a friend. Overwhelmed with sorrow—for her colleague, for his widow, for their newborn—she burst into tears. Her friend looked at her angrily. "Where was he when he was killed?" she asked. On the barricades, replied Berina. "Yes, but on which side?" pressed the friend. Berina sighed. With the Serbs, she said. "Are you out of your mind?" her friend cried. "He was there with a weapon that could have killed your husband!"

Then Berina understood. "It was them or us," she said. And she stopped crying.

SUPERFACTIONS ARE INCREASINGLY a threat even to stable democracies. For more than five decades, India, the world's largest democracy, has succeeded despite widespread poverty, illiteracy, immense ethnic diversity, and a struggling economy. Hindus comprise the vast majority of India's population—around 80 percent. Muslims constitute about 14 percent, while Christians, Sikhs, Jains, Buddhists, and nonreligious people together make up the remaining 6 percent of the country. A strictly secular state whose constitution guarantees freedom of religion helped a diverse population live in relative peace. But this began to change in 2014, when a right-wing Hindu nationalist political party, the Bharatiya Janata Party, came to power. Frustrated over the economy and the corruption of the ruling party, known as Congress, Indians had voted overwhelmingly for change.

The 2014 election was the first time that any single party had won a majority in India in thirty years. The leader of the BJP was Narendra Modi, who was named prime minister. Modi, who as a youth had served as a foot soldier for the RSS—a paramilitary organization dedicated to the idea that all Indians belonged to a Hindu race—immediately embraced an identity-based political agenda. He pursued his party's hard-line vision of an exclusionary Hindu nation, granting key government positions to extremists, including Yogi Adityanath, the chief minister of Uttar Pradesh, India's largest state. This was a man who had called Muslims a "crop of two-legged animals." Modi went on to put extremists in charge of cultural and educational institutions, where they were able to change place names and control school curricula, effectively writing Muslims out of India's cultural history. In 2019, he rescinded special status for Jammu and Kashmir, India's only majority-Muslim region. He also created a path to Indian citizenship that excluded Muslims.

India fits into a pattern that is proliferating around the world. One of the great worries of the twenty-first century is not only that democracy is declining, but that it is declining in some of the largest democracies around the world. Whereas politics in these places once revolved primarily around differing visions of governance—taxes, the social safety net, healthcare, education—politicians and their parties are increasingly coalescing around identity: religious views, racial backgrounds, urban and rural values. Ethnonationalist leaders have risen to pull citizens away from secular social ideals toward identity politics. They have done this, in part, to exploit the human tendency to band together and protect their own during times of rapid change and uncertainty. As factors like anocracy and factionalization increase—no longer just in former autocracies but also now in weakening democracies—so too do the number of places where civil war might erupt.

Nowhere is this shift more evident in democracies than in the rise of predatory political parties. In India, Modi has ruled in favor of Hindu interests at the expense of the country as a whole, tightening his political power by attacking three core components of India's electoral democracy: free and fair elections, freedom of speech, and freedom of association. Modi has used state powers to investigate and arrest opposition leaders on trumped-up charges of bribery and corruption. His government declared its intention to black-list journalists who distributed "fake news"—meaning stories critical of the administration—and has enforced laws against large gatherings. When both Muslims and progressive Hindus took to the streets to protest against his citizenship law, Modi had his security forces unleash a brutal crackdown.

Despite all this, Modi and his BJP party's popularity increased, allowing them to win the 2019 general elections with an even larger absolute majority than in 2014. This is because he knows how to foster, and take advantage of, growing superfactions in his country, playing up external threats and stoking nationalism to create alarm. In New Delhi, neighborhoods that were once integrated are now splintering along religious lines. Hindu mobs have beaten Muslims in the streets with sticks. Though the economy has not improved under his tenure, as he promised it would—unemployment is at a forty-five-year high—Modi has received especially high levels of support from upper-caste Hindus, and from citizens in those parts of India that have experienced tensions between Hindus and Muslims. The violence, which Modi appears to encourage, serves his party by alarming more moderate voters and convincing them that his claims about Muslims are true. It also conveniently diverts attention from the economy.

This pattern is repeating itself in democracies the world over. In Brazil, former army captain Jair Bolsonaro won the presidency in 2018 by capitalizing on an urban-rural divide that was exacerbated by race and class. Bolsonaro launched his campaign against a backdrop of unrest—the popular former president, Luiz Inácio Lula da Silva, was convicted on charges of corruption, there was an economic downturn,

and gang killings were surging—by appealing to the fears of
Brazilians in order to win. According to Brazil's most recent
census, the country had shifted away from being majority
white (today, 52 percent of Brazilians are African, Asian, Indigenous Indians, or multiracial), and Bolsonaro exploited
this racial fault line by invoking the specter of lawlessness.
His vitriol for minorities could be found in all of his propos-
als. He sent forces into largely Black and mixed-race slums to
curtail crime, supported police responsible for homicides
while on duty, encouraged land development in areas populated by Indigenous communities, and denounced university
quota systems for Black and ethnic Brazilians. He even referred to African refugees coming to Brazil as "the scum of
the earth." The strategy succeeded. Bolsonaro eventually secured the presidency thanks to the votes of white men and
wealthy Brazilians.

For average citizens, ethnic and racial propaganda can
often feel like the ramblings of idiosyncratic radicals who
simply have an ax to grind. Many dismiss the diatribes—on
talk radio, partisan TV networks, in tweetstorms—as mere
rhetoric or entertainment. When Radovan Karadžić warned
on Bosnian TV that "one constitutional nation is going to
disappear," many residents of Sarajevo rolled their eyes. "We
called him a crazy psychiatrist and a clown," said Berina. But
the fault lines these entrepreneurs seek to cleave can then
reveal themselves, swiftly and surprisingly, as intractable:
with a surprising election, and an unexpected takeover.

Daris often thinks back on all the propaganda of those
days, and the alarmism that Milošević promoted among
Serbs. "I didn't know at the time that this was a big, big danger," he said. "We were all just good citizens, following what
we believed. It was when everyone split, gravitating toward

their own group, that I realized this hadn't happened in [a matter of] days and months. It had been happening over years." Indeed, citizens do not organize themselves into narrow, self-serving factions overnight. Often, they are unaware that the factionalism is even happening; they are certainly unaware of how dangerous it can be. They think they are ensuring their survival, defending their families and communities from emerging threats, pursuing what they believe is rightfully theirs—what is good for them and their country.

When war erupted, Daris and Berina were so shocked that they thought the conflict would be short. After electricity and water had been shut off for two weeks in Sarajevo, Berina left with the couple's two babies to stay in Macedonia near her brother. She packed few clothes because she thought she would be gone only a couple of weeks. But she and Daris would not see each other for three years, and Berina would never return to Sarajevo. It was not until the end of December 1994 that their application for refugee status to the United States was approved. By then, their homes in Sarajevo had been taken and there was no going back. In February 1995 they arrived in the United States, five months before the genocide of eight thousand Muslim men and boys in Srebrenica and its surroundings.

"I couldn't believe it," said Daris. "The war is a surprise to me even now." But outside observers had seen the warning signs of Yugoslavia's collapse several years earlier. In October 1990, the CIA issued a report predicting that Yugoslavia would fall apart within two years' time, and that a civil war was a distinct possibility. One reason, the agents noted, was that its citizens were steadily organizing themselves into separate ethnic factions. Their prognosis proved right. Large-scale war broke out a year and a half later.

They were right about something else: that the Serbs would be the instigators. The document made clear that Milošević and Serbian extremists would be the masterminds of the violence and they would use nationalism to mobilize the Serbs behind them. Average citizens may not foresee civil war or anticipate who is likely to start it. In fact, oftentimes they are looking in the wrong direction, as ethnic entrepreneurs try to place the blame on some other group to deflect attention from themselves. But experts who study civil war know where to look—and it is often not the group most people would suspect.

CHAPTER 3

THE DARK CONSEQUENCES OF LOSING STATUS

Datu Udtog Matalam was someone that everyone loved in central Mindanao, a mixed Muslim-Catholic region in the southern Philippines. To Muslims, he was a World War II hero who had fought against the Japanese, a wise religious leader, and a fair arbiter of disputes among the local people. To the Catholics who had settled in the area from the north, he was known for his commitment to uniting the two groups and maintaining peace. No one expected him to help start one of the world's most persistent civil wars.

Matalam was born at the turn of the twentieth century in a small river town about two days by canoe from Cotabato City, the capital city on the coast. As the son of the region's sultan, Matalam became a "datu" (chief), in keeping with the Muslim community's tradition of inherited leadership. The Philippines was still a U.S. colony, and like others in his position, Matalam served as both a traditional leader to the locals and as a representative of the Manila-based national government. In 1914, he rose to assistant superintendent, overseeing Muslim activity in the farming community, and then to school inspector, ensuring that Muslim children were enrolled in colonial schools. Matalam was part of the first generation of datus who accepted colonialism. Indeed, he built his career by working with colonial administrators rather than against them.

Following his service in World War II, Matalam was appointed governor of Cotabato, the third largest administrative region in lush, tropical Mindanao. But even as he established himself as a strong and efficient administrator, keeping the province fiscally sound, the world was changing around him. In the past, outsiders hadn't interfered much with the Moro people, as those native to the region are called. The population was sparse, and the locals were known as fierce and well-armed fighters. They were hard to subjugate. In 1946, the Philippines became independent, and Catholics increasingly began to migrate to Mindanao from the more populous north, encouraged by the central government, which wanted to develop Mindanao's rich land for the economic benefit of the nation as a whole. The government transferred legal ownership of the best agricultural land to Catholic settlers and gave them loans to grow crops, along with other assistance not granted to local inhabitants. Many Muslims were physically thrown off land they had occupied for generations. So many Catholics migrated to Mindanao to take advantage of these benefits that by 1960, Catholics greatly outnumbered indigenous Muslims living in most parts of the region. Matalam went along with this, reaping the political and financial rewards of Manila's favor. Meanwhile, a new generation of datus emerged. Unlike Matalam and his peers, these rising leaders had been born in the postcolonial era. They had some college education, usually acquired in Manila, and most were professionals (lawyers or educators). They were also more likely to have Catholic, not Muslim, wives. Their connection to Mindanao and its culture was not as strong.

And then in 1965, Ferdinand Marcos ran for president. After winning a bitter election in 1965, Marcos, a Catholic, moved to replace opposition officeholders with those who were loyal to him. Matalam went from a career as a revered provincial leader, a man at the center of power and influence, with deep knowledge of Muslim people and their culture, to a man with no power at all.

Matalam's loss of political stature became painfully clear when an off-duty agent working in the Justice Department shot Matalam's firstborn son in the summer of 1967. It was a terrible blow, made even worse when his colleagues failed to offer condolences. In a society where family and communal ties meant everything, Matalam understood that this was a deep insult. Matalam reacted by establishing the Muslim Independence Movement several months later, on May 1, 1968. He published a manifesto calling for all Muslim areas in the southern Philippines to secede and form their own "Republic of Mindanao and Sulu."

The Moro people had a long history of demanding independence; in 1935, decades after the United States had claimed the Philippines, more than a hundred leading datus and local Muslim leaders sent a written declaration to Washington insisting on eventual separation from the country. They feared that they would lose their religion and culture within the much larger Catholic population and wanted to be free to worship and live as they saw fit. "Once our religion is no more," they wrote, "our lives are no more." Matalam's manifesto, however, caused a spiral of fear-driven responses. Throughout the Philippines, the press carried headlines like "War Brews in Cotabato." Marcos sent troops to the area. And some Catholic families chose to sell their property and leave Mindanao in anticipation of a Muslim uprising.

Matalam bowed out of the Muslim Independence Movement fairly quickly and instead retired to his farm. But the creation of the MIM had the unanticipated effect of inflaming both Muslims and Catholics, setting off a dangerous dynamic that propelled the country toward war. By early 1969, the MIM was training Muslim guerillas, likely financed by the Malaysian government, and by March 1970, sectarian violence had begun to break out. Catholic gangs began assaulting Muslim farmers and burning their homes, which provoked Muslims to retaliate. From there, conditions worsened, with Muslims accusing the government of encouraging Christian violence and Muslims forming their own armed bands. It was the classic "security dilemma," in which people, fearing violence, arm themselves in self-defense, but in the process convince their enemy that they want war.

But what really tempted all-out conflict was Marcos's decision to declare martial law in September 1972. The president portrayed the order as necessary to prevent further violence between Catholics and Muslims, but in fact he was using the unrest in the south to consolidate his own power. Marcos demanded that all Filipinos turn in any weapons within a month, including the swords and knives that were culturally important to Muslim men. Anyone who attempted to resist would be "annihilated."

A few days before the weapons deadline, hundreds of armed Muslims attacked Marawi City, just north of Cotabato. About five hundred to one thousand Muslim rebels simultaneously attacked Mindanao State University, the provincial headquarters of the Philippine national police, and the Pantar Bridge, which connected Mindanao to the neighboring province. This was the first time the rebels fought as the newly constituted Moro National Liberation Front (MNLF), a more extreme militant group that had split off from the MIM. The rebels failed to spark a popular uprising, but they fled to the southern part of the island, where they reconsolidated and continued the war, now using guerrilla tactics. The group first attacked government forces, then widened its targets to include civilians, as well as Roman Catholic bishops and foreigners who the group kidnapped for ransom.

Over the years, the group has spawned numerous offshoots, often battling with an even more militant radical Islamist group, the Moro Islamic Liberation Front (MILF). Almost every president since Marcos has attempted to end what has become one of the world's longest civil wars, offering various degrees of autonomy for the region. In most cases, the government has not delivered on its promises, and various Moro groups have continued to fight, leading to the deaths of more than one hundred thousand people.

WHAT EXPLAINS THE revolt of the Muslims in Mindanao? Part of the answer lies in the fact that the Philippines was becoming more of an anocracy. When Marcos took office in 1965, he inherited a political system that was almost democratic (with a polity score of +5). In the space of four years, he eroded it to the point where it was firmly in the anocracy zone (+2), and close to the tipping point for civil war. He did this by weakening individual and minority rights, expanding the power of the government, diminishing the rule of law, curtailing the independence of the judiciary, and removing numerous checks on presidential power. The Philippines had also become highly factionalized. Since the end of World War II, politics in the country had been dominated by local political clans (Catholics in the north and Muslims in the south) competing with each other for patronage from Manila.

And yet, there are lots of disgruntled ethnic groups living in factionalized anocracies, and most do not rebel. For example, Ethiopia has more than eighty different ethnic groups, practicing at least five major religions. But only a handful have ever organized to take on the government. And Indonesia is one of the most ethnically diverse countries in the world, with over 360 tribal and ethno-linguistic groups, yet only four—the Ambonese, the East Timorese, the Acehnese, and the Papuans—have ever taken up arms. What is it about some groups that make them so motivated to fight?

Over the past three decades, scholars have zeroed in on an answer, drawing on several large datasets on nearly a century of civil wars. One of the first things they found, perhaps unsurprisingly, was that the groups that turn violent generally feel left out of the political process. They have limited voting rights and almost no access to government positions; they tend to be excluded from political power. But the most powerful determinant of violence, researchers discovered, was the *trajectory* of a group's political status. People were especially likely to fight if they had once held power and saw it slipping away. Political scientists refer to this phenomenon as "downgrading," and while there are many variations on the theme, it is a reliable way to predict—in countries prone to civil war—who will initiate the violence.

The Moro people of Mindanao had been gradually disempowered over the course of colonial rule and then again after they were incorporated into the Philippines. They had once governed their home region; their datus, sultans, and rajahs had made and enforced the laws, determined how land would be allocated, and decided which cultural practices would be honored. It was only after the Philippine government began to encourage the much larger Catholic population to migrate to Mindanao—displacing the Muslim locals—that the violence began. Matalam and many of his fellow Muslims were being downgraded, and the evidence of their lost status in terms of land ownership, job opportunities, and political power was all around them. They were losing their livelihood and their culture to people they saw as interlopers on their land.

Many modern civil conflicts follow this pattern. A study of eastern European countries over most of the twentieth century by Roger Petersen, a political scientist at MIT, found that a loss of political and cultural status fueled conflict in that region. Donald Horowitz, the political scientist at Duke who has studied hundreds of ethnic groups in divided societies, found the same thing. The ethnic groups that start wars are those claiming that the country "is or ought to be theirs." Downgrading helps to explain why it was the Serbs and not the Croats or Bosniaks who started the civil war in Yugoslavia. Like the Moro people of Mindanao, the Serbs saw themselves as the rightful heirs to their country. They had once ruled themselves. They were the largest ethnic group in Yugoslavia when it was created, and they occupied most of the high-ranking positions in the Yugoslav military and bureaucracy. The Serbs initiated violence in Croatia and then Bosnia because they understood that they would lose significant power if both regions were allowed to secede. The Sunnis started the war in Iraq because they, too, had lost power after the American invasion. The Moro people, the Serbs, the Sunnis—all of them were downgraded, and all of them turned to violence.

Downgrading is a psychological reality as much as it is a political or demographic fact. Downgraded factions can be rich or poor, Christian or Muslim, white or Black. What matters is that members of the group *feel* a loss of status to which they believe they are entitled and are embittered as a result. In case after case, resentment and rage appear to drive a faction to war. The Stanford scholars Fearon and Laitin found that when the Sinhalese of Sri Lanka tried to make Sinhala the official language of the state, it "immediately caused a reaction among Tamils, who perceived their language, culture, and economic position to be under attack." There is almost always a sense of injustice, a belief that whoever is in power doesn't deserve to be there and has no right to that exalted position. Downgrading is a situation of status reversal, not just political defeat. Dominant groups go from a situation where, one moment, they get to decide whose language is spoken, whose laws are enforced, and whose culture is revered, to a situation where they do not.

Human beings hate to lose. They hate to lose money, games, jobs, respect, partners, and, yes, status. The psychologists Daniel Kahneman and Amos Tversky demonstrated this in a series of experiments in which they asked subjects if they would be willing to accept a gamble where they had a 50 percent chance of winning, say, $100, but an equal chance of losing $100. They found that most people refuse the gamble. The reason? Human beings are loss averse. They are much more motivated to try to reclaim losses than they are to try to make gains. People may tolerate years of poverty, unemployment, and discrimination. They may accept shoddy schools, poor hospitals, and neglected infrastructure. But there is one thing they will not tolerate: losing status in a place they believe is theirs. In the twenty-first century, the most dangerous factions are once-dominant groups facing decline.

THE PEOPLE OF Abkhazia, in Georgia, can trace their history in the region back to the sixth century B.C. They consider themselves the Indigenous people of the Caucasus and have no homeland outside of Georgia. Their small slice of this region, which lies just south of Sochi, is strikingly beautiful—mountains rising out of the emerald green waters of the Black Sea. Abkhazians have experienced periods of autonomy, but these have been followed by longer periods of conquest. Their rulers have included the Roman Empire, the Byzantine Empire, neighboring Georgians, the Ottomans, and the Soviet Union. Despite these occupations, Abkhazians have retained their distinct culture, in part through an unwritten code of ethnic lore called *apsuara* ("Being Abkhazian"), which is passed down from generation to generation.

The twentieth century nearly brought the death of that culture. The first threat came when Joseph Stalin tried to wipe out ethnic Abkhaz rule by executing the Abkhaz elite, imposing elements of Georgian script on the native language, and moving tens of thousands of ethnic Georgians into Abkhazia. In the late 1980s, a second threat emerged when the Soviet Union began to dissolve and Georgians pushed for independence. Like the Moro people in the Philippines, Abkhazians feared that Georgians would remove the protected minority status they had secured after Stalin's death.

When that fear came true, they took up arms. In July

1992, a little more than a year after Georgia gained independence, the Abkhazian people rebelled against incursions on their culture and language by declaring their own independence, triggering a conflict in which Abkhazian fighters, with Russian military support, sought to cleanse the region of ethnic Georgians. Thousands of Georgians and Abkhazians were killed, with many more wounded and displaced. By the end of the conflict, Abkhazians, who had once composed 19 percent of the local population, made up half of it. Control of the region was once again theirs.

Groups like the Abkhazians are what experts call "sons of the soil," and many of the downgraded ethnic groups that go to war fit this mold. They are indigenous to a region or play a central role in its history. They think of themselves as the rightful heirs to their place of birth and deserving of special benefits and privileges. These groups are dominant because of majority status or because they inhabited or conquered the territory first. They consider themselves the "native" people, and all others who have settled there, or whose mother tongue is not the territory's main language, are declared "outsiders." In one study of civil wars since 1800, ethnic groups that fall into the "sons of the soil" category rebelled at a rate of 60 percent, roughly twice the rate (28 percent) of those that did not. These groups are dangerous because they tend to be more capable of organizing a resistance movement, and their sense of grievance can be overwhelming. Both are primary factors in who sparks civil wars.

In their dominance, sons of the soil can easily lose sight of their privilege because it is so pervasive; it just seems natural. Their elders are the leaders of the country or their region; they make political decisions for the population as a whole. Their language is the "official"—and often only—state language. It is their cultural practices and symbols that are celebrated, their holidays that are recognized, their religious schools that get preferential treatment. But when a new group begins to arrive in large numbers, the ground shifts. Outsiders bring their own culture and their own languages. In time, they can swamp the local population. Papuans, for example, lived their whole lives in the rich forests of Western New Guinea, entirely self-sufficient politically and economically. All this changed when they were forced to join Indonesia, and migrants from Java, Sulawesi, and Bali began to move in. In 1965, Indigenous Papuans formed the Free Papua Movement, seeking independence. In 1971, the group declared a "Republic of West Papua" and drafted a constitution. And in 1977, the group began a low-intensity guerrilla war, first targeting the main foreign-owned copper mine in the region, and then expanding to attack Indonesia's military and police, along with non-natives living in West Papua. Since the war began, an estimated one hundred thousand Papuans have died.

Native speakers of a country's official language enjoy a huge economic advantage over citizens whose language is not recognized by the state. Francisco Franco, dictator of Spain from 1939 to 1975, understood this. One of the ways Franco consolidated power was to elevate Castilian over other languages, declaring it Spain's only official tongue. He then banned citizens from speaking Basque, Catalan, Galician, or any other language in public. Newborns were not allowed to be given regional names, and dialects were no longer allowed to be taught in school or used to conduct business. Language, it turns out, is strongly tied to the identity of a nation, and it determines whose culture ultimately dominates. One of the main fears of ethnic Russians in the

Donbas region of Ukraine was that the new nationalist government would make Ukrainian the official language of the state to the exclusion of Russian. It's hard to compete for well-paying jobs if you don't speak the language. Controlling access to education, especially higher education, is another way to elevate one ethnic group over another. The same is true of access to civil service jobs, which are some of the most steady and lucrative positions in a country. When people face the loss of such privileges, they can become deeply aggrieved and motivated to resist.

In democracies, sons of the soil groups are most commonly downgraded by simple demographics—some combination of migration and differences in birth rates. Democratic elections are ultimately head counts, and, as Donald Horowitz observed, "numbers are an indicator of whose country it is."

In Assam, a mountainous region of northeast India known for its tea plantations, local Assamese (who were predominantly Hindu) watched as ethnic Bengalis (who were predominantly Muslim) immigrated into their area from neighboring Bangladesh starting in 1901, steadily increasing their numbers throughout the century. The first migrants were brought in by the British colonial government intent to settle the sparsely populated and fallow land. Britain encouraged two types of Bengalis to migrate: low-skilled farmers who were predominantly Muslim, and educated Bengali Hindus who could help Britain administer the government as civil servants. But migration continued even after India became independent in 1947, to the increasing dismay of the Assamese. Between 1971 and 1981, the region took in as many as 1.2 million migrants, the highest influx of immigrants per capita of any region in India.

The local Assamese grew increasingly worried. Their first concern was cultural. As more and more immigrants arrived from Bangladesh, Bengali increasingly became the language of choice—at home, in business, and in government—and Bengali culture became a more prominent part of everyday life. The Assamese didn't want to become a linguistic minority in their own homeland. The second concern was political. The Assamese won control over the regional government when the British left, and they knew they would be able to maintain power only if they remained a majority of the population. The influx of immigrants threatened to turn them into a minority and end their control over the state. The third concern was economic. Assam was far less populated than neighboring Bangladesh, and much of the land was unoccupied and ripe for new settlers. The migrant farmers quickly began to cultivate and occupy these lands, while the better educated Bengali Hindus gained coveted jobs in the bureaucracy. As time passed, these immigrants enjoyed a higher standard of living than the native Assamese.

The Assamese responded by organizing and creating an ethnic faction that attempted to exclude Bengalis and Muslims from what they saw as their rightful space. Assamese political leaders made Assamese the official language of the state in 1960, making it harder for Bengali speakers to compete for state jobs. They also made it the language of instruction in state schools, creating an additional barrier for Bengalis. Finally, Assamese were given preferential treatment in state administrative jobs. But the migrants kept coming. And when Assam's election commissioner reported an unexpectedly large increase in new names on the electoral rolls (most of them Bengalis) prior to the 1979 parliamentary elections, the Assamese suddenly saw their worst fears confirmed: By allowing these immigrants to enter the country and vote, the national government in Delhi—over a thousand miles away—appeared to be encouraging the transformation of Assam.

For the first time in its history, the proportion of Bengalis was increasing, while the proportion of Assamese was declining. Bengalis had long outnumbered Assamese in the region's major cities, where Bengali had become the dominant language. In the words of Myron Weiner, late professor at MIT and an expert on anti-immigration movements, "For the Assamese, the towns of Assam had become centers of alien life and culture." But the change was now evident in the rural areas, as well, leaving no place untouched.

The surge in new voters revealed not only that the region's demographics were rapidly changing, but that the political landscape was likely to change as well. One of the main problems for the Assamese was that it was quite easy for foreigners to become citizens and vote. At the time, India granted citizenship to three categories of people: those who were born in the country, those who had at least one parent who was born in the country, and those who had lived in India for at least seven years. So if someone had entered Assam illegally from Bangladesh but had lived there for almost a decade, he or she could become a citizen. Not surprisingly, India's dominant political party—the Congress Party—encouraged both legal and illegal immigration because many of these foreign nationals, including many Bengalis, supported the party; the Assamese did not.

For the Assamese, fixing the problem was difficult. It was not clear how the government, even if it were willing, could reliably determine who of the many foreign-born Bengalis were legal: India did not have a single identity card that included citizenship status, and large numbers of mostly poor people did not even have birth certificates. Legal Bengalis were indistinguishable from non-legal Bengalis.

The Assamese responded by organizing a resistance movement.

In 1979, student leaders from Assam's middle class created the All Assam Students' Union (AASU), which articulated a new set of demands: Foreign nationals who had arrived between 1951 and 1961 would be given citizenship. The many immigrants who had come between 1961 and 1971 would be relocated to other parts of India but would not be given citizenship. Everyone who had arrived after 1971 would be deported. It was, in effect, a form of ethnic cleansing, whereby the Assamese would ensure their political and cultural dominance. (Their goal was ostensibly to expel "illegal immigrants," but Bengalis as a whole—whether legal or illegal—were targeted.) The government ignored these demands, leading to the formation of an even more radical group—the United Liberation Front of Assam (ULFA)— which used militia techniques to target civilians through bombings and assassinations of officials and businessmen. The ULFA even threatened secession. But the governing Congress Party had no incentive to deport Bengalis—who tended to vote for Congress Party candidates—or even restrict immigration. It certainly had no incentive to grant independence.

The leaders of the AASU—who were mostly urban, middle-class, and well educated—used fear and xenophobia to convince rural Assamese that Bengali immigrants were taking valuable land and jobs, creating an undue burden on resources, and exhausting the farmlands. They called immigration "an invasion" and portrayed the movement as a struggle for cultural, political, and demographic survival. Conspiracy theories proliferated that Bangladesh was encouraging migration in order to eventually make Assam part of their state.

At first, the targets of Assamese ire—Bengali immigrants, both Hindu and Muslim—remained quiet, despite increasing acts of violence against them. But by 1980, they had begun to form their own groups to oppose deportation. The All Assam Minority Students Union (AAMSU) was formed in May 1980, demanding that all immigrants who had come to Assam prior to 1971 be granted citizenship and that harassment against minorities stop. Violent clashes broke out between AASU and AAMSU supporters, and there were reports of terrorist attacks on state officials and state property.

A critical moment in the lead-up to more organized violence was the 1983 election. Would the government compromise with the resistance movement and remove post-1971 immigrants from the electoral rolls, as the Assamese had demanded? When the government announced that it would continue to use the electoral rolls from 1979—those that included post-1971 immigrants, who the Assamese considered illegal—violence escalated. Assamese leaders called for a boycott of the election, and fighting broke out. According to Sanjib Baruah, an expert on Assam, the violence reflected the belief that the election was Assam's "last struggle for survival."

Manash Firaq Bhattacharjee, a young Bengali boy who was attending school at the time in the town of Maligaon in central Assam, recalls what it was like. There were roadside memorials on the road to Assamese "martyrs" that included signs written in Assamese saying, "We will give blood, not country." There were also torchlit marches at night by the local Assamese. "We would sit in the darkness listening to them chant 'Foreigners get out' as they passed by our house."

Violence reached its peak on February 18, 1983. At eight in the morning, local peasants and farmers from the area around a town called Nellie surrounded several Muslim villages, pounding drums and chanting "Long Live Assam." Using machetes, spears, and homemade guns, they massacred as many as four thousand Bengali immigrants. Most of the people killed were women and children because, unlike the men, they could not outrun their attackers. Hundreds of thousands of additional individuals fled, many ending up in refugee camps.

The Nellie massacre, as it came to be called, was the desperate act of a downgraded population, one that felt threatened by a new demographic reality.

ECONOMIC FACTORS HAVE long confounded researchers who study civil war. Early statistical analyses seemed to find a correlation between per capita income and violence, and the wars themselves seemed to bear this out: Citizens in poor countries were much more likely to fight than citizens in rich countries. But when scholars took into account measures of good governance—including citizen participation, the competitiveness of elections, and constraints on the power of the executive—economic variables became much less important. Income inequality, which many considered a red flag for war, proved to be the opposite. As James Fearon wrote in a 2010 report for the World Bank, "Not only is there no apparent positive correlation between income inequality and conflict, but if anything, across countries, those with more equal income distributions have been marginally more conflict prone."

This does not mean that economic factors are irrelevant or that income inequality doesn't matter. After all, the economy plays a huge role in determining which ethnic groups feel left behind or diminished. Economic inequities seem to aggravate existing anger and resentment. They also make it easier for those with wealth to suppress those without. The citizens living in the Donbas region of eastern Ukraine lost their president in 2014 at the same time that they were losing manufacturing jobs. They were both politically excluded and uncertain about their economic future. The Assamese saw better jobs being given to newcomers. Similarly, the Moro people did not rise up until the government expropriated Muslim-owned lands and transferred them to Catholic settlers and foreign-controlled plantations. Local Muslims were politically powerless to respond. "Loggers came to despoil our beautiful hills and mountains," complained one Moro leader in 1992. "They were followed by permanent settlers. And together they drove us . . . deep into the forest."

Economic discrimination need not be deliberate for resentment to be felt. Modernization, the process by which rural, traditional societies are transformed into urban secular ones, favors citizens with the education and skills to compete in a mechanized world. Globalization has shifted manufacturing jobs to less developed countries while benefiting service-oriented workers (who happen to be disproportionately women). Sons of the soil tend to be disproportionately affected by these tectonic shifts: They frequently live in rural areas, far from a country's economic, cultural, and political centers. They also tend to be poorer and less educated, and so more vulnerable to competition. The advantage they originally had—of being first on the land—not only disappears; it becomes a handicap. As the world moves on without them, they feel forgotten and ignored.

In the lead-up to the Yugoslavian civil war, Serbs in Bosnia were poorer than the region's Croats and Bosniaks and had long resented the greater wealth of their city-dwelling compatriots. Serbs were looked down upon as being quasi-peasants, even though they were the more politically and militarily powerful group in a larger Yugoslavia. The Moro people were hurt economically by the loss of their land, but also because they could not compete with the better educated migrants moving in.

Indeed, immigration is often the flashpoint for conflict. Migrants come into a country and compete with poorer, more rural populations—sons of the soil—fueling resentment and pushing these groups toward violence. It is especially alarming, then, that the world is entering an unprecedented period of human migration, in large part due to climate change. As sea levels rise, droughts increase, and weather patterns change, more and more people will be forced to relocate to more hospitable terrain. By 2050, the World Bank predicts, over 140 million "climate migrants" will likely flee Southeast Asia, sub-Saharan Africa, and Latin America. Experts have also warned that climate change is likely to lead to scarcity of resources, which could also fuel conflict. The Syrian war is an early example of this. Between 2006 and 2010, Syria experienced a devastating drought that, combined with the government's discriminatory agricultural and water-use policies, resulted in significant crop failures. In search of opportunity, roughly 1.5 million people—mostly Sunni—migrated from the countryside to

Syria's cities. In the capital city of Damascus, the center of Christian Alawite power, these Sunnis were viewed as enemies of President Bashar al-Assad, and before long felt discriminated against because of their religion, creating resentment. When the government began to award water well-drilling rights on a sectarian basis, that anger intensified, accelerating the march to war.

Climate change will likely lead to a greater number of natural disasters that will disproportionately affect poorer, rural groups and create economic crises. It is during these times that citizens will feel the pain of discriminatory political and economic policies and inept governments most acutely. A 2016 study published in the *Proceedings of the National Academy of Sciences* found that armed conflict was more likely in ethnically fractionalized countries after climate-related disasters. Between 1980 and 2010, conflicts in almost a quarter of these countries coincided with climatic calamities that acted as threat multipliers. If a country was already at risk of civil war, natural disasters tended to make things worse. In a world where drought, wildfire, hurricanes, and heat waves will be more frequent and more intense—driving greater migration—the downgraded will have even more reasons to rise up.

CHAPTER 4

WHEN HOPE DIES

Irish Catholics in Northern Ireland were used to loss. It started when the Anglo-Normans invaded their land in the twelfth century, continued through centuries of British colonization, and escalated in the seventeenth century when Britain encouraged Scottish Protestants to sail across the North Channel and settle there. By 1652, all Catholic-owned land had been confiscated, and by 1690, Ulster-Scots—as the Scottish Protestants were then called—were a majority of the population in the north.

The most painful loss came in 1922, when Irish Catholics who lived in the north were not given independence with the rest of Ireland. Britain created the Irish Free State—a newly independent country—but left the six counties of the north under British control. Even worse, Westminster revised the borders of Northern Ireland to ensure that Protestants—who identified as British—would make up two-thirds of the population. This meant that Protestants, not Catholics, would dominate the region's new semi-autonomous government, controlling education, law, social services, industry, and agriculture—and Westminster was happy to allow them to rule as they pleased so long as they maintained law and order. Not only were the Irish Catholics of the north cut off from the rest of Ireland, but they were now a minority in their own native land. By the time Northern Ireland was created, their "conquest" by foreign interlopers was complete.

Protestants proceeded to enact a series of undemocratic laws designed to exclude Irish Catholics from power and deny them the best jobs, the best land, and the best homes. Northern Ireland, according to Sir James Craig, its first prime minister, would be "a Protestant state" whose chief aim was to serve the interests of the Ulster majority. One person, one vote did not exist in Northern Ireland despite it being part of the United Kingdom. In order to vote in local government elections, a person had to own a home, an arrangement that disproportionately benefited Protestants. Protestant-dominated city councils determined how housing was allocated; they favored Protestants and made Catholics wait years to own property. The councils also controlled government jobs, and Catholics often only had to mention their name or address to be rejected. Gary Fleming, an Irish Catholic, explained the system: "It was basically designed to treat my parents, me, the rest of my family and our families to come, as second-class citizens." So while Irish Catholics in the newly independent Irish Free State to the south enjoyed freedom and equal rights before the law, Irish Catholics in Northern Ireland did not. Instead, they saw their circumstances decline over time, and they grew bitter.

Britain's decision to let Protestants rule Northern Ireland as they liked allowed them to create a partial democracy that excluded one-third of the population. Irish Catholics did not have the same right to compete for power as Protestants. They were not offered the same protections or given the same resources. The system also had a larger effect. By favoring Protestants, it created two superfactions, because Catholics and Protestants in Northern Ireland were also divided politically, economically, and geographically. Protestants voted almost exclusively for unionist parties that wanted to remain part of the United Kingdom. Catholics voted almost exclusively for nationalist parties that wanted to become part of Ireland. Protestants dominated the professional and business classes, owning the majority of businesses and large farms. Catholics tended to be unskilled laborers working on the docks or in construction or on small farms. Catholics were poorer than Protestants and lived in separate enclaves in cities and separate regions in the country, and people from both communities sent their children to segregated schools. If you asked Protestants why Catholics were poorer, they generally believed it was because Catholics were lazy, irresponsible, and had too many kids. They did not think that systemic discrimination was to blame. But if you were Catholic, you understood that a vicious cycle had taken hold.

By mid-century, Northern Ireland had all the underlying conditions for civil war: partial democracy, competing identity-based factions, and a deeply rooted native population that was excluded from politics. But Catholics had felt the sting of discrimination and poverty for years—since 1922, in fact—and had resisted violence. They believed and hoped that their lives would improve.

That all changed in the summer of 1969. On August 12, more than ten thousand Protestants marched along the edge of the Bogside, an overcrowded working-class Catholic neighborhood in Derry, a town on Northern Ireland's northwestern border. Hundreds of Protestants joined the march every year to commemorate the 1689 Siege of Derry, when

Protestants repelled the attack of the deposed Catholic monarch James II. This year's march, however, was meant to be particularly provocative. The Protestants wanted Irish Catholics—who were increasingly protesting against discrimination—to know their place. The marchers passed by the neighborhood as the men, women, and children from the Bogside watched. Pennies were thrown at the Catholic onlookers. Stones were thrown at the marchers. Soon, the Protestant-dominated Royal Ulster Constabulary (RUC), arrived and forced their way into the streets of the Bogside using batons and armored vehicles. The Catholics of the Bogside fought back, inspired in part by the civil rights protests in the United States. They continued to throw rocks at the police and the marchers as they entered the neighborhood. Soon they began to hurl homemade petrol bombs from roofs in what quickly became a riot. Residents of the Bogside weren't surprised when the RUC returned the next day in combat gear and gas masks and blanketed the neighborhood with tear gas, and when the "B Specials"—masked paramilitary forces made up entirely of Protestants—were deployed to the scene. The Catholics knew the lengths to which Protestant leaders would go to hold on to their power.

On the third day of the riots, three hundred British soldiers arrived in Derry. Northern Ireland's Protestant prime minister had requested them, fearing that his police were losing control. This was the first time London had directly intervened in Ireland since the island was partitioned, and the Catholics of the Bogside were thrilled. They welcomed the soldiers, convinced that they would protect them from the Protestant mobs and police forces. But that's not what happened. The citizens of the Bogside soon understood that the British soldiers were there to help the Protestants, not the Irish Catholics. The soldiers were brutal, engaging in counterinsurgency tactics, conducting raids and searches of Catholic homes, and clashing with demonstrators. They treated the Catholics as the enemy, not as citizens with equal rights.

By the time a truce was called three days later, more than a thousand people had been injured, buildings had burned, and six people had been killed in riots that had broken out around the country (five in Belfast and one in Armagh). The Battle of the Bogside was the end of Irish peace. Catholics quickly organized protests around the region, and both sides became increasingly paranoid about the other's intentions. According to journalists Patrick Bishop and Eamonn Mallie, "Catholics were convinced that they were about to become victims of a Protestant pogrom; Protestants that they were on the eve of an IRA insurrection." British troops attempted to disarm Irish neighborhoods in Belfast, and the Irish responded with more riots. The Provisional Irish Republican Army (IRA)—an Irish Catholic paramilitary organization—was formed to defend Catholic areas, but by October 1970 it had gone on the offensive. Initially it set off bombs in shops and businesses, but then it started to target British soldiers. It wanted Britain and its army out.

On January 30, 1972, a little more than two years after the first battle in the Bogside, British soldiers once again forced their way into the neighborhood. This time—on a day that has become known as Bloody Sunday—they shot twenty-six unarmed civilians, fourteen fatally. Irish Catholics had been peacefully protesting the Ulster government's decision to jail Catholics without trial. British soldiers responded by shooting protesters in the back as they attempted to run away. "The Troubles," as the civil war came to be called, had begun.

CATHOLICS DIDN'T WANT war. They had peacefully protested for decades to try to gain fair political representation and equal treatment in Northern Ireland. They had written letters, formed civil rights associations, and demonstrated in the street. They had held open-air meetings, sit-ins, and at one point in 1968 occupied Northern Ireland's parliament in Belfast. In January 1969, they had organized a "Long March" from Belfast to Derry modeled on the march from Selma to Montgomery in the United States. But Protestants, through it all, had shown no interest in compromise. Nothing changed.

Before British soldiers arrived, Catholics had hoped that London's more democratic government would rein in the worst tendencies of Northern Ireland's Protestants. They knew that the region's Protestants were determined to exclude them from power, but they also believed that Britain's leaders were better, and fairer, than their own highly partisan, pseudo-democratic leaders. The British had not been the best overseers—they had been absentee rulers, distracted by other parts of their empire—but Catholics trusted that at the end of the day, the British would protect them.

The counterinsurgency tactics of the British soldiers revealed the truth, and it was at this point that the Catholics lost hope. By the time British soldiers began to bash heads in the Bogside, it was clear that peaceful protests would not work. All attempts to change the system, according to former Sinn Féin president Gerry Adams, "had failed." Catholics saw that the British soldiers viewed them as separate and distinct—not to mention a threat because of their large numbers. The soldiers came to protect the Protestants, relative newcomers in a land the Irish had inhabited for millennia. Once Britain took the side of the Protestants and targeted the Catholics, hope died. It was all the evidence they needed to finally understand: Without violence, their fate was sealed.

Scholars know where civil wars tend to break out and who tends to start them: downgraded groups in anocracies dominated by ethnic factions. But what triggers them? What finally tips a country into conflict? Citizens can absorb a lot of pain. They will accept years of discrimination and poverty and remain quiet, enduring the ache of slow decline. What they can't take is the loss of hope. It's when a group looks into the future and sees nothing but additional pain that they start to see violence as their only path to progress.

People are fundamentally hopeful. They want to believe that their life, no matter how bad, will get better with effort. Hope makes the present more bearable and creates incentives for even the downtrodden to work within a system rather than burn it down. But hope requires uncertainty. Citizens can be hopeful because they don't know how the future will unfold and, in their minds, they can anticipate something better. Irish Catholics were hopeful because they believed the British government would eventually step in to help them. Once British batons came out, there were no more illusions. Hope shrinks in the face of blatant government brutality. The Moro people of Mindanao lost hope that life would get better when President Marcos declared martial law and forcibly took their land and weapons. And the Catholics of Northern Ireland lost hope for peaceful reform when British soldiers treated them as intruders on their own soil.

As groups lose faith in the existing system, extremists often step in to offer an alternative. In Northern Ireland, it was the Provisional IRA. "People were in a hopeless situation until then," said the influential Irish republican Danny Morrison, "and the IRA provided people with hope."

NO ONE EXPECTED a civil war in Syria. Syrian citizens had quietly watched as Arab Spring protesters flooded the streets in Tunisia, Egypt, Libya, Bahrain, and Yemen, demanding change. They had seen Tunisia's president, Zine al-Abidine Ben Ali, step down weeks after protests began, and Egypt's longstanding dictator, President Hosni Mubarak, resign in the face of demonstrations. But they did not immediately join them because their own president, Bashar al-Assad, had masterfully used fear and intimidation to divide Syrians and aggressively suppress dissent.

And yet, the underlying conditions were there. Assad consistently promised his people that he would reform but then failed to deliver. He cemented sectarian politics by favoring his own Alawite tribe over the larger Sunni majority. This disparity—between Alawite and Sunni, rich and poor, urban and rural—revealed itself during a drought between 2006 and 2010. Most Syrians were Sunni and lived in the rural east of the country, but they were ruled by a wealthy urban Alawite elite who lived along the Mediterranean coast. When hundreds of thousands of rural Sunnis streamed into the poorer neighborhoods of Syria's cities in the wake of the drought, Assad and the government did little to help them. Sunnis living in these new "misery belts" watched as government services and jobs were funneled to Alawite neighborhoods at their expense. They watched as government security forces harassed anyone who stepped out of line. (Youths in Daraa, inspired by other Arab awakenings, had been rounded up, tortured, and killed after writing in graffiti: "The people want the fall of the regime.") Still, the uprisings in other countries gave Sunnis hope. If Tunisians, Egyptians, and Libyans could protest against their dictators, maybe they could, too.

When the protests began on March 15, 2011, Syrians were optimistic. They believed that their protests would work just as the protests in Tunisia and Egypt had worked. Initially, their demands were modest. They wanted the freedom to express themselves, the freedom to form opposition groups, and freedom from arbitrary arrest and detention. But the demands became more ambitious over time. Soon the protesters were demanding improved education, an end to sectarian discrimination in employment, and an end to pervasive government corruption.

Daraa, a city in southwestern Syria about a ten-minute drive to Jordan and a half-hour drive to Israel, became the early center of protests, sparked by the murder of the young graffiti artists. (When the children's parents went to the station to inquire about them, they were told: "Forget about your children. Make more. And if you don't remember how, bring us your wives and we'll show you.") On March 18, after coordinating on Facebook, Sunnis gathered at a mosque, one of the few places off-limits to military intelligence services. *"Hurriyeh, Hurriyeh!"* ("Freedom, freedom!"), they cried. They didn't hide their faces or their phones as they videotaped the scene. They were confident that they would be safe inside the mosque. As they exited, thousands of demonstrators were waiting outside to join them. They weaved their way through the streets toward the regional government headquarters. They were tasting freedom for the first time and it was exhilarating.

But soon the protesters were met by Assad's police and civil defense forces, who shot tear gas at the crowd. The protesters responded by throwing rocks. Tear gas and rocks, tear gas and rocks. In the late afternoon, the protesters began to see men without identification, wearing masks and black clothing. They were part of Assad's elite security force, the General Security Directorate, and their goal was to disperse the crowd. At first, they fired their weapons into the air, but when that failed, sharpshooters started to pick off demonstrators one by one. The Sunnis sought refuge in a nearby mosque, which they turned into a hospital and meeting place. They wrote out their demands on white bedsheets that they hung outside the building. They still had hope that Assad would negotiate.

On the night of March 23, five days after the protests began, the lights in Daraa suddenly went out and cellphone service was cut. Soldiers armed with assault rifles stormed the mosque and opened fire on the peaceful protesters. Dozens were killed. A doctor and a paramedic who rushed over in an ambulance were killed by sharpshooters stationed outside. Sunnis across Syria responded to the attack by organizing protests across the country. "We were only chanting in the streets," said one man in Aleppo. "We could have chanted for the rest of our lives without anyone even paying attention to us. But when the regime started attacking us, a lot of people who were on the sidelines started to join and protest, too. Because of the blood. Blood is what moves people."

It didn't take long for the Sunnis to lose hope. Syrians hadn't known how President Assad would respond to the protests, but they believed he would be open to reform.

After all, he was soft-spoken and erudite, had been partly educated in Britain, and claimed he was a new breed of reformist Arab leader. It was reasonable to think that he would be willing to compromise. But Assad's response removed any doubt about his intentions. A week later, on March 30, he appeared on television to address Syrians for the first time since protesters took to the streets. A physician named Jamal gathered with a group of doctors and nurses in front of a TV in a hospital in Hama with a mix of anxiety and hope. Advisers to the president had hinted that Assad was planning to announce reforms and that imprisoned Daraa protesters would be released. Instead, Assad blamed the uprising on "terrorists" with extremist motives who were being supported by Syria's enemies. He offered no concessions. "If you want war," he said, looking straight into the camera, "we are ready for war." Jamal and his colleagues, even those who supported Assad at the time, were shocked. "We couldn't believe what we were hearing," he said.

Assad's belligerence set off an even greater surge of protests. The speech, according to Middle East expert David W. Lesch, was "the one that sent Syria in a trajectory toward a catastrophic war." The demonstrations grew, becoming larger and angrier, and police and security forces became increasingly violent, beating protesters, firing live ammunition, and arresting tens of thousands of people. By the end of April, Daraa became one of the first cities to be surrounded by the Syrian army. Tanks were brought in and snipers were placed on rooftops. Security forces were dispatched to confiscate food and shut off power. Protesters responded by arming themselves. By June, some security officers had begun to defect, refusing to kill civilians, and by the end of July, a group of these officers announced that they had formed the

Free Syrian Army (FSA). By September 2011, government troops repeatedly had to fend off rebel militia attacks. Sunnis had hoped that their protests would lead to a better life. But Assad's speech and his brutal crackdown on Sunni citizens destroyed their faith in the future.

Protests per se don't lead to civil war. In fact, protests are fundamentally about hope. Average citizens leave their homes and go out into the streets with sheets and placards and begin to chant because they believe their government will listen to them and their lives will improve. If people thought their government would shoot at them, they would either stay at home—too afraid to act—or they would come out guns blazing. Going out in the street with nothing but a cellphone is an act of optimism. It means that citizens still believe that the system will correct itself. If Assad had reformed in the face of protests, Sunnis would have packed up their signs and returned home.

It's the failure of protests that eliminates hope and incentivizes violence. That's when citizens finally see that their belief in the system has been misplaced. In Israel, Palestinians engaged in nonviolent protests for years—participating in mass demonstrations, work stoppages, strikes, and boycotts—but made no progress in negotiations with the government. The result? "People exploded," said Radwan Abu Ayyash, a Palestinian journalist. This helps explain why violence tends to escalate in the aftermath of failed protests. Protests are a last-ditch effort to fix the system—the Hail Mary pass for optimists seeking peaceful change—before the extremists take over.

This is why civil wars are often preceded by years of peaceful protests. It's not that protesters transform themselves into soldiers. It's that the more militant members of an unhappy group come to feel that no other option exists and begin to mobilize armed resistance. "Remember," Brendan Hughes, a member of the Provisional IRA, pointed out, "Irish people for hundreds of years have campaigned, fought elections, have tried every method to bring about their just aims. And every single time, the reaction from the British has been with violence." It was only when peaceful protest didn't work that the more extreme members of the faction were able to gain the upper hand. That's when the kidnappings, assassinations, and bombings began. The most violent phase of the Arab-Israeli conflict—the second intifada—began only after the Camp David talks between Israeli prime minister Ehud Barak and Palestinian leader Yasser Arafat broke down in 2000. Algerians, for their part, had long engaged in general strikes, boycotts, and protests against systematic discrimination by the French before more militant citizens turned to terror. Failed protests are a sign that moderates and their methods have failed.

Both democracies and autocracies can handle protests with relative ease. When demonstrations broke out in Tiananmen Square in 1989, the Chinese government could carefully monitor student leaders, wiretap their meetings, and identify, capture, and punish anyone who participated in the protests. The government was also able to declare martial law and send as many as 250,000 soldiers to Beijing. Protests in the face of such overwhelming authoritarian power have great difficulty gaining ground. Healthy democracies are also less likely to experience failed protests since the system itself creates multiple avenues for compromise and accommodation.

But protests can be particularly destabilizing in anocracies, which are often too weak institutionally to root out extreme elements and respond in a measured way, and too fragile and unstable to guarantee real political reform. Countries in the middle zone provide the perfect conditions for the formation of violent extremist groups.

Protests can also cause problems in countries whose populations have factionalized. According to Erica Chenoweth, an expert on nonviolent resistance at Harvard, governments are more likely to negotiate—and less likely to crack down—when a protest group includes a wide assortment of a country's population. The larger and more mainstream a protest group, the more likely it is to gain support from politicians. Ethnic or religious factions, especially superfactions, are not diverse—they represent one element of society and thus create fewer incentives for the government to compromise. One of the reasons why the civil rights movement in the United States was successful was that it was a true coalition. It included powerful allies in government, including President Kennedy and Attorney General Robert F. Kennedy, as well as white liberals across the country. The same was not true of the Black Panthers, who were hunted down by the FBI in part because they were an exclusively African American organization. Ethnically exclusive factions that are out of power are easy to ignore politically. And they are easier to punish.

Protests are a warning sign. They indicate that citizens believe their system still works but is troubled. Since 2010, protests have surged around the world. There have been more protests in the last ten years than at any time since data began to be collected in 1900. In 2019 alone, political protests erupted on every continent and across 114 countries, including Chile, Lebanon, Iran, Iraq, India, Bolivia, China, Spain, Russia, the Czech Republic, Algeria, Sudan, and Kazakhstan. Protests have increased the most in the countries deemed "free" by the nonprofit research institute Freedom House, including the liberal democracies of Western Europe and the United States.

What's disturbing is that these protests are failing at a higher rate than ever before. In the 1990s, peaceful protests had a 65 percent success rate, meaning that they resulted in the overthrow of a government or the gaining of independence. But since 2010, the success rate has dropped to 34 percent. "Something has really shifted," acknowledged Chenoweth. And this leaves the world's oldest and freest democracies increasingly vulnerable.

FAILED PROTESTS CREATE dangerous moments in a country ripe for civil war. Elections can have the same effect. Ivory Coast's transition to democracy and its series of early elections in the 1990s provide a good example. After gaining independence from France in 1960, the country was ruled by President Félix Houphouët-Boigny until 1993. Papa Houphouët, as he was affectionately called, helped to develop the coffee and cocoa industries. He also instituted a system of quotas designed to prevent any one ethnic group from politically dominating the others. The result was an economically prosperous and politically stable country.

All that changed when the country held its first multiparty election in 1990 and politicians, including President Houphouët-Boigny, began to use ethnic identity to generate political support. The president ran against the opposition leader Laurent Gbagbo, who accused Houphouët-Boigny of favoring the interests of his tribe, the Baoulé. The Baoulé were one of Ivory Coast's largest ethnic groups and were concentrated in the south of the country. Houphouët-Boigny's party, in turn, accused Gbagbo's party of representing the interests of foreigners and ethnic groups from the north. Ethnic factionalism continued to plague the 1995 elections, with the opposition boycotting what they said were unfair electoral policies. Those in power excluded members of the opposition faction from government and further aggravated the north-south divisions in the country. Citizens of the north eventually rebelled in September 2002, in large part because they were excluded from power.

Elections are potentially destabilizing events in highly factionalized anocracies—especially when a downgraded group loses. In a study of global conflict between 1960 and 2000, researchers found that ethnic groups were more likely to resort to violence after they had lost an election. Elections preceded the civil war in Burundi in 1993, when the minority Tutsis—who controlled most of Burundi's military—revolted after losing in the country's first multiparty presidential and legislative elections. Ukraine's civil war began in 2014 immediately after Petro Poroshenko won a special election designed to replace President Yanukovych, who was forced to resign in the face of mass protests. Yanukovych's Russian-speaking supporters in eastern Ukraine reacted by declaring independence and taking up arms. And in the United States, it was the election of President Abraham Lincoln, the first president able to win power without the support of Southern Democrats, that convinced Southerners to secede.

Like protests, elections per se are not dangerous. In fact, most citizens are eager to participate in elections, seeing them as a hallmark of a democracy. Over 80 percent of Ivory Coast's citizens participated in the elections that preceded its civil war. The same was true in Burundi, where over 93 percent of registered voters participated in their 1993 election. Elections give people hope. They focus citizens' attention on the long game; people believe that even if they lose today, they could win tomorrow. And the more hopeful citizens are about the future, the more likely they are to try to peacefully work within the system.

But if the losing side believes that it will never gain or regain power, then hope disappears. America's 1860 election was devastating to Southern Democrats because a candidate was able to win the White House without a single electoral vote from the once-powerful South. Republicans—whose platform included abolishing slavery—no longer needed to cater to Southerners in order to win office.

Elections provide important information about the future and thus reduce uncertainty. First, they shed light on a group's ability to compete. Two consecutive losses indicate that a party does not have the votes to gain control and is thus likely to be excluded from power. Elections can be particularly destabilizing in winner-take-all systems. Presidential majoritarian systems are heavily biased in favor of the majority group in a country; if one party or faction cannot gain the support of a majority of citizens, it will never gain power. The Ivory Coast has the same presidential system as the United States, where the president gains power based on majority rule and is not only the head of state but also the head of government and the commander in chief of the armed forces. Winning an election in this type of system is particularly consequential. Afghanistan, Angola, Brazil, Burundi, Indonesia, Nigeria, the Philippines, Rwanda, and Venezuela all have the same type of presidential system, and all have experienced a high degree of political violence. One study revealed that all of the democracies that experienced civil war between 1960 and 1995 had majoritarian or presidential systems. None of them were based on proportional representation.

Ethnic factionalization in majoritarian systems makes elections even more fraught. When citizens coalesce around an ethnic faction, their electoral support becomes fixed and predictable. Everyone knows the likely result of an election because they can look at the country's demographics and accurately guess how people will vote. Unless demographics change, the political system changes, or the faction becomes more inclusive, there is little reason to hope that political outcomes will be different.

Elections also provide information about the ruling party's willingness to play fair. They reveal whether those in power are truly committed to democracy. If one side can manipulate the results of an election, and democratic checks and balances are too weak to enforce a peaceful transfer of power, then hope in fair competition is lost. The 1948 elections for a new assembly in Algeria was so heavily and openly rigged by French settlers to guarantee their victory that the phrase *election algerienne* became synonymous with unfair elections. A fraudulent election shows excluded groups that they have no conventional means to gain or regain access to authority now or in the future. The ability to rig an election makes a mockery of hope.

Elections themselves can lead to factionalization, encouraging politicians to "play the ethnic card"—a strategy whereby they consciously generate deep feelings of ethnic nationalism and grievance in order to mobilize the support necessary to bring themselves to power. The campaigning that leads up to an election also provides the critical infrastructure for rebellion, which requires groups to pull less politically engaged citizens into a larger movement. Campaigning for office is the process of uniting people under a particular ideology to compete for political power. In some ways, it is the peaceful precursor to armed mobilization. Once elections take place, party leaders have a ready-made band of supporters, some of whom may be willing to fight. The line separating an organized political faction from an armed faction can be dangerously thin—particularly in countries where weapons are easily accessed and distributed.

Elections can strengthen a country, bringing citizens together in a meaningful act of civic duty. They can renew faith in institutions and reaffirm the power of a person's vote. But they can also provide painful evidence of a group's declining status, causing its members to lose hope for future representation—and convincing them they have nothing to lose by fighting.

CIVIL WAR IS sometimes traced to a single incident: a trigger. Sometimes it's an election, sometimes a failed protest, sometimes a natural disaster. In the Philippines, it was the isolated massacre of Muslim army recruits by other service members. In Lebanon, it was the killing of a Christian man on his way to his son's wedding. Guatemala's civil war escalated in part after a devastating earthquake revealed just how inept and corrupt the government was. But these flashpoints have long backstories. Most of the time, civil wars start with small bands of extremists—students, exiled dissidents, former members of the military—who care more deeply about power and politics than the average citizen.

The men, women, and children who rioted in the Bogside didn't start Ireland's civil war. The war was started by the radicals who created the Provisional Irish Republican Army. The founders of the paramilitary group, including Seán Mac Stíofáin, Seamus Twomey, and Joe Cahill, had met for decades before planning their first attack. In the American Civil War, so-called Minute Men militias—who modeled themselves after the Revolutionary War–era patriots—began to crop up throughout the South as early as the 1830s, decades before the Civil War broke out. These militias were organized by small groups of radical secessionists, almost all of whom were white plantation owners, who wanted to build support for Southern independence. It took them years to rally the white working class to their cause. Even in Syria—which most people think of as an explosive civil war that emerged from the Arab Spring protests—the organizers of the Free Syrian Army had been meeting in Turkey for almost six months before they started to fight. By the time average citizens are aware that a militant group has formed, it is often older and stronger than people think.

Governments can become inadvertent recruiters for militant groups. Multiple studies have found that if a government responds with brutal force to the early mobilization of an extremist group, local support for even unpopular groups increases. A government's attack on its own citizens has the power to transform the man on the street into a radical. Abu Tha'ir, an engineer in southwestern Syria, described how this worked in Daraa. When government forces stormed the al-Omari mosque after the city's lights were shut off, killing dozens of Syrians, local villagers heard about the shooting and came to Daraa to beg for peace. Instead of ignoring them, or talking with them, the security forces opened fire, slaughtering civilians from every village in the region. "If I ever write a book about this," Abu Tha'ir said, "I'll call it *How to Spark a Revolution in One Week.*"

Early militants, of course, know that civilian deaths at the hands of the government can tip conflicts into all-out war; they see the opportunity in a harsh government response and plan accordingly. Hamas has stored weapons in schools, mosques, and residential neighborhoods, goading the Israeli military to bomb them. Carlos Marighella, a Brazilian Marxist revolutionary, urged fellow militants to target government forces in order to provoke a violent reaction. He believed that if the government intensified its repression against Brazilians, arresting innocent people and making life in the city unbearable, citizens would turn against it. In Northern Ireland, Tommy Gorman, a member of the IRA, recalled that the British Army and government, with their harsh tactics, "were our best recruiting agents." And in Spain, the violent separatist group ETA was not particularly popular with Basque citizens until President Franco allowed the Germans, during the Spanish Civil War, to viciously bomb Basque villages. According to one expert on the Basques, "Nothing radicalizes a people faster than the unleashing of undisciplined security forces on its towns and villages." That's why civil wars appear to explode after governments decide to play hardball. Extremists have already embraced militancy. What changes is that average citizens now decide that it's in their interest to do so as well.

Violent extremists can also take advantage of peaceful protest movements to sow chaos. Erica Chenoweth calls these people violent conflict entrepreneurs. They try to hijack a social movement by nudging it toward violence. Partly this is designed to provoke a harsh counterattack by the gov-

ernment, but partly it is designed to generate fear and insecurity among the protesters themselves, convincing more
moderate members that they need to take up arms. Suddenly, average citizens are seeking the services of extremists,
certain that those pursuing peaceful means cannot protect
them. Leaders may not even be aware they are creating this
security dilemma. When Tudjman redefined Serbs as a minority within Croatia and asked them to take an oath of
loyalty, he likely didn't understand the degree to which this
made Serbs fearful and pushed them into the waiting arms of
Milošević. In the face of such fears, the more radical members of the group often win.

So why wouldn't governments, especially democratic
governments, yield to protesters if it helped them avoid war?
One answer is that some governments believe their very survival is at stake. From Assad's perspective, democracy in Syria
would have paved the way for Sunni rule, leaving him and
his Alawite supporters pariahs or worse. Assad had seen what
had happened to Saddam Hussein in Iraq and Muammar
Gaddafi in Libya when they stepped down from power. He
was not going to do the same.

Other leaders of multiethnic countries become convinced that only conflict can hold the country together. In a
study of self-determination movements between 1955 and
2002, I found that leaders were less inclined to negotiate—
and more likely to fight—in nations with multiple potential
separatist groups. If a leader believed that granting independence to one group would lead others to make their own
demands—setting off a secessionist chain reaction—then
fighting would help deter future challenges. Indonesia's harsh
response to East Timor's declaration of independence, which

killed an estimated 25 percent of East Timor's population, was made in part to dissuade the country's many other ethnic groups from demanding independence as well.

Key government constituencies—a ruling elite, a voting base, the military brass—can also nudge a country toward conflict. Leaders who are beholden to any or all of these groups might find themselves taking, rather than giving, orders. The French government chose not to grant Algeria independence without first fighting a war because politically powerful French settlers living in Algeria, together with the support of French army officers, rejected compromise. (French Algerians controlled the interior ministry, which controlled the police.) Communist Party leader Zhao Ziyang had favored compromising with the Tiananmen Square demonstrators, but Communist Party hard-liners threw him out of power—claiming he was being soft—and instead pursued a military response.

Ignorance can also lead governments to overreact, triggering wider conflict. Studies have shown that governments are especially likely to over-respond in regions where a weak on-the-ground presence has left them out of touch and stripped of influence. According to Jonathan Powell, the chief British negotiator on Northern Ireland, the British "really had no idea what was going on in Northern Ireland. . . . Their intelligence was out of date. They locked up the wrong people." But by resorting to violence, the British not only destroyed Catholics' faith in the possibility of reform, they delivered them into the open arms of the Provisional IRA.

It's never clear how a government is going to respond to sustained protests. Emotions run high, unexpected events occur. Intransigence and fear set in. People on both sides demand and seek revenge. That's why the early acts of terror by members of a downgraded group are often more dangerous than people realize. Violence entrepreneurs are playing a bigger game. And in the early decades of the twenty-first century, these extremists who hope to provoke war have an extraordinarily powerful new weapon at their disposal. It's cheap, it's fast, it's remarkably good at generating anger and resentment, and most people are not yet fully aware of its peril: social media.

CHAPTER 5

THE ACCELERANT

An hour into our drive we realized we were being followed. The gray sedan could have stopped us anytime. Our little Toyota couldn't go more than 30 miles an hour, as we were maneuvering around potholes, bicyclists, and pedestrians. When we got to our destination—an old colonial town north of Mandalay known for its lush gardens, cool mountain air, and military base—a man in military uniform was waiting: "What is your name?" "Where do you come from?" "Why are you here?"

My husband, young daughter, and I were in Myanmar to witness what many thought would be a remarkable transformation. It was 2011 and Myanmar's military junta, which had ruled the country with a heavy hand for decades, had just agreed to transition to civilian rule. The ruling generals would allow elections to be held and they agreed to free the famed opposition leader Aung San Suu Kyi. If all went well, life would change dramatically in this beautiful country and it would become more free, more prosperous, and more benevolent to its citizens.

But we were also full of trepidation, driven by an uneasy feeling that Myanmar could just as easily be on the verge of political upheaval. If real elections were held, and Aung San Suu Kyi became the equivalent of prime minister, Myanmar would likely become an anocracy fairly quickly. The military would be the biggest losers in the transition, relinquishing dictatorial control and unrestrained access to the state's coffers. I also worried about the rise of factions, especially a Buddhist faction. Myanmar (formerly called Burma) had a history of ethnic conflict, especially between its majority Buddhist population and its Muslim minority. The fraught relationship dated back to the British occupation of the country, which lasted from 1826 to 1948. During this time, Indian and Muslim skilled workers immigrated to Burma to work for British-controlled industries. Many Buddhist natives—Myanmar's sons of the soil—felt marginalized, particularly in regions that absorbed many immigrants. The Buddhists were left out of the new industrial economy and relegated to lower-paying agricultural work. In the 1930s, radical Buddhist nationalists started campaigning against Muslims and calling for a "Burma for the Burmans." Ever since then, Indian Muslims and the Rohingya people—Muslims from the Arakan region—had been continuously discriminated against, demoted from citizenship, denied legal representation, and forced into labor camps. When rebel groups tried to resist, the government used the struggles and protests to justify crackdowns. An opening up of the political system to competition could create even more incentives for Buddhists to flex their political muscle and exploit this divide.

A year after our visit, however, there was reason to be optimistic about Myanmar's democracy. The government agreed to a cease-fire with separatist rebels from the Karen ethnic group, it released hundreds of political prisoners, and

Aung San Suu Kyi's party won parliamentary elections in a landslide. Even the country's censorship laws were loosening.

During our trip, the only internet access I'd been able to find was on a computer in the old British colonial hotel in dusty downtown Yangon. Most of the time the connection failed. When I showed people my iPhone, their faces went blank; they had no idea what it was. But in 2011, the new government significantly reduced internet restrictions. Soon, Facebook launched in the country. By 2015, when Aung San Suu Kyi was set to be named state counsellor, Myanmar had gone from a country in which only 1 percent of its citizens had internet access—the lowest in the world except for North Korea—to one where 22 percent did. It seemed like an enormous leap forward.

Instead it was a disaster in the making. In 2012, a group of Buddhist ultranationalists, many of them monks, took to Facebook to target Muslim populations throughout Myanmar. They blamed them for local violence, and described them as invaders of the region and a threat to the Buddhist majority. The posts, which went viral, included comments like "Just feed them to the pigs." Group pages proposed massive rallies demanding that the Rohingya be deported from the country. The tech giant quickly became the country's most popular social media platform—and the primary source of digital news. Before long, Myanmar's military leaders were using it to post hate speech and false news stories; fear served to buttress their influence and power at a time when they otherwise might have lost it. Government leaders, not wanting to antagonize the military, supported these stories, with officials creating thousands of fake accounts that spread disinformation, blaming the "Bengalis"—as they called the

Rohingya, whom they considered illegal immigrants—for violence and crimes.

Violence first broke out in the Rakhine state between Buddhists and Muslims in June 2012 when eighty thousand Muslims were reported "displaced." Less than a year later, the world began to hear reports of ethnic cleansing campaigns against the Rohingya. The initial violence appeared to be perpetrated by local mobs of Buddhists, as government security forces stood by and watched. Rakhine men (Buddhists) used Molotov cocktails, machetes, and homemade weapons to attack villages throughout the region. Sometimes the soldiers joined in. Though it seemed evident that the violence was being stoked by the falsehoods circulating on Facebook, the government refused to acknowledge that the Rohingya Muslims even existed. Journalists who reported on ethnic cleansing and military crimes were imprisoned. Others who tried to get Facebook to intervene were stonewalled. In 2013, Aela Callan, an Australian documentary film student at Stanford who had captured the violence on-screen, reached out to Elliot Schrage, the vice president of communications and public policy at Facebook. She presented her project revealing the connection between hate speech and the Rohingya genocide, but Facebook turned a blind eye. A year later, a Norwegian phone company named Telenor entered the market in Myanmar, letting its cellphone purchasers use Facebook without paying any data charges, massively increasing the platform's reach.

In the years that followed, dozens of journalists, companies, human rights organizations, foreign governments, and even citizens of Myanmar continued to alert Facebook to the unchecked spread of hate speech and misinformation on the platform. But Facebook remained silent, refusing to acknowledge the problem. Violence began to escalate in October 2016 when the military intensified its campaign against the Rohingya, murdering, raping, and arresting them, and even burning their homes. By December 2016, hundreds had been killed and thousands more had fled. But the real genocide began in August 2017, when the Myanmar military, along with Buddhist mobs, began mass killings, deportations, and rapes. By January 2018, an estimated 24,000 Rohingya people had been killed, with an additional 18,000 Rohingya women and children raped or sexually assaulted. Another 116,000 were beaten, 36,000 were thrown into fires, and approximately 700,000 of the nearly one million estimated Rohingya had been forced to flee. It was the largest human exodus in Asia since the Vietnam War.

The world looked to Aung San Suu Kyi, the Nobel Peace Prize winner who had championed democracy, for a response. But she did not acknowledge the violence, claiming instead that photos of Rohingya fleeing western Myanmar were fake. On Facebook, she wrote, "We know very well, more than most, what it means to be deprived of human rights and democratic protection." All the people in Myanmar, she insisted (on a phone call to Turkish president Erdoğan), were entitled to protection. The Rohingya situation, she continued, was the result of "a huge iceberg of misinformation" rather than anything real.

EVERY YEAR SINCE 2010, the world has seen more countries move down the democratic ladder than up it. This backsliding has occurred not just in places where democracy is new, but also in wealthy, liberal countries whose longtime democracies were once considered sacrosanct. Some elected leaders have attacked free speech and remade their constitutions to concentrate power in their own hands. Others have attempted to undercut representative elections. All have tried to convince their citizens of the need for more autocratic measures. V-Dem, the Swedish research institute, collects detailed data on the different types of democracies around the world and then rates them on a 100-point scale with 100 being the most democratic and 0 being the least. According to the institute, Spain has suffered one of the worst declines in Western Europe, followed by Greece, Germany, France, the United Kingdom, Ireland, and Austria. Nordic countries, the most liberal in the world, have also dropped since 2010: Denmark, the number one ranked democracy for most of the past hundred years, has been downgraded 10 points on V-Dem's scale; Sweden has been downgraded 35. The swift rate of democratic decay around the world has been so rapid that V-Dem issued its first "Autocratization Alert" in 2020.

For a while, at least, the one glaring exception to this trend was Africa. Over much of the past decade, sub-Saharan Africa was the only part of the globe where democracy continued to expand rather than contract. Burkina Faso experienced its first-ever democratic transition in 2015 after twenty-seven years of uninterrupted semi-authoritarian rule. Sierra Leone transitioned to democracy in 2018 when the ruling party stepped down after being defeated by the opposition. The Ivory Coast held its first postcolonial internationally supervised and most inclusive election in 2015. And after two decades of military rule, Gambia transitioned to democracy in 2017.

Africa was an outlier in another way, too: Over this same

period, its countries experienced the least amount of internet penetration anywhere in the world. North Korea had the very lowest in 2016, but the next twelve countries—including Eritrea, Somalia, Niger, the Central African Republic, Burundi, Chad, and the Democratic Republic of Congo—were all in Africa. Access to the internet began to increase in Africa in 2014, when social media became a primary means of communication. Facebook, YouTube, and Twitter made inroads in sub-Saharan Africa starting in 2015, and as they did, the level of conflict began to rise. In Ethiopia, for example, longstanding tensions between Tigrayans and Oromos began to boil over in 2019 when a series of fake videos claimed local officials were arming young men. The conflict had been escalating since 2018 as Ethiopia transitioned to a new democratically elected government. According to one analyst, this coincided with "a rapid increase in access to the internet, where Facebook dominates." And hate speech promoted on social media in the Central African Republic has recently been stoking divisions between Muslims and Christians there. In 2019, the democracy ratings on V-Dem for sub-Saharan Africa began to decline like everywhere else in the world.

It's not likely to be a coincidence that the global shift away from democracy has tracked so closely with the advent of the internet, the introduction of smart phones, and the widespread use of social media. The radically new information environment in which we live is perhaps the single biggest cultural and technological change the world has seen in this century. Facebook was initially hailed as a great tool of democratization. It would connect people, encourage the free exchange of ideas and opinions, and allow news to be curated by citizens themselves rather than major news outlets. It seemed like the perfect tool to put power in the hands of the people. Dissidents had a new way to organize and communicate, which promised to usher in a new era of freedom and reform. Facebook became the world's most popular platform in 2009. By 2010, YouTube, Twitter, WhatsApp, and Instagram were all popular and growing. By 2013, 23 percent of Americans received at least some of their news from social media. By 2016, over 62 percent of Americans did. Today it's over 70 percent.

But social media platforms have proven to be a Pandora's box. The age of information sharing has opened up unmitigated, unregulated pathways to the spread of misinformation (which is erroneous) or disinformation (which is intentionally misleading). Charlatans, conspiracy theorists, trolls, demagogues, and anti-democratic agents who had previously been shut out of the media environment—or at least had great difficulty gaining a mass audience—suddenly gained traction. According to Kate Starbird, a cofounder of the Center for an Informed Public and professor at the University of Washington, "The problem of misinformation was relatively very small back in 2009, and in fact, we talked about it: 'Oh, don't worry too much about it. Most of the information we see is true and from people who are well-meaning.'" But within five years, the amount of false information on social media platforms had skyrocketed. As social media penetrated countries and gained a larger share of people's attention, a clear pattern emerged: ethnic factions grew, social divisions widened, resentment at immigrants increased, bullying populists got elected, and violence began to increase. Open, unregulated social media platforms turned out to be the perfect accelerant for the conditions that lead to civil war.

The problem is social media's business model. To make money, technology companies like Facebook, YouTube, Google, and Twitter need to keep people on their platforms—or as they call it, "engaged"—for as long as possible. The longer users remain online—clicking on links about kittens, retweeting stories about celebrities, or sharing videos—the more advertising revenue the companies receive. Longer engagement also allows companies to gather more behavioral data about their users, which makes it easier to target ads, which brings in even more money. In 2009, Facebook introduced the "like" button, a feature that told the company which posts were most popular with its users. That same year—the year before democracies started to decline—Facebook introduced a second innovation: an algorithm that used a person's previous likes to determine the posts they would see. Google, which owns YouTube, soon followed.

It turns out that what people like the most is fear over calm, falsehood over truth, outrage over empathy. People are far more apt to like posts that are incendiary than those that are not, creating an incentive for people to post provocative material in the hopes that it will go viral. With the introduction of the like button, individual Facebook users were suddenly being rewarded for posting outrageous, angry content whether it was true or not. Studies have since shown that information that keeps people engaged is exactly the type of information that leads them toward anger, resentment, and violence. When William J. Brady and his colleagues at NYU analyzed half a million tweets, they found that each moral or emotional word used led to a 20 percent increase in retweets. Another study by the Pew Research Center showed that posts exhibiting "indignant disagreement" received nearly twice as many likes and shares as other types of content. And

Tristan Harris, an American computer scientist and a former ethicist at Google, explained the incentives in a 2019 interview with *The New York Times*: "If I'm YouTube and I want you to watch more, I'm always going to steer you toward Crazytown."

Worse, the behavioral algorithms began creating self-reinforcing, increasingly outlandish information silos that led users down dangerous paths: toward conspiracy theories, half-truths, and extremists seeking radical change. These recommendation engines, as they are called, ensured that users were channeled toward more narrow and more extreme information. If a user "liked" a post on a police officer helping a kitten, say, Facebook would funnel additional posts to the user on police benevolent associations, then pro-police stories, then increasingly more fanatical material. Walter Quattrociocchi, a computer scientist at Sapienza Università di Roma, analyzed fifty-four million comments over four years in different Facebook groups. He found that the longer a discussion continued, the more extreme the comments became. One study found that YouTube viewers who consume the kind of "mild" right-wing content created by provocative talk show host Joe Rogan, whose audience in 2020 was 286 million, are often pulled into much more radical alt-right content. The study concluded that YouTube is "a radicalization pipeline."

It's this business model of engagement that makes social media so terrifying to those of us who study civil wars. The current model doesn't care if the information it disseminates is true or not, just that it is all-absorbing. And the big technology companies—who are now the new gatekeepers of news and information—have no incentive to restrict who uses their platforms or what they say. In fact, it is in the interest of their shareholders to disseminate engaging information as widely as possible.

If you are an extremist and you want to proselytize, social media is the perfect tool. This was certainly the case in Myanmar, where extremists like radical Buddhist monk Ashin Wirathu found an eager audience for his anti-Rohingya views. After being imprisoned for his extreme views during the military's rule, Wirathu emerged after 2013 as a radical cult figure, gaining thousands of followers inside and outside religious communities. Wirathu traveled around the country "preaching" against the Muslim problem in Myanmar and calling for greater military intervention. (In 2019, the government charged him with sedition because he claimed that Aung San Suu Kyi was not being harsh enough with the Muslim "invaders.")

In 2018, Facebook finally admitted that it had contributed to community violence in Myanmar after a series of high-profile reports and stories directly connected the platform to the 2017 genocide. CEO Mark Zuckerberg promised to do everything in the company's power to stop the flow of hate speech and misinformation. The company hired three Burmese-speaking representatives, who ultimately removed 484 pages, 157 accounts, and 17 groups. Most activists and human rights groups felt this was grossly inadequate.

It was also too late to stem the tide. Military leaders who were blocked from Facebook turned to Twitter, where anti-Islamic and anti-Rohingya tweets had begun to proliferate. In one of the hundreds of new Twitter accounts discovered by Reuters in the summer of 2017, one person expressed a common sentiment: "There is no Rohingya in Myanmar, they are only illegal immigrants and terrorists." But Twitter also declined to take down most of the posts. The consensus today is that none of the social media platforms did nearly enough to address how their platforms were being used to eradicate a minority group in this small southeast Asian country.

The Myanmar military's violent campaign against the Rohingya was not a civil war. The Rohingya were not able to organize or fight back. This was a one-sided attack by the government and by Buddhist citizens against a minority group. It was a form of ethnic cleansing; an extreme example of the kind of conflict happening all over the world, aided by the megaphone that ethnic entrepreneurs have been given on social media to incite fear and violence. By the spring of 2018, Facebook's dominance over Myanmar's national conversation was so complete that when President Htin Kyaw resigned from his post, he chose to make his announcement not on television or radio, but on Facebook.

Sadly, civil war might be coming to Myanmar, nonetheless. Several months after Aung San Suu Kyi's party won an overwhelming victory in the November 2020 elections, the military staged a coup—claiming election fraud—ousting her and other opposition leaders. Protesters and police clashed in the streets in the spring of 2021, the two sides inflamed by years of division that was sown in large part by social media. The military quickly began to crack down on peaceful protesters, shooting civilians in the street, beating and throwing protesters in jail, and grabbing suspected leaders from their homes at night. Even though Facebook barred Myanmar's military from its platform and also blocked advertisements from military-owned businesses, the generals' personal pages channeled copious amounts of propaganda to rationalize the coup and rally low-ranking officials.

The last weekend of March 2021 was the bloodiest to

date. One of the local leaders of the protest, Soe Naing Win (an alias), who lives on the outskirts of the city of Yangon, cried when interviewed by an American journalist. Nonviolent protest wasn't working, he told the reporter. "If diplomacy fails, if the killings continue, the people of Myanmar will be forced to defend themselves." Soe Naing Win revealed that he had already begun training to fight. Civil war, he said, was going to happen.

RODRIGO DUTERTE WAS a nobody—the mayor of a city in Mindanao known as "the fruit basket of the Philippines"— when he decided to run for president in 2015. He had little money and little political support. But he knew enough to hire Nic Gabunada, a marketing consultant, to build a social media army that might help get him elected. Gabunada allegedly paid hundreds of social media influencers to praise Duterte and criticize his opponents, then popularize hashtags to draw attention to these posts.

Duterte used the platforms to exploit and amplify discontent with the Philippine government. He criticized the media as an arm of the political elite, questioned institutions, and painted the political establishment as corrupt. He stoked citizen fears of drugs proliferating, and made the case for a police crackdown to restore order. Facebook was essential to Duterte's win in 2016: Over 97 percent of Filipinos who are online are on the platform, leading Bloomberg journalist Lauren Etter to describe the Philippines as "prime Facebook country."

At the start of Duterte's campaign, Duterte was the only candidate to attend a forum for college voters organized by Maria Ressa, a renowned Filipino journalist and founder of

Rappler, the Philippines' largest online news source. Immediately, Duterte focused on reaching out to young people via their primary platform: Facebook. He reimagined his campaign, amplifying people who spread fake news and rumors about his opponents.

The strategy worked. Duterte won the majority of votes in greater Manila, the Cebuano-speaking regions in the south, and Mindanao—home of the long-aggrieved Moros. Exit polls showed that he had gained the support of young, well-educated voters who were tired of both the status quo and the corrupt political elite. Even though his campaign budget was much smaller than his opponents', Duterte became the sixteenth president of the Philippines in 2016.

It's become a pattern: social media as the vehicle that launches outsiders with autocratic impulses to power, riding a popular wave of support. We've seen it with Erdoğan in Turkey and Modi in India. It also potentially helped bring Mariano Rajoy of Spain to power. All were social media savvy dark horse candidates. Rajoy won a surprise victory in Spain in 2016 after carefully targeting Facebook users who had previously voted for his opponent. Social media offers these candidates not only an unregulated environment but also multiple platforms from which to disseminate information and propaganda (candidates can reach different audiences on YouTube, Twitter, and Facebook). In the past, if a politician wanted to influence voters, they had to go through gatekeepers: party leaders and major networks and newspapers. Social media has allowed any candidate and any party—no matter how fringe—to circumvent these controls.

But it's not just about exposure. The algorithms of social media mean that these outsiders can capitalize on the best drivers of engagement—fear and outrage—to disseminate lies about their opponents and a country's institutions to a mass audience. According to a 2017 report by Freedom House, disinformation campaigns influenced elections in at least seventeen countries that year. Sudan's government created an internal unit within its National Intelligence and Security Service that employed "cyber-jihadists" who created fake accounts that then infiltrated popular groups on Facebook and WhatsApp. They then wrote favorably about government policies while denouncing any journalist critical of the regime. As the report documented: "Government agents in Venezuela regularly used manipulated footage to disseminate lies about opposition protesters on social media, creating confusion and undermining the credibility of the opposition movement ahead of elections. In Kenya, users readily shared fake news articles and videos bearing the logos of generally trusted outlets such as CNN, the BBC, and NTV Kenya on social media and messaging apps in advance of the August 2017 election."

This isn't the first time in modern history that populists with anti-democratic leanings have come to power. It is also not the first time that democracies have experienced backsliding. What's different is the mechanism: Before, autocracy came about when military generals launched coups. But now it's being ushered in by the *voters themselves*.

This is happening in large part because social media allows candidates to sow, or capitalize on, doubts that citizens might have about democracy as a form of government. Disinformation campaigns can be used to attack institutions, undermining people's trust in representative government, a free press, and an independent judiciary, reducing tolerance and support for pluralism. They can be used to stoke fear, which helps get far-right, law-and-order candidates elected.

Finally, they can cause citizens to question the results of an election, claiming fraud and convincing at least some voters that the election has been stolen. To make good decisions about candidates in democracies, voters must have good information, and social media has flooded voters with bad information. As people lose faith in the democratic process, they are more apt to support an alternative system—and to willingly place power in the hands of the charismatic individuals who promise protection and a certain future.

This is what Duterte did when he broke almost every democratic norm in the country. It's also what Bolsonaro has done in Brazil. Like Duterte, no one thought Bolsonaro had a chance to win the presidency; a poll of Brazilian voters in 2014 by Fadi Quran (an activist and campaign director) found that 66 percent of them had no intention of voting for him. He was perceived as too right-wing and too inexperienced. But Bolsonaro used what little money he had to place ads on Facebook and YouTube—the first Brazilian candidate to campaign via social media. His early YouTube videos and Facebook posts were brutal attacks against his opponents. He compared former president Dilma Rousseff to the Boston marathon bombers. He created a video where he claimed that Rousseff's secretary of policies for women, Eleonora Menicucci, was (bizarrely) both a communist and a Nazi, and an embarrassment to the country. In some videos, he called for extreme forms of political torture, and in others for the return of a military dictatorship.

Slowly, the videos started gaining more likes, more views. At first, they simply peddled conspiracy theories, but over time, they began to feature the ideas of the global alt-right. Like other populist leaders, Bolsonaro positioned himself as an outsider who was fighting for the people of Brazil against a crooked political elite. As Bolsonaro faced greater scrutiny from traditional media, he relied more on social media to communicate directly with ordinary Brazilians, calling the old media corrupt and full of lies. Six months after he began his social media campaign, he won the presidency. Almost 90 percent of people who voted for Bolsonaro had read and believed these stories. Today, he continues to communicate frequently with supporters on WhatsApp and Twitter, often in ALL CAPS. For the past few years, Bolsonaro has hosted a weekly YouTube and Facebook Live session, streaming live videos for his over ten million followers.

One might think the move away from democracy would make these leaders unpopular, but by the time they consolidate power, they have successfully wielded their favorite means of communication—social media—to convince voters that anti-democratic measures are needed to preserve the country's peace and their own prosperity. Duterte has hired hundreds of individuals, many from China (Duterte is an avid supporter) to create fake social media accounts, where they continue to harass critics and post messages that praise the president. It is estimated that of all Twitter accounts that mention Duterte, 20 percent are in fact bots. By October 2020, Duterte's approval rating was 91 percent.

Something similar has happened in Hungary, where President Viktor Orbán has also become more popular over time, not less. In Europe, right-wing anti-immigrant parties such as the Alternative für Deutschland in Germany, the Lega Nord in Italy, the Vlaams Belang in Belgium, the Front National in France, and the Freiheitliche Partei Österreichs in Austria have all seen their support increase in recent years. The way social media is structured is Darwinian—it is the survival of the fittest, where the most aggressive and most brazen voices drown out everyone else. And in the contest between liberal democracies and authoritarian regimes, social media is inadvertently helping the autocrats win.

SOCIAL MEDIA DOESN'T just drive countries down the democratic ladder. It also heightens the ethnic, social, religious, and geographic divisions that can be the first step in the creation of factions. This is, of course, because myth, emotion, and the politics of grievance—all of which drive factionalism—make for incredibly engaging content. Social media algorithms encourage this divisive content. They segregate people by design, driving those whose values or opinions differ into ever-diverging realities, tearing societies apart.

Sweden, for example, is not known for far-right nationalist politics. In fact, it's known for just the opposite: a progressive political culture and generous welfare system. Sweden's population has always prided itself on what it sees as "Swedish Exceptionalism," a dedication to community, equality, and mutual concern. Swedes actually have a name for it—*folkhemmet,* which means "the people's home."

But on September 9, 2014, a former neo-Nazi party became Sweden's third largest party in parliament. The fact that Sweden, of all the Western democracies, had embraced a racist, xenophobic party was so surprising that Jo Becker, a *New York Times* journalist, decided to spend months investigating how it happened. The party, known as the Sweden Democrats, was founded in 1988 by a chemist who had joined the Waffen SS during World War II. In 2005, party leader Jimmie Akesson set out to reform the party's image, swapping swastikas and combat boots for suits and ties and reorienting the group from Nazism toward populism. (Members are no longer allowed to wear Nazi uniforms to meetings.) But the party had a problem: Swedish newspapers, television stations, and radio shows refused to run their ads. The postal service often refused to deliver its mass mailings. The party wasn't growing. Most citizens didn't even know it existed.

The internet changed that. As Becker discovered, in 2009, Akesson, a former web designer, began to focus on building an online presence. He created multiple Facebook pages, which allowed him and other party leaders to communicate directly with their followers. They then created two news websites, *Samhällsnytt* (News in Society) and *Nyheter Idag* (News Today), where they published far-right stories related to daily events. Though much of the information—about immigrants, about the far left—was deliberately misleading, it quickly found an audience. Becker noted that, in 2018, the vast majority (85 percent) of election-related junk news in Sweden came from these two websites, plus a third called *Fria Tider* (Free Times). More than a million Swedes viewed these sites weekly—about the same number of readers as Sweden's two largest newspapers. In 2010—a mere year after switching to an online campaign—the party gained seats in Sweden's parliament for the first time. By 2014 it was the third-largest party in parliament. Nine years was all it took.

The Sweden Democrats insist that they are not neo-Nazis. Their leaders will tell you that they are normal working-class people who care about the social changes happening in Sweden. They certainly look respectable. Members of the party are striking for their clean-cut blazer-wearing appearance. But the language they espouse online tells a different story. This is an identity faction that sees its historical rights at stake, a faction that actively seeks to define itself in relation to a lesser "other" and exclude them from the *folkhemmet*. On its websites, you will find stories about Muslim immigrants committing crimes, Muslim immigrants brutalizing animals, and Muslim immigrants refusing to conform to Western laws. You will read that "foreign burglars were arrested following tips from an attentive neighbor," accompanied by a clearly staged photograph. The party emphasizes the need to return Sweden to a simpler and happier time. The goal is to restore "the national home."

Social media is every ethnic entrepreneur's dream. Algorithms, by pushing outrageous material, allow these nationalist extremists to shape people's toxic views of "the other"—an ideal means of demonizing and targeting racial minorities, and creating division. Ethnic entrepreneurs use it to craft a common narrative, a story that people can get behind, and they encourage followers to go down the rabbit hole. Swedish YouTubers like Vedad Odobasic, who goes by the name "Angry Foreigner" (he is white and originally from Bosnia and Herzegovina), creates videos that are radically anti-immigrant. One is called "Interviews: Victim of Multiculturalism." Another is "Tourists Aren't Safe in Sweden." His videos have garnered more than thirty-three million total views. Another Swedish YouTuber, Lennart Matikainen, hosted a show on Swebbtv, a conservative YouTube and "news" platform that advocated far-right policies and conspiracy theories. YouTube took the platform down in 2020 for violating community guidelines. However, Matikainen's own personal account has over six million views.

Over the last ten years, ethnic entrepreneurs have emerged and thrived in countries around the world, aided by social media. In India, Modi has used every page from the ethnic entrepreneur playbook to denigrate non-Hindus. He does this by communicating directly with his forty-seven-million-plus followers on Twitter, Facebook, and YouTube. (In March 2020, Modi had the third-highest number of Twitter followers of any politician in the world, after former president Barack Obama and then-president Donald Trump.) He frequently uses social media to communicate "Hindutva"—the movement to prioritize Hindu teachings in Indian culture. Modi has been helped in his efforts by lesser ethnic entrepreneurs who are just as media savvy. TV presenter Arnab Goswami has peddled misinformation and hate speech in support of Modi, while famous yogi Baba Ramdev has used his platform to inflame the Hindu nationalist base—and sell his Ayurvedic products.

In Brazil, YouTuber Nando Moura has embraced Bolsonaro-supporting conspiracy theories and paranoid far-right rants to grow his audience, which now numbers about three million people. In the United Kingdom, YouTuber and social media influencer Paul Joseph Watson, who has an audience of 1.88 million subscribers, has said that Islam glorifies sexual assault and accuses refugees of carrying "parasitic disease."

If Milošević were alive today, he would adore social media, using it to celebrate the mythology of a greater Serbia on Twitter or Facebook. He would like fake videos of Albanians starting riots. He would share stories of Croats taking Serb jobs. He would retweet conspiracy theories about Bosnians abusing Serb children. He would hire a team of trolls to disseminate his calls for "unity" and spread disinformation about his opponents. And the algorithms of social media would reward him: with more followers, more likes, and perhaps even more money.

In the world's democracies, where the principles of free

speech and representative voice historically worked against demagoguery to promote healthy public discourse, the reach of today's ethnic entrepreneurs is staggering. That they've been helped by social media is clear in a democracy like France, where the far-right political party known as the National Rally (formerly the French National Front Party), was once dismissed as a fringe movement, its leader Jean-Marie Le Pen a peddler of ugly rhetoric about immigrants and the supremacy of French culture. Now, under the leadership of Le Pen's daughter, Marine, the party has spread its message—exploiting and inflaming racial tension—with the most sophisticated social media operation of any major political party in France. (Le Pen has fifteen permanent staffers who carry out research, craft memes, and coordinate the party's attempts to discredit opponents on social media.) Despite losing the 2017 runoff election and being investigated for misuse of EU funds, by 2019, Le Pen had secured twenty-two seats for her party in the EU parliament, more than Macron's, and landed a seat in France's parliamentary assembly.

It used to be that far-right parties were unelectable in liberal democracies. But the story of fear and grievance told by ethnic entrepreneurs—the myths and losses of sons of the soil—prove irresistible to an audience made captive by social media. "Right-wing populism is always more engaging," one Facebook executive has noted. According to the same executive, populism triggers reactions that are "incredibly strong" and "primitive" by appealing to emotionally charged subjects like "nation, protection, the other, anger, fear." In Sweden, the stories on *Samhällsnytt* and *Nyheter Idag* were designed with this in mind: to create fear for Swedes' safety, for the safety of their families, and for their culture and society. If these websites were your main sources of news—surfaced and reinforced by algorithms—you would quickly come to believe that Sweden was falling apart and that immigrants and the far left were to blame. It would be nearly impossible for anyone to persuade you otherwise.

People don't realize how vulnerable Western democracies are to violent conflict. They have grown accustomed to their longevity, their resilience, and their stability in the face of crises. But that was before social media created an avenue by which enemies of democracy can easily infiltrate society and destabilize it from within. The internet has revealed just how fragile a government by and for the people can be.

IT WAS EASY for Shane Bauer, a thirty-three-year-old Berkeley grad with an unkempt beard, to join one of America's largest militia groups. All he did was go on Facebook and begin to like the many militia sites that popped up. Bauer wanted to join a militia group not because he believed he or his family needed protection. Bauer was an award-winning journalist—and in 2016 he wanted to investigate what was going on behind the scenes in the militias emerging across America.

He liked three different groups: the Three Percenter Nation, the Patriotic Warriors, and the Arizona State Militia. If you like these pages, Facebook then automatically generates additional suggestions of other militia pages. (When I searched Facebook for "Arizona state militia," it gave me a choice of five different Arizona militias to join.) Facebook does all the work connecting you with any community you're interested in—even the most extreme.

Bauer liked all these pages. But to be accepted to the private Facebook groups, he had to convince the owners that he was sincere. So he opened a Facebook account and began to post negative material about Barack Obama and memes about American flags. He wrote blog posts about the threat of Syrians traveling to Mexico in order to more easily cross the border illegally into the United States. He then sent dozens of friend requests to people he found on the Facebook pages of different militias. "Within a couple of days I had more than 100 friends," he reported. Shortly after that, Bauer saw the Three Percent United Patriots' private Facebook group called "Operation Spring Break." When he requested and received access, he learned about an upcoming event—a border protection operation along Arizona's border with Mexico. According to information posted on Facebook, all Bauer had to do was show up with his own weapons, medical supplies, and body camera. That's exactly what he did.

There's no better way to organize people today than social media—especially if those people are feeling aggrieved or threatened. It is how the Arab Spring protesters organized in 2011, how the 2017 Women's March came together, and how the Black Lives Matter movement initially gained traction. But when this power to draw like-minded people intersects with extremist, outrage-driven narratives—and a thirst for violence—it creates a powder keg. Members of nascent movements now use the internet to find one another, to organize, to disrupt peaceful protests, and to equip themselves for a cause. They can now easily share information on how to make bombs and use secure online chats to contact foreign military advisers with combat experience. In addition, Facebook hosts "sprawling online arms bazaars, offering weapons ranging from handguns and grenades to heavy machine guns and guided missiles." J. M. Berger, a longtime expert on violent extremism, has followed the progression of white nationalist groups on social media since 2012, when most of these groups had only a few followers. Four years later, most had increased their followers by over 600 percent. And by 2018, according to Berger, "hundreds of thousands of new and legacy racist extremists had flooded the platform." Since 2018, the number of white nationalist groups has dropped somewhat, although overall membership in such organizations does not appear to have declined, suggesting that there's consolidation happening, as popular groups—such as the Proud Boys—beat out smaller competing ones.

The world saw the organizing power of social media with the rise of the Islamic State, which has used websites, chat rooms, and sites like Twitter to disseminate propaganda that radicalizes individuals in the comfort of their living rooms. It has convinced at least thirty thousand citizens from about one hundred different countries to join its battle in Syria. Social media has been so instrumental for these purposes that, as one Islamic State defector noted, its practitioners are rewarded accordingly. "The media people are more important than the soldiers. . . . Their monthly income is higher. They have better cars. They have the power to encourage those inside to fight and the power to bring more recruits to the Islamic States."

It used to be that one of the main challenges violent extremist groups faced was how to raise money, especially if they did not control territory. But apps now make it easy to transfer money instantaneously across borders, making even the smallest fringe groups viable. Vera Mironova, a Russian American academic, asked one of the founders of a new rebel group formed in Syria in 2011—Mahgerin al-Allah—

how they acquired funding. "The first thing I did when I took this job," he explained, "was to make a YouTube video about the group. I asked group leaders to gather as many people as they could . . . to show how big the group was; bring all the weapons and cars they had . . . to show that they were well equipped; and wear uniforms and stand in military formation. I just had to show that they were professional." The group received financial support from a wealthy Syrian living in the Persian Gulf.

Once you have people organized and radicalized, social media itself offers the very match that lights this powder keg. The collective fear and sense of threat created by extremist videos and rhetoric shifts power to those itching for a fight. According to Erica Chenoweth, these violence entrepreneurs almost always try to interject themselves into nonviolent resistance movements and push these movements to the extreme—and the easiest way to do this is social media, where they can agitate and provoke to great effect. This appears to be what happened with the "yellow vest" protest movement in France, when outside radicals and agitators joined its Facebook groups in order to advocate for violence. According to Renée DiResta, an expert on the abuse of information technology, these are the "people who are more likely to set things on fire."

Ultimately, it's the algorithms of social media that serve as accelerants for violence. By promoting a sense of perpetual crisis, these algorithms give rise to a growing sense of despair. Disinformation spread by extremists discredits peaceful protesters, convinces citizens that counterattacks by opposition groups are likely, and creates a sense—often a false sense—that moderates within their own movement are not doing enough to protect the population, or are ineffective and weak compared to the opposition. It's at this point that violence breaks out: when citizens become convinced that there is no hope of fixing their problems through conventional means.

Fueled by social media, they come to believe that compromise is simply not possible.

CHAPTER 6

HOW CLOSE ARE WE?

Wearing winter coats and MAGA hats, the crowd of Trump supporters began to gather at the Ellipse, a park just south of the White House, early on the morning of January 6, 2021. They had traveled to Washington from every corner of America. As they waited for the president to appear, they surveyed their country's venerated ground: the Washington Monument to the south; the Lincoln Memorial to the west; the Capitol to the east. The lawn where they stood had once served as a campsite for Union troops. This was fitting because they too—they told themselves—were patriots. They loved America too much for it to be taken away.

By noon, when President Trump came out to address them, the "Save America" rally had swelled to several thousand. The crowd was restive. In the weeks since the presidential election in November, Trump had refused to concede that he'd lost to Democrat Joe Biden, insisting instead that widespread voting fraud had cheated him of his rightful landslide victory. Democrats, he claimed, had worked behind the scenes, state by state, to ensure his loss. After the election, Trump had rallied an army of lawyers to contest the results, and he had bullied governors and election officials to try to alter vote counts. He had also asserted, falsely, that Vice President Mike Pence had the power to overturn the votes of the electoral college. But his efforts had gone nowhere, and that morning, as he stood before his supporters, lawmakers were gathering at the Capitol to certify Biden's victory.

This did not have to be, Trump told his supporters. Standing on a dais, surrounded by American flags, he told his listeners he was not giving up. Congressional Republicans could still overturn the vote, he claimed. For more than an hour, supporters listened with a mix of adoration and pride, their anger and energy growing with Trump's every word. They waved flags with his name, and placards with his rallying cry: "Stop the Steal." As he stood looking at them, chants of "USA, USA, USA!" broke out across the crowd.

Trump was delighted. Grassroots groups, along with Republican funders and operatives, had helped to organize the rally, and Trump had done his part to ensure a large turnout, tweeting on December 19: "Big protest in D.C. on January 6. Be there, will be wild!" On the first day of the new year, he'd tweeted again: "The BIG Protest Rally in Washington, D.C., will take place at 11.00 A.M. on January 6th. Locational details to follow. StopTheSteal!" Trump became even more insistent when Vice President Pence signaled he would not interfere with the certification. On January 4, at a rally in Georgia, Trump declared: "If the liberal Democrats take the Senate and the White House—and they're not taking this White House—we're going to fight like hell. . . . We're going to take it back!"

"Today is not the end!" the president shouted into the

crowd on the Ellipse. "It's just the beginning!" The crowd contained a mix of people: veterans, business owners, real estate agents, grandfathers, mothers, a state legislator, a former Olympian, members of the Proud Boys wearing orange hats. Most were white. Most were men. Some wore T-shirts that said "God, Guns, and Trump." Others carried Bibles. (At a rally the night before, pastor Greg Locke had told the crowd that God was raising up "an army of patriots.") To the approving roar of his listeners, Trump urged his followers to march to the Capitol and press lawmakers to do what was right. "We're going to try to give them the kind of pride and boldness that they need to take back our country," he said. And then he pledged to join them.

In fact, he returned to the White House. But his supporters knew what to do: For weeks, spurred by Trump's tweets, they had been preparing for this moment on Facebook and Parler, a right-wing social networking service. There they had coordinated their travel as they shared their fury over the "stolen" election. They had outlined the best streets to take to the Capitol to avoid the police, and shared advice about what equipment and tools to bring to break into the building. Some of the more extreme voices online had called for the arrest of Pence, House Speaker Nancy Pelosi, and other lawmakers. Many came armed for battle, wearing bulletproof vests, carrying gas masks and zip ties (to use as handcuffs), and loaded handguns.

Political violence had long been encouraged as legitimate by their leader himself—as far back as 2016, in fact, when he'd run his presidential campaign against Hillary Clinton to chants of "Lock her up!" While campaigning, Trump had discovered that crowds became delighted at his belligerence. Months before the 2016 election, Trump told supporters in

Cedar Rapids that he would cover their legal fees if they tussled with people protesting his campaign rallies. That same month, when a rally in Las Vegas was disrupted by a heckler, Trump crowed: "I'd like to punch him in the face, I'll tell you." Later, Trump stunned the nation by hinting that gun owners could prevent Clinton from becoming president. "If she gets to pick her judges, nothing you can do, folks. Although the Second Amendment people—maybe there is, I don't know."

The presidency had emboldened him. Six months into his tenure, when white nationalist demonstrators converged in Charlottesville and a counterprotester was killed, Trump had shrugged off the violence, saying there were "very fine people" on both sides. And though he'd decried the rioting in cities such as Minneapolis and Portland during Black Lives Matter protests in 2020, he'd then escalated tensions by calling protesters "terrorists" and threatening to unleash federal agents on them. That spring, as the COVID-19 pandemic forced states to shut down businesses, he'd called on "patriots" to "liberate Michigan" by going to the state's capitol and demanding that Governor Gretchen Whitmer, a Democrat, lift restrictions. After photos circulated online of armed protesters staring down at Michigan lawmakers in the Senate chamber, Trump praised them on Twitter, again calling them "very good people."

Trump's supporters at the higher echelons—Republican lawmakers, evangelical leaders, conservative media elites— had for years dismissed the rhetoric, insisting that he was just a bombastic, charismatic leader. But to the crowd standing on the Ellipse that January morning, the president's words were not an abstraction. He was giving them a mission: to save the integrity of their glorious Republic. "If you don't fight like hell," he told them, "you're not going to have a country anymore."

They were streaming toward the Capitol before he'd even finished his speech. They didn't bother with side roads, instead marching along Pennsylvania and Constitution avenues and straight down the Mall, taking selfies and videos of one another. The night before, someone had placed pipe bombs at the nearby headquarters of the Republican National Committee and the Democratic National Committee. Converging on the Capitol, they surrounded the building, looking for a way to enter and interrupt the count of the electoral college votes. Some wore tactical gear; some wielded automatic weapons. They carried Confederate flags, American flags, flags that said "Fight for Trump" and "Veterans for Trump," and "Jesus Saves" signs. A fake gallows was erected.

On the west side, the mob quickly knocked barricades over, violently clashing with police officers. Others scaled walls. Still others sprayed chemical agents and broke windows. Some climbed window-cleaning scaffolding to the second floor. On the east side, they breached the largest barricade. Ten minutes after Vice President Pence and the rest of the Senate were hustled off the Senate floor, Trump tweeted, "Mike Pence didn't have the courage to do what should have been done to protect our Country and our Constitution." Energized, the protesters finally broke down the main door on the west side. Pushing their way into the rotunda, they chanted the names of their targets: Pelosi, Schumer, Pence.

As police barricaded the House chamber and lawmakers scrambled to evacuate, protesters streamed through the hallways, taking more selfies. They were confident, unafraid. They walked through the Capitol as if they belonged there, deserved to be there, and would be protected by the law. They had nothing to hide, nothing to fear. They ransacked offices, smashed furniture, stole a podium with the seal of the Speaker of the House, stole laptops and a framed photo of the Dalai Lama. They defaced statues and ripped Chinese art off the wall. They live-streamed themselves to the world: breaking into the House chamber, invoking God from the Senate dais, and posing next to a life-sized statue of Gerald Ford on whom they had placed a red MAGA hat and a "Trump 2020 No More Bullshit" flag. They were exultant. They were the true American patriots saving the Republic from a stolen election.

At around three P.M., Trump tweeted: "No violence!" But by then it was too late. One rioter had already been fatally shot. Another had been crushed by the mob. Numerous police officers had sustained physical injuries. The siege would last more than four hours, and by the end, five people would be dead. At 4:17 P.M., after multiple pleas by his staff and by President-elect Biden, Trump tweeted a video. He had watched the siege on television from his dining room off the Oval Office. "It was a landslide election, and everyone knows it," he announced. But it was time to go home, he told the rioters. "We love you, you're very special."

A couple of hours later, he tweeted again. This time, he excused the riot, claiming that it was the natural consequence of an election victory being stripped away from "great patriots" who had long been mistreated. "Remember this day forever!"

LIKE ALL AMERICANS, I was shocked by what happened on January 6. But it was, at the same time, deeply familiar. President Trump's defiance after losing the 2020 election reminded me of other presidents, from Nicolás Maduro, who in the months before Venezuela's 2015 election declared he would not relinquish his post no matter the outcome, to Laurent Gbagbo, who refused to concede after Ivory Coast's 2010 election because he claimed it was stolen. Venezuela slid toward authoritarianism; the Ivory Coast descended into civil war. A part of me did not want to accept the implications of what I was seeing. I thought of Daris, from Sarajevo, who, even years later, still struggled to understand how the people of his multicultural, vibrant country had turned so violently on one another. *This is America,* I thought. *We are known for our tolerance and our veneration of democracy.*

But this is where political science, with its structured approach to analyzing history as it unfolds, can be so helpful. No one wants to believe that their beloved democracy is in decline, or headed toward war; the decay is often so incremental that people often fail to notice or understand it, even as they're experiencing it. If you were an analyst in a foreign country looking at events in America—the same way you'd look at events in Ukraine or the Ivory Coast or Venezuela—you would go down a checklist, assessing each of the conditions that make civil war likely. And what you would find is that the United States, a democracy founded more than two centuries ago, has entered dangerous territory.

The first condition—how close we are to anocracy—is best understood through our polity index score, which, as you'll recall, places countries on a fully autocratic to fully democratic scale of −10 to +10. The middle zone covers the −5 to +5 zone. Polity data has been collected on the United States since 1776. The last time America was an anocracy was between 1797 and 1800, when it was rated a +5, mostly for its limited political competitiveness (the Federalists had dominated government since their party's inception in the 1790s). America's polity ranking increased to +6 in March 1801 with the inauguration of Thomas Jefferson, a Democrat-Republican, and then increased to +10 in 1829 with the inauguration of Andrew Jackson, a Democrat.

In the years that followed, the country experienced only two large dips in its polity rating. The first happened in 1850, when Southern Democrats were pursuing take-no-prisoner politics against Northern Republicans in the years that led to the Civil War; the U.S. polity score dropped as low as a +8. It did not recover until 1877, when the heavily disputed election of 1876 was settled. The second dip came during the civil rights era of the 1960s and early '70s, when mass demonstrations increased, Martin Luther King, Jr., and Robert F. Kennedy were assassinated, President Richard Nixon began to pursue more predatory tactics, and the government began to direct violence against its own people. Once again, American democracy was downgraded to a +8. Civil rights legislation, the Watergate investigation, and Nixon's resignation brought it back to a +10.

And then it dropped again: In the wake of the 2016 presidential election, America fell to a +8. There are four major factors that the Polity Project uses to assess democracy: how free elections are from government control, how constrained the executive branch is, how open and institutionalized political participation is, and how competitive the recruitment for the presidency is. Though international observers deemed the 2016 election free, they decided it was not entirely fair: Election rules had been changed as a result of partisan interests, and voting rights were not guaranteed for all citizens. In addition, U.S. intelligence agencies detailed a systematic online campaign by Russian agents to interfere in the election.

Within months of his inauguration, Trump and the Republican Party also began to erode the constraints on the executive branch. Trump unilaterally purged government figures he found disloyal and leveraged bureaucratic operations to benefit his administration and punish opponents. As his tenure progressed, he sought to expand executive powers, refused to release his tax returns, instituted a rash of executive orders, and pardoned guilty friends of crimes. America had become an "imperial presidency"—as presidential historian Arthur M. Schlesinger, Jr., once put it—with its president ruling by executive order rather than consulting with Congress.

In 2019, after Trump refused to cooperate with Congress, especially during its impeachment inquiry, America's democracy score dropped to a +7. Congress has the right to investigate and oversee the executive branch; as William P. Marshall, a law professor at the University of North Carolina, has noted, "We're supposed to be in a system of checks and balances, and one of the biggest checks that Congress has over the executive is the power of congressional oversight." But the White House refused to turn over any information, sued to block subpoenas, and instructed officials to ignore the subpoenas they did receive. Republicans in both the House and the Senate, meanwhile, willingly followed the president's lead, allowing the executive branch to run roughshod over their own branch.

The year 2020 brought crises that would have stressed

even the most robust democracy: a global pandemic, a teetering economy, and riots in the streets over systemic racism, sparked by police killings of Black citizens. But rather than shore up citizens' trust in their country's institutions, Trump deliberately undermined them. He challenged governors who tried to contain the spread of COVID-19 by turning shutdown measures into a political issue. (In April 2020, he tweeted: "LIBERATE MICHIGAN! LIBERATE MINNESOTA! LIBERATE VIRGINIA!, and save your great 2nd Amendment. It is under siege!") As Black Lives Matter protests roiled the country, he attacked city mayors for being ineffectual and threatened to use government force against protesters. He then wielded it for his own purposes: On June 1, Trump had police officers use an irritant (likely tear gas) to clear out hundreds of peaceful protesters in Lafayette Square for a photo op. "If a city or state refuses to take actions that are necessary to defend the life and property of their residents," he told journalists, "then I will deploy the United States military and quickly solve the problem for them." As he reached the end of his term, he sowed distrust in the election by undermining voting by mail. He then questioned the peaceful transfer of power, a hallmark of American democracy, and attempted to overturn the results of the election. This led to America's polity score dropping from a +7 to a +5, the lowest score since 1800.

The United States became an anocracy for the first time in more than two hundred years. Let that sink in. We are no longer the world's oldest continuous democracy. That honor is now held by Switzerland, followed by New Zealand, and then Canada. We are no longer a peer to nations like Canada, Costa Rica, and Japan, which are all rated a +10 on the polity index.

There is some good news. A few of the guardrails that protect democracy remained firm in the face of challenges. Though Trump and the Republican Party filed more than sixty lawsuits claiming election fraud in swing states, more than fifty of those were dismissed or denied (the handful that did make it through were overturned in higher courts). The Supreme Court, which has a majority of conservative judges, also rejected Trump's election challenge. Republican state officials on the receiving end of the president's bullying—Trump threatened to sideline Arizona's governor for certifying election results and pressured Georgia's secretary of state to "find" the votes he'd need to win—held their ground.

So, too, did the military. Trump catered to America's generals throughout his time in office, but rather than validate his bids for more power, they distanced themselves from his agenda at key moments. In 2020, Secretary of Defense Mark Esper refused to use active-duty troops to control Black Lives Matter demonstrators (he was later fired). And on January 3, 2021, the ten living former defense secretaries, including James Mattis, Mark Esper, Dick Cheney, and Donald Rumsfeld, issued a statement in *The Washington Post* making clear that they would defend the Constitution, not the president. They concurred with a statement made months earlier by General Mark Milley, chairman of the Joint Chiefs of Staff: "There's no role for the U.S. military in determining the outcome of a U.S. election."

There are other reasons for hope. On January 6, after the Capitol was again secure, members of Congress immediately returned to work. They certified the results of the election, ensuring a peaceful transfer of power and safeguarding the rule of law. The FBI immediately launched investigations into the rioters, filing its first conspiracy charge against the leader of the Oath Keepers. The agency vetted National Guard troops in charge of security at the inauguration, and the Pentagon ramped up efforts to eliminate far-right extremism within its own ranks. Biden and his vice president, Kamala Harris, were sworn into office. It is thanks to the peaceful transfer of power and the new administration's subsequent respect for the rule of law that America's polity score rose to +8.

Still, we cannot ignore what happened, or the speed at which it happened. Americans are used to thinking of their democracy as the best in the world—we've even exported our Constitution to countries in eastern Europe and Latin America—but we transitioned from a full democracy to an anocracy in just five years. That's not quite as fast as the countries that have found themselves in civil wars (they usually see a six-point or more drop in their polity score within three years), but it's close. "A drop of five points is considered borderline," Monty Marshall has noted, and it signals potential "regime change." In the words of Anna Lührmann, the deputy director of the V-Dem Institute, the democratic decay in the United States has been "precipitous" and, at least in the U.S., "unprecedented."

A partial democracy is three times as likely to experience civil war as a full democracy. Recall, too, that the risk of civil war for a decaying democracy rises significantly soon after it enters the anocracy zone. A country standing on this threshold—as America recently was—can easily be pushed toward conflict through a combination of bad governance and increasingly undemocratic measures that further weaken its institutions. The question for America moving forward is whether voters can be persuaded that their democracy works (and is critical to their safety)—and whether leaders will choose to reinstate its guardrails.

JAMES MADISON AND Alexander Hamilton believed that if American democracy were to die, it would happen at the hands of a faction. The greatest threat to the republic, wrote the authors of the Federalist Papers, was not an outside adversary but a homegrown group ravenous for control. Given the chance, the leaders of such a faction—"adverse to the rights of other citizens or to the permanent and aggregate interests of the community"—would consolidate power and elevate their own interests over the public good. The type of faction the founders saw as the greatest threat was based on class; they worried that property owners might seek to concentrate political power to protect their wealth and prevent its redistribution. The Madisonian model of creating separate, powerful branches of government—executive, legislative, judicial—was designed to counteract this threat.

What America's eighteenth-century leaders couldn't have predicted was that the factionalization they feared would be rooted not in class but in ethnic identity. That's because in 1789, at least at the federal level, all American voters were white (and all of them were men). Today, the best predictor of how Americans will vote is their race. Two-thirds or more of Black, Latino, and Asian Americans consistently vote for Democrats, while roughly 60 percent of white Americans vote for Republicans. That represents a dramatic shift from the middle part of the last century, when the ethnic minority vote was split roughly between the two parties, and most white working-class Americans tended to vote Democratic.

In fact, as late as 2007—the year before Barack Obama was elected president—whites were just as likely (51 percent) to be Democrats as they were Republicans. Today, 90 percent of the Republican Party is white.

The shift toward identity-based politics began in force in the mid-1960s, when Lyndon Johnson—the bawdy, bigoted, and politically savvy Texan—betrayed white southerners by backing the Civil Rights Act. Voters in the eleven former Confederate states had been faithful Democrats for over a hundred years, still angry that Republican president Abraham Lincoln had refused to accept secession. But Johnson's legislation, in 1964, led to a seismic change. ("I think we just delivered the South to the Republican Party for a long time to come," Johnson said to his special assistant, Bill Moyers.) Though the Democrats won the presidency that year in a landslide, Johnson's Republican rival, Barry Goldwater— who opposed the Civil Rights Act—was the first Republican candidate to win all of the Deep South's electoral votes since Reconstruction. Richard Nixon, a former presidential candidate himself, had already seen the implications from afar. As he told a reporter for *Ebony* magazine in 1962, "If Goldwater wins his fight, our party would eventually become the first major all-white political party. And that isn't good."

It didn't take long, however, for Nixon to change his mind. Running for president in 1968, Nixon decided to capitalize on racial resentment himself, leveraging white fear with calls for "law and order" and a pledge to fight the "war on drugs." This so-called Southern Strategy helped the GOP win the presidency and later retake the Senate after being out of power for almost thirty years. Future Republican candidates would rely on similar appeals to win the presidency, though always with coded language, whether it was Ronald Reagan shaming "welfare queens" or George H. W. Bush disparaging Willie Horton. George W. Bush's campaign was accused of spreading rumors of John McCain fathering an illegitimate Black child.

Over the following decades, other identity markers became politicized. Religion was next. In an effort to secure the support of evangelical leaders and their increasingly mobilized flock, Republican elites staked out more and more pro-life positions. People like Jerry Falwell, Sr., the leader of the Moral Majority, a political organization associated with the Christian right, grew increasingly powerful. Democrats, seeing a chance to win over more atheists, agnostics, and culturally liberal voters, came out more and more in favor of women's rights and access to abortion. By the early twenty-first century, if you were Christian or evangelical, you had little choice but to vote Republican. Early partisan divides on abortion were followed by increasingly polarized positions on gay rights and eventually transgender rights. Wealthy Republicans used these issues to capture the white working-class vote, and they largely succeeded, even though voting Republican was often not in workers' economic interest. Moral imperatives and cultural identities were now, more than ever, driving voting patterns. White evangelicals now represent two-thirds of the Republican Party. By contrast, non-Christians—including agnostics, Jews, and Muslims—represent half of the Democratic Party.

By appealing to their core policy concerns like gun rights and by playing on their anxieties about immigration and America's changing racial demographics (whites are projected to be in the minority by 2045), Republicans have been able to win over larger and larger shares of the white rural vote. Likewise, the Democratic Party has become an increasingly urban party by doing essentially the opposite—trying to reduce violence by restricting access to guns and embracing the diversity that is reshaping urban America. Today, the rural-urban divide is really a divide between citizens whose orientation is national and citizens whose orientation is global.

By the time Obama came into office, political division had become deeply intertwined with a host of ethnic and social identities. Your group affinities—who you liked and who you didn't—were becoming much more important politically than how you felt about policy and whether, for example, you favored higher or lower taxes or supported school choice. This phenomenon was epitomized by the inordinate attention Obama received not for his policy positions but for identity-related concerns, such as whether he was a Muslim (he was not) and whether he was a citizen (he was). The result was two tribes that increasingly fought over almost everything—and were increasingly willing, especially on the Republican side, to subvert democracy to win.

All of this was exacerbated by social media. Just as the two parties were diverging on identity, Twitter exploded, Facebook went mainstream, and social media became an ever present part of our lives. Critically, a network of gleeful ethnic entrepreneurs realized that they could gain ratings and influence by emphasizing this division. Media titans whose bottom lines were enhanced by each of those clicks fed us more and more polarized content. Savvy TV personalities like Tucker Carlson and Sean Hannity were only too happy to spread conspiracy theories and use hatred and division to increase their own ratings. They were joined by conspiracy theorist Alex Jones, who promoted distrust of the political system altogether; by 2010, *The Alex Jones Show* was attracting two million listeners each week. Keith Olbermann, for his part, stirred up left-leaning voters.

Into this political morass stepped the biggest ethnic entrepreneur of all: Donald Trump. And in his bid for power, he quickly realized that appeals to identity could galvanize his political base. He had already, in the past, made a racist crusade of questioning Obama's birthplace. Now he embraced identity politics explicitly and with gusto. He painted Black Americans as poor and violent. He referred to Mexicans as criminals. He spoke of Christian values, despite numerous accusations of sexual assault. He called women "horseface," "fat," and "ugly." Once sworn into office, he quickly instituted a travel ban on Muslims, and called Haiti, El Salvador, and African nations "shithole" countries. His policies were nativist policies: He started building a "big, beautiful wall" along the border with Mexico, pulled out of international agreements, and started a trade war against China. Trump retweeted a video of a retiree in Florida chanting "white power." And he threatened to veto a defense spending bill in order to protect the legacy of Confederate generals on U.S. Army bases.

In all of these ways, Trump was encouraging ethnic factionalism. It's exactly what Tudjman did when, as part of his plan to become president of an independent Croatia, he began to consolidate Croatians into an ethnic faction in 1989. It is what Hutu extremists did when they characterized Tutsis as cockroaches and Hutus as the chosen people. It's what President Henri Konan Bédié did in the Ivory Coast in the mid-1990s, when he reversed his pro-immigrant policies to gain more votes from native citizens. And it is what Modi in India still does, when he promotes an India primarily for Hindus.

No Republican president in the past fifty years had ever pursued such an openly racist platform, or championed white, evangelical Americans at the expense of everyone else. At first, it wasn't clear that the Republican leadership would go along—during his own presidential campaign, Texas senator Ted Cruz blasted Trump, calling him "utterly amoral"—but in Trump they saw a way to enact their own agendas. This included tax cuts for the rich, business deregulation, and environmental rollbacks. With Trump in the White House and Republicans controlling the Senate, the party could also stack the Supreme Court and the judiciary more generally with conservative judges who could potentially stymie democratic initiatives for years to come. Though gerrymandering was a tactic on both sides, Republican governors and Republican state legislatures have made concerted efforts to enact voter ID laws, purge voter rolls, limit polling stations and hours, and even withhold food and drink from people waiting in lengthy voting lines.

As you'll recall, the level of factionalism in a country is based on a five-point scale, with 5 being the least factional and 1 being the most (a 3 puts a country firmly in the danger zone). In 2016, the United States dropped to a 3—factionalized—and it remains there today, alongside Ukraine and Iraq. (The United Kingdom also fell to a 3 in 2016.) We've seen this level of political factionalism only twice before: In the years before the Civil War, which were marked by the intransigence of Southern Democrats and their willingness to exclude non-whites from equal protection under the law; and in the mid-1960s, when the country was roiled by civil rights demonstrations, the Vietnam War, and a corrupt government intent on crushing the anti-establishment movement. Both times, the country's political parties had radically different visions of America's future: What could the country be? What *should* the country be?

The same is happening today. Just as in the past, one group is increasingly becoming more radical, more willing to use extralegal measures, and more violent in the pursuit of its vision. Today, the Republican Party is behaving like a predatory faction. In a 2019 survey that asked nearly two thousand experts to rate the world's political parties, the GOP was rated most similar to radical right anti-democratic parties such as Turkey's Justice and Development Party (known as the AKP) and Poland's Law and Justice Party (known by its acronym PiS). It is primarily ethnic and religious based. It has supported a populist who pursued white nationalist policies at the expense of other citizens, and it has elevated personality above principle. The annual Conservative Political Action Conference (CPAC) in February 2021 showcased a golden statue of Donald Trump; a poll of attendees revealed that 68 percent of them wanted Trump to run again, and 95 percent wanted the GOP to pursue Trump's agenda and policies moving forward.

Republicans are now in a state of desperate survival politics where they are playing to an increasingly rabid base just to hold on to their seats. Nowhere was this more evident than after the 2020 election, when Republican politicians openly supported—or tacitly approved—Trump's claims of fraud, against all evidence. Ted Cruz went on Fox News's *Sunday Morning Futures with Maria Bartiromo* to talk about voter fraud. On January 6, as Trump supporters were cheering at the Ellipse, Republican senators Ted Cruz, Mike

Braun, John Kennedy, Ron Johnson, Steve Daines, James Lankford, Marsha Blackburn, and Bill Hagerty made a final attempt to overturn the votes. One hundred and thirty-nine Republican members of the House of Representatives (66 percent) voted against certifying Joe Biden as president. Two House members—Mo Brooks from Alabama and Madison Cawthorn of North Carolina—had spoken at the rally on the Ellipse. It was James Madison and Alexander Hamilton's worst fear: the dismantling of democracy by a faction's cynical bid for power.

FOR AMERICA'S FIRST 219 years, every president was a white man. So was almost every U.S. senator, representative, Supreme Court justice, and cabinet member. That the early founders had sanctioned mass genocide of Native Americans, or that many of them were slaveholders, were inconvenient chapters in a mythic narrative of freedom and unbound opportunity. Serbs had their Battle of Kosovo, Russians had Kievan Rus (the belief that mother Russia originated in Ukraine), Spaniards had the Reconquista, which claimed their land for Catholics. We had our Pilgrims seeking a new life. According to our founding story, it was the manifest destiny of our people—at least those who were white and Protestant—to expand across the continent and harvest its riches.

The election of Barack Obama, a dark-skinned president with a Muslim middle name, shattered that myth. His victory was clear evidence that America's demographics and balance of political power were changing. Americans not only had their first Black president, but the majority of Obama's cabinet was non-white as well. The seismic change reflected in the faces of the new administration was confirmed by the 2012 Census Bureau population estimate, which revealed that, for the first time, a majority of babies born in the United States were non-white. Hispanic and Asian populations had grown by 43 percent in the previous ten years, while the white population had grown by just 6 percent. By around 2045, minorities in America will likely outnumber the white majority. The census, according to Andrew Cherlin, a sociologist at Johns Hopkins University, was a "watershed moment. It show[ed] us how multicultural we'[d] become."

In 2015, Lin-Manuel Miranda, a composer from New York City of Puerto Rican and Mexican descent, premiered *Hamilton* on Broadway. All the founding fathers were played by people of color. It was a smashing success. But for those who had once felt secure in America, it signified a radical departure from tradition. Many white citizens, particularly those in rural areas, were already feeling left behind economically. Since 1989, the quality of life for the white working class with no college education had been declining according to almost every measure: Their share of income had fallen, their homeownership and marriage rates had plummeted, and their life expectancy had dropped. (The same was not true of working-class Latinos or Black families, or of households headed by white college graduates; living standards for these groups remained steady or improved slightly between 1989 and 2016.) Increasingly open global trade had hollowed out U.S. manufacturing. Citizens of Homestead, Pennsylvania, and Youngstown, Ohio, saw union jobs at the local steel mills disappear, then the steel mills shut down entirely. They saw their children go off to foreign wars and come back to minimum wage jobs with no benefits. They were losing friends to opioid addiction or suicide.

Working-class whites had been hailed as the backbone of America, their ways and values memorialized in Norman Rockwell paintings. And now, it seemed, the government was abandoning them. Global trade agreements were signed that benefited coastal elites and city dwellers at their expense. Immigration continued, and allowances were made for illegal immigrants. To whites experiencing real economic and social decline, the U.S. government was like the Indian government that encouraged Bengalis to migrate to Assam, the Indonesian government that encouraged Javanese to migrate to West Papua, or the Sri Lankan government that had encouraged the Sinhalese to migrate to Tamil regions. White Americans were seeing young people from countries like India and China—whose first language wasn't English, whose religion was not Christianity—get lucrative tech jobs and live an American dream that no longer existed for them.

Trump intuitively understood that this deep feeling of alienation could carry him to power. And so he didn't just focus on division, denigrating Muslims or Black Americans as the "other." He also emphasized the downgrading of the former white majority—America's own sons of the soil. Like other ethnic entrepreneurs before him, he put the grievances of white, male, Christian, rural Americans into a simplified framework that painted them as victims whose rightful legacy had been stolen. He spoke often about what was being taken away: religious rights, gun rights, job opportunities. His campaign slogan promised a return to glory: "Make America Great Again." In him, people saw someone unlike any other candidate, someone who recognized their lives. In January 2017, in his inaugural address, he described their experience as an "American carnage." "Their pain is our pain," Trump told the nation. "Their dreams are our dreams, and their success will be our success."

In the United States, white Americans are now dispro-portionately concentrated in rural areas throughout the Northeast, Midwest, and mountain states, while non-whites tend to be concentrated in urban areas, the South, and along the coasts. This urban-rural divide has become a critical fea-ture in other far-right movements, such as in Turkey and Thailand, where the territorial distribution of power and economic resources increasingly lies in the major cities, which also tend to be more multicultural than the more ho-mogenous rural regions. Movements that are geographically concentrated and predominantly rural are more likely to mobilize violent resistance because it's easier to recruit sol-diers, collect funding, and evade police in areas far from the capital. This was true of the Sunnis in Syria, the Moro peo-ple in Mindanao, and Papuans in West Papua. Extremists exist in American cities, but they are more often located in rural areas—areas that also contain a higher percentage of military veterans and where gun culture has strong roots.

The grievances of sons of the soil are often deeply felt, if not always legitimate. It's what makes the appeals of political leaders such as Trump so effective. The leaders of the Provi-sional IRA tapped into Irish Catholics' genuine anger at eco-nomic and political discrimination at the hands of Protestants. The leaders of Hamas tapped into Palestinians' deep resent-ment at losing their land. The Republican Party, by embrac-ing white Americans' grievances, has become like other political parties that have championed sons of the soil move-ments around the world: the Serbian Radical Party in Yugo-slavia, the Islamic Party of the Philippines in Mindanao, the

Tamil National Alliance in Sri Lanka, and the far-right parties that have emerged in Europe. The Sweden Democrats campaigned, and won votes, on the issue of immigration. After Europe's Syrian refugee crisis, in 2015, Germany's populist Alternative für Deutschland (AfD) went from a failed party to the country's second largest. And Austria's Freedom Party, after struggling in the early 2000s, had enormous success in the 2017 election with its anti-immigration platform. It now shares power with the center right.

Trump's emphasis on grievance has been amplified by other ethnic entrepreneurs, whose conspiracy theories and half-truths have fed a vulnerable audience that was already convinced it was under attack. Breitbart News, led by Trump's chief campaign strategist Steve Bannon, emphasized what Bannon called "alt-right" news. This included a focus on the perils of immigration and the coming of American sharia. Mike Cernovich, a social media personality, gained hundreds of thousands of followers on Twitter and had Fox pick up his stories by spreading conspiracy theories such as Pizzagate, which claimed that Democrats were Satanists and pedophiles.

Social media algorithms—and Trump's rapid-fire tweeting—have reinforced the sense of aggrievement among white conservatives. A 2016 study by researchers at Princeton and New York University found that self-identified conservatives and Republicans were more likely to share false news than Democrats and liberals. Researchers at the University of Oxford similarly found that conservatives were far more likely than liberals to spread information that is intentionally misleading or not true. This pattern was present in the most recent 2019 election in the United Kingdom. Claire Wardle, a leading expert on social media, found that the Conservative Party was running ads in which 88 percent of the content was labeled as misleading by a fact checker. The same was not true of other parties.

Trump showed future candidates how to lock in a subset of white voters and rally them to go to the polls. One particularly compelling study showed that the best predictor of voters who switched from Obama to Trump was not a change in financial well-being—which had little impact on candidate preference—but instead concerns about status threat, including deep anxiety about the rise of a majority-minority America. Justin Gest showed that the best way to predict Republican support was simply to ask white working-class Americans how much power and status they felt they had lost in the past few decades. White Americans who perceived that they were losing power voted overwhelmingly Republican. In another study, researchers found that by experimentally triggering threats to whites' social standing, they could greatly increase whites' support for punitive policies against minorities.

Almost everyone who scored highest on a widely respected racial resentment measure voted for Trump in 2016, while almost everyone on the opposite end of the scale supported Hillary Clinton. Even after taking into account partisanship, whites' resentment at Black gains and Black demands for equal rights had an oversized impact on the vote. According to one analysis, Republicans with high racial resentment scores were about 30 percent more likely to support Trump than their less aggrieved Republican peers. Perhaps most convincing are studies showing that attitudes on race strongly predict party defections. Those who are racially resentful today are especially likely to become Republicans tomorrow.

The scholars who created the racial resentment scale argue that the racial views of white Americans have changed radically over the last half century. The United States, they write, has shifted from a nation where most of the population believed that racial minorities were inferior to one where many Americans believe that all races are equal but resent African Americans and other minorities for demanding too much in the way of special favors and accommodations. Along with being anti-Black, these attitudes are fueled by reverence for rugged individualism: Racially resentful whites feel that, by asking for government support and protection, Blacks are not adhering to values associated with the Protestant work ethic. In the 2016 American National Election Study, about 40 percent of Americans (and almost 50 percent of white Americans) could be categorized as racially resentful—figures that suggest this new, more subtle form of prejudice is widely held. Remember, it's not the desperately poor who start civil wars, but those who once had privilege and feel they are losing status they feel is rightfully theirs.

People throughout history have spent a lot of time and energy justifying their claims to a place. American Southerners did this after the Civil War: Unwilling to accept the reality of defeat, groups such as the United Daughters of the Confederacy, the United Confederate Veterans Association, and the Ku Klux Klan carefully crafted a narrative of a genteel South whose culture and way of life had been destroyed by the money-grabbing, industrial North. Symbols of the Confederacy—memorials, plantations, flags—advanced the "Lost Cause" narrative: a nostalgia for a better, simpler time in America, when the South's dominance was uncontested.

Trump spun a similar narrative in the wake of his 2020

presidential loss. Just as the Confederates clung to the story of the Lost Cause—the South had better men, they were never truly defeated—so, too, did Trump, insisting that he hadn't really lost and, more critically, that the election had been stolen from its true heirs. After the attack on the Capitol failed to produce the results he wanted, Trump's myth would offer him and his followers just the story line they needed. They didn't shut out immigrants; they just made them play by the rules. They weren't intolerant; they honored God. They weren't extremists; they were patriots who cared about their country. *That's* what they were fighting for.

THE 2020 ELECTION was devastating for Republicans. They turned out in record numbers for an incumbent president, but still lost the White House by more than seven million votes. Two months later, a pair of Democratic victories in Georgia, a key flip state in the presidential election, made the new vice president, a Black and South Asian woman from California, the deciding vote in the Senate.

A movement turns to violence when all hope is lost. As the storming of the Capitol made clear, citizens on the right are not just resentful of their declining status, they now believe that the system is stacked against them. Everyone they trust—from Fox News to their senators—has told them so. In a poll conducted days after the Capitol siege, nearly three-quarters of likely Republican voters continued to doubt the presidential election results. Polls also revealed that 45 percent of Republicans supported the attack on the Capitol. And more than six months after the election, a majority of Republicans surveyed still claimed that the election had been stolen and that Donald Trump was the true president. The peaceful inauguration of President Biden did not change their views.

Americans across the political spectrum are becoming more accepting of violence as a means to achieve political goals, not less. Recent survey data show that 33 percent of Democrats and 36 percent of Republicans feel "somewhat justified" in using violence. In 2017, just 8 percent of people in both parties felt the same way. Another recent survey found that 20 percent of Republicans and 15 percent of Democrats say the United States would be better off if large numbers of the other party *died*. But when does sporadic violence escalate into civil war? How do you pinpoint the moment when hope is lost?

The CIA has been studying this question for decades, in an effort to quell insurgencies around the world—in effect, to stop civil wars before they start. Though the agency's mission is to provide intelligence about foreign countries, a declassified report from 2012 sheds light on how homegrown extremism tends to evolve. Most insurgencies, the report notes, "pass through similar stages of development during their life cycle." In the pre-insurgency phase, a group begins to identify a set of common grievances and build a collective identity around a gripping narrative—the story or myth that helps them rally supporters and justify their actions. They begin to recruit members, some of whom even travel abroad for training. They begin to stockpile arms and supplies.

The United States probably entered the pre-insurgency phase in the early 1990s, with the formation of militias in the wake of the deadly standoffs at Ruby Ridge in Idaho—when federal agents killed right-wing activist Randy Weaver's wife and son—and the fifty-one-day siege in Waco, Texas, which left eighty dead, including twenty-two children, after the Branch Davidians set fire to the compound as the FBI attempted to raid it. By the mid-1990s, militias were active in virtually all fifty states, peaking just after Timothy McVeigh killed 168 people in Oklahoma City in the deadliest domestic terror attack in U.S. history. The number of militias in the United States began to grow again in 2008, when Barack Obama was elected president. Prior to 2008, only about 43 militias existed; by 2011, there were 334.

Today's militias are different in nature from those in the past. In the 1970s, most violent extremist groups in the United States were left leaning. Today, less than a quarter are. During Obama's presidency, the country began to see an increase in far-right organizations plotting racially motivated attacks. About 65 percent of far-right extremists in the United States today have white supremacist elements. These groups are, in the words of the FBI, "motivated by a hatred of other races and religions," and they have more guns and more members than militias of the past. A subset—29 percent—are also part of the sovereign citizen movement, which rejects the authority of the federal government. Two of the most high-profile militias in the United States, the Oath Keepers and the Three Percenters, were founded after Obama became president, out of the belief that the federal government was "working to destroy the liberties of Americans." A more recent addition is the anti-immigrant, all-male Proud Boys. As of March 2021, ten people associated with the Oath Keepers have been arrested for helping to organize the January 6 siege of the Capitol. More troubling, members of all three organizations had been actively communicating in the lead-up to January 6, suggesting a possible alliance. According to JJ MacNab, one of the world's experts on extremist organizations, "You have had distinct groups in the past—sovereign citizens, tax protesters, militia, survivalists, Oath Keepers, Three Percenters—and I think they are just becoming one big messy family right now."

Right-wing terrorism used to rise and fall depending on who was president: It decreased when a Republican was in the White House and increased when a Democrat was in power. President Trump broke the pattern. For the first time, violent right-wing groups increased their activity during a Republican administration. The president encouraged the more extreme voices among his supporters rather than seeking to calm or marginalize them. To these followers, Trump's 2016 victory wasn't the end of their fight; it was the beginning. As Trump put it in his first presidential debate against Democrat Joe Biden, they were to stand back and stand by.

The second stage of insurgency, which the CIA calls the incipient conflict stage, is marked by discrete acts of violence. Timothy McVeigh's attack in Oklahoma City could be viewed as the very earliest attack, in some ways years before its time. The insurgents' goal is to broadcast their mission to the world, build support, and provoke a government overreaction to their violence, so that more moderate citizens become radicalized and join the movement. The second stage is when the government becomes aware of the groups behind these attacks, but according to the CIA, the violence is often dismissed "as the work of bandits, criminals, or terrorists." Timothy McVeigh seemed to many Americans a lone wolf actor. But McVeigh and his accomplice, Terry Nichols, were suspected members of the Michigan Militia. In 2012, the number of right-wing terrorist attacks and plots was fourteen; by August 2020, it was sixty-one, a historic high.

The open insurgency stage, the final phase, according to the CIA's report, is characterized by sustained violence as increasingly active extremists launch attacks that involve terrorism and guerrilla warfare, including assassinations and ambushes, as well as hit-and-run raids on police and military units. These groups also tend to use more sophisticated weapons, such as improvised explosive devices, and begin to attack vital infrastructure (such as hospitals, bridges, and schools), rather than just individuals. These attacks also involve a larger number of fighters, some of whom have combat experience. There is often evidence "of insurgent penetration and subversion of the military, police, and intelligence services." If there is foreign support for the insurgents, this is where it becomes more apparent. In this stage, the extremists are trying to force the population to choose sides, in part by demonstrating to citizens that the government cannot keep them safe or provide basic necessities. The insurgents are trying to prove that they are the ones who should have political power; they are the ones who should rule. The goal is to incite a broader civil war, by denigrating the state and growing support for extreme measures.

Where is the United States today? We are a factionalized country on the edge of anocracy that is quickly approaching the open insurgency stage, which means we are closer to civil war than any of us would like to believe. The siege on the Capitol has made it impossible for the government to dismiss the threat that far-right groups pose to the United States and its democracy. January 6 was a major announcement by at least some groups—such as the Oath Keepers—that they are moving toward outright violence. Many in the crowd declared this intention with black signs and T-shirts that said "MAGA Civil War January 6, 2021." In fact, the attack on the Capitol could well be the first of a series of organized attacks in an open insurgency stage. It targeted infrastructure. There were plans to assassinate certain politicians and attempts to coordinate activity. It also involved a large number of fighters, some of whom have combat experience. At least 14 percent of those arrested and charged are thought to have connections to the military or law enforcement.

As Tim Alberta, chief political correspondent for *Politico,* tweeted after the insurrection: "The stuff I've heard in the last 72 hours—from members of Congress, law enforcement friends, gun shop owners, MAGA devotees—is absolutely chilling. We need to brace for a wave of violence in this country. Not just over the next couple of weeks, but over the next couple of years."

We do not yet know whether the attack on the Capitol will be replicated or become part of a pattern. If it does, Americans will begin to feel unsafe, unprotected by their government. They will question who is in charge. Some will take advantage of the chaos to gain through violence what they couldn't gain through conventional methods. That's when we'll know we've truly entered the open insurgency stage. For now, one thing is clear: America's extremists are becoming more organized, more dangerous, and more determined, and they are not going away.

CHAPTER 7

WHAT A WAR WOULD LOOK LIKE

On the morning of Tuesday, November 14, 2028, Wisconsin House Speaker Justin Lawrence steps to the podium to call the state legislature to order. Before he can speak, a bomb explodes, shattering the enormous skylight and showering the ornate second-floor room with shards of glass. Amid the smoke and splintered furniture, the mangled bodies of twelve legislators lie on the red carpet—among them Lawrence, nearly ten feet from where he'd been standing. A security guard, covered in blood, also lies motionless on the floor. Two thousand miles away, another bomb explodes in the state capitol in Salem, Oregon. Reports circulate of large explosions in or around capitol buildings in Denver, Atlanta, Santa Fe, and Lansing, Michigan. People are already on edge, with fires raging in California and several Category 4 hurricanes having hit the East Coast in quick succession, causing catastrophic damage.

As word of the bombing spreads, Americans stop what they are doing to watch the news and frantically scroll through their social media feeds. No one understands what is happening, or whether they can even trust what they're seeing. One video, apparently from inside a large auditorium at the University of Texas in Austin, shows students screaming and running. It's blurry, but it looks like there's a body in a pool of blood on the stage. It's later revealed that someone opened fire in the school's largest lecture hall, killing the head of the biology department as he was teaching a class on molecular immunology. Videos stream in from all across the country with scenes of blood and chaos. It seems like everything is exploding at the same time.

James Demick, CNN's chief news correspondent, reports that seven state capitol buildings have been hit. CNN has also received reports that, earlier in the day, Secret Service agents foiled plans to assassinate President-elect Kamala Harris as she gave a speech announcing her intention to ban assault weapons, and Fox News reports that another failed assassination attempt targeted the Democratic governor of California.

By the next morning, Americans have a better sense of the extent of the damage. Wisconsin's Democratic governor and attorney general, a Republican, are in critical condition, and it's not clear whether they will survive. Unexploded bombs have been discovered in Topeka, Salt Lake City, Phoenix, and Albany. The main courthouse in downtown Philadelphia has also been hit, killing four judges, and has been closed indefinitely. Looting has begun.

It is unclear who is behind the attacks or why these targets were chosen. In fact, the range of methods and weapons—an army grenade in Denver, a car bomb in Santa Fe—suggests that multiple groups are behind it. But no one comes forward. Instead, stories quickly emerge and spread on Rumble, Gab, and MeWe, as well as Telegram, Facebook, and Twitter, that a left-wing group—Blacks for Anarchy ("blaKx")—is to blame, and that this is part of a coordinated attack by minorities to take over the country. Viral YouTube videos show Black youths throwing bricks through store windows and setting cars on fire. In one particularly disturbing video, a Black Lives Matter leader threatens further violence and calls on Black Americans to "prepare for the war we all know we need to fight." QAnon's network is on fire with rumors that blaKx is working with Mexicans, Salvadorans, Puerto Ricans, and Muslims, and that professors at America's elite universities are directing the movement behind the scenes. That afternoon, YouTube announces that the Black Lives Matter video is a deepfake, and takes it down after 3.7 million views.

Three days later, an anonymous fourteen-page manifesto, called "Cast off the Yoke," appears on 8kun. The language, rambling and combative, celebrates the carnage, and appears to take credit for some of it, insisting that violence is an overdue corrective to the "radical-left politics" of America's cities, which are ruled by a "corrupted, self-hating elite" that is "killing the country in darkness with their silent blades." The manifesto repeats conspiracy theories that have circulated on Telegram in the past few years: that Democrats, supported by immigrants and Jews, plan to confiscate all guns, abolish local police and declare martial law, turn churches into abortion clinics, and seize land from white farmers to hand over to Black families as reparations. They must be stopped, the user declares, before they take over the country and turn the United States into a mixed-race, secular, socialist state. The next day, authorities trace the 8kun account to the Countrymen, a right-wing militia. The two competing narratives—is the country under siege from the left or the right?—are almost impossible to sort out, but the FBI determines that the Countrymen are almost certainly behind the attacks.

Government offices, schools, places of worship all close—everything grinds to a halt. People stay at home, afraid to shop or go to work. Americans across the country wait for help. President-elect Harris calls for calm and tries to dissuade her party from sending in federal troops, fearing it would just incite more violence by groups she believes are already anti-government. Congress is deadlocked.

Over the next ten days, sporadic attacks continue, this time in Los Angeles, Boston, Tallahassee, Miami, and New Orleans. The scope is widening, too, with attacks on schools, churches, and big-box stores. People feel as if their government has collapsed. Jennifer Lawson, a working mother who lives in Maplewood, New Jersey, appears in an interview on CNN. Staring into the camera with tired, glazed eyes, she says, "I feel like no one is there for me and my family. I have no idea who to trust."

Militias grow more visible, often claiming to be neighborhood watchmen, but in fact selectively harassing young Black men, Latinos, and Asians. They have even begun to threaten National Guard troops, judges, politicians, and police officers that they can't persuade to join them. They seem determined to take control of local governments and limit the federal government's ability to enforce any laws the militants dislike. Black-clad men with automatic weapons force abortion clinics to close and intimidate customers who frequent minority-owned shops. No one stops them.

Americans on the left begin to form their own militias to protect their families and neighborhoods. Local law enforcement and federal agents increasingly fade into the background, becoming secondary players in a larger contest between local militias as more and more Americans are forced to choose with which group to align.

On January 13, 2029, a week before the inauguration, supporters of soon-to-be President Harris march in Detroit, demanding even stricter gun control legislation and the deployment of federal troops to safeguard their city. But another crowd has also gathered near the capitol. The militiamen include individuals who appear not to speak English, some of whom have insignias associated with the AfD in Germany and the far-right Russian Imperial Movement (RIM). Soon drones can be heard overhead, whirling ominously above the protesters. As pro-Harris demonstrators advance down the street, the militiamen step into their path. The pushing and jostling starts almost immediately. "Go back to Portland!" someone is heard to yell. "This is a true-Patriot state!" A rock flies through the air and a nearby storefront shatters. People are climbing over cars. Firecrackers explode.

Suddenly, someone fires two shots, and the crowd scatters. Undercover federal agents step in. They spray tear gas into the hyped-up crowd, and then fire rubber bullets into a group of militiamen who appear to have started the shooting. Videos of bleeding militiamen quickly reach the internet. Angry supporters erupt into side streets, taking baseball bats to windshields as they flee. A "Black Lives Matter" flag is set on fire and thrown through a car window; the vehicle is engulfed in flames. Twelve-year-old Emma Jones, the daughter of one of the militiamen, is rushed to the hospital with burn wounds. The next day, she dies in the intensive care unit. Across the Midwest, her name becomes a rallying cry for white nationalists, who accuse "radical left crazies" of stoking violence. The hashtag #Fight4Emma goes viral, spreading on social media. On YouTube, QAnon influencers warn followers that the Storm has finally arrived.

On Twitter, Senate Majority Leader John Cornyn and

other prominent Republicans call for national unity. But it doesn't rise above the cacophony of competing messages: *The radical left is taking over the country. White nationalists plan to kill any minorities who protest. The government is colluding with the right. The government is colluding with the left. The government is doing nothing.* Gun and ammunition sales spike. Canned goods fly off grocery shelves.

After nine consecutive nights of protests and riots, Detroit residents begin to flee the city. The streets are choked with smoke. "My daughter's afraid to sleep at night," says Anna Miller, who has lived in the city for thirty years. Detroit's faith leaders call for peace and healing. But the violence doesn't subside; it spreads to Milwaukee, Philadelphia, and Atlanta. "We don't want a fight," says Elijah Lewis, a protester from Milwaukee, "but if Harris doesn't step up, I just don't see what else we can do."

WHEN WE IN the United States think of civil war, most of us think about our country's first Civil War, which lasted from 1861 to 1865. We picture officers on horseback, and blue-and gray-clad infantrymen charging each other on enormous battlefields. We see in our minds the photograph of President Lincoln at Antietam, consulting with officers outside a Union tent in his long coat and stovepipe hat. Or we remember Pickett's Charge, commemorated in paintings, when a mass of Confederate soldiers attacked a wall of Union soldiers on the last day of the Battle of Gettysburg. We think of bodies littered upon empty fields. We think of muddy embankments and cannons.

A civil war like this, we conclude, could not happen

again. For one thing, the U.S. government and its military is much stronger today. The U.S. military was weak in 1860, with only sixteen thousand soldiers spread out over the enormous continent; most of them, in fact, were stationed west of the Mississippi, to neutralize the "threat" posed by Native Americans. Today, the U.S. military has about 1.3 million soldiers under arms, an additional 900,000 in reserve, and roughly 450,000 in the National Guard. It also has the ability to move these soldiers quickly to problem areas. It was not crazy for Confederates to think they could take on the American military in 1860. It is crazy for militias to think that today.

There's also the matter of geography. By 1861, Confederates were unified in their decision to secede; the leaders of all eleven states of the South agreed to create their own separate country. This was possible, in part, because the states were concentrated geographically in a single region. Most of the South's citizens supported secession; by 1861 there was very little disagreement about what they should do in the wake of Lincoln's election. Today, by contrast, would-be secessionists are dispersed around the country, and attempts to separate— from the Alaskan independence movement to the Cascadia secessionist movement (which would join Oregon and Washington State with British Columbia)—seem far-fetched. There are also large and powerful pockets of left-leaning citizens living in urban areas of even the most conservative states, which means that a sizable contingent of citizens would oppose such a move.

But to think this way—to think of civil war only in these terms—is a failure of the imagination. That's because civil wars look entirely different today. Those who wage war against their governments in the twenty-first century tend to avoid the battlefield entirely; they know they will almost certainly lose in a conventional war against a powerful government. Instead, they choose the strategy of the weak: guerrilla warfare and terrorism. And, increasingly, domestic terror campaigns are aimed at democratic governments.

Terror can be effective in democracies because its targets—citizens—have political power: They can vote against politicians who are unable to stop the attacks. The Provisional IRA, Hamas, and the Tamil Tigers all believed that the more pain they inflicted on average citizens, the more likely governments would be to make concessions to the terrorists in exchange for peace. Either way, extremists benefit: They either convince the incumbent leader to pursue policies more favorable to the extremists (no gun control, stricter immigration policies), or they convince enough voters to elect a more extreme leader who is ideologically closer to them. Terror is also surprisingly easy to pull off in democracies, where there is more freedom of movement and less surveillance. There are also numerous constitutional constraints against labeling domestic groups terrorists, giving them more leeway than foreign terrorists would have.

If America has a second civil war, the combatants will not gather in fields, nor will they wear uniforms. They may not even have commanders. They will slip in and out of the shadows, communicating on message boards and encrypted networks. They will meet in small groups in vacuum-repair shops along retail strips, in desert clearings along Arizona's border, in public parks in Southern California, or in the snowy woods of Michigan, where they will train to fight. They will go online to plan their resistance, strategizing how to undermine the government at every level and gain control of parts of America. They will create chaos and fear. And then they will force Americans to pick sides.

EXTREMISTS TYPICALLY FIND inspiration for their beliefs in certain canonical texts. The members of al-Qaeda had Osama bin Laden's thirty-page manifesto, titled *Declaration of War Against the Americans Occupying the Land of the Two Holy Places.* The Nazis had Adolf Hitler's *Mein Kampf,* which he published in 1925, fourteen years before the German army invaded Poland. Libyan terrorists would refer to Muammar Gaddafi's *Green Book*—an homage to Mao's *Little Red Book*—which laid out Gaddafi's radical vision for remaking Libyan society.

In the United States, there is *The Turner Diaries,* which the FBI has called the "bible of the racist right." The book is a fictional account of an Aryan revolution that overturns the U.S. government. But the narrative—written in 1978 by William Pierce, who led the National Alliance, a neo-Nazi group—offers a playbook for leveraging racial resentment into a race war, offering a specific picture (terror attacks, mass casualty bombs) for how a band of fringe activists could take down the federal government and "awaken" other white people to the cause. Its themes—the media can't be trusted, the feds are coming for your guns, violence is inevitable—form a "heady heroic narrative that appeals to would-be rebels, patriots, and martyrs for a cause," as journalist Aja Romano has noted. "It teaches its adherents not just to adopt the mentality that they are at war with progressives, but that a real-life war is inevitable."

The Turner Diaries has directly inspired far-right terrorism. Pages from the book were found in Timothy McVeigh's truck after his attack on the Alfred P. Murrah Federal Building in Oklahoma City. Both Patrick Crusius, the alleged El Paso Walmart gunman, and John Timothy Earnest, accused of shooting up a synagogue in Poway, California, echoed ideas from the book in their manifestos. And the influence of the book was evident during the Capitol insurrection. It describes bombing FBI headquarters, attacking the Capitol building, and instituting "the Day of the Rope," in which "race traitors"—including politicians, lawyers, TV newscasters, judges, teachers, and preachers—are strung up on a gallows. In one video from January 6, 2021, a Proud Boy can be seen telling a journalist to read *The Turner Diaries.*

But there is also *Siege,* by neo-Nazi James Mason, a fan of cult leader Charles Manson. In the 1980s, Mason—who is still alive—wrote a series of newsletters for the American Nazi Party, in which he advocated murder and violence to create the kind of chaos that would destabilize the U.S. government. Mason's writings were then collected into a book. As reported by ProPublica, Mason encouraged his disciples to launch a clandestine guerrilla war to bring down "the System." He envisioned a mobile, decentralized White Liberation Front that would execute "hit-and-run" raids while hiding out "in wilderness areas." Mason even publicized what Americans were likely to experience first. "If I were asked by anyone [for] my opinion on what to look for," he writes, "I would tell them a wave of killings, or 'assassinations' of System bureaucrats by roving gun men who have their strategy well mapped-out in advance and well-nigh impossible to stop."

In 2017, a new 563-page edition of *Siege* was released, and in June 2020, *The Turner Diaries* was number 46 on Amazon's "Bestselling Literature" list. You could purchase both books on Amazon, where the site's recommendation engine would suggest you also purchase *White Power, Hunter* (an action novel about race), *Mein Kampf, Revolt Against the Modern World,* and *International Jew.* (Amazon is the biggest distributor of self-published books and as such has become a popular site to sell and distribute far-right material.) This changed only after the attack on the Capitol in January 2021, after which Amazon removed *Siege* and *The Turner Diaries* from its site.

Increasingly, civil wars involve some type of ethnic cleansing, and—thanks in part to these texts—there is every reason to suspect that this is where an escalating campaign of far-right terror in the United States would lead. In their quest to reset the country's social order, terrorists would aim to turn citizens against the federal government; convince moderates to accept the new status quo; intimidate minorities into remaining silent; and deter new immigrants from coming. They would also try to persuade regular Americans that they'd be safer if certain people—minorities, liberals, anyone deemed a "socialist"—left their cities and their states, creating a set of white ethno-states in the rural heartland.

Consider the recent decision made by the town clerk in Stratton, Vermont, to use the following language on the cover of the town's annual report: "You came here from there because you didn't like there, and now you want to change here to be like there. We are not racist, phobic or anti-whatever-you-are, we simply like here the way it is and most of us actually came here because it is not like there, wherever there was. You are welcome here, but please stop trying to make here like there. If you want here to be like there you should not have left there to come here, and you are invited to leave here and go back there at your earliest convenience." Internal migration alters the ethnic and religious makeup of an area, often in ways that local inhabitants don't like, and ethnic cleansing—whether forceful or subtle—is designed to roll it back.

Citizens almost never believe that ethnic cleansing could happen in their country—remember Daris and Berina in Sarajevo. But this is where a document by Gregory Stanton, the president of Genocide Watch, proves extremely useful. The document, titled "The Ten Stages of Genocide," argues that countries go through eight steps before they reach genocide, and forcibly moving minorities out of a region is one of them. The Indian government, in an attempt to ensure that Hindus would be a majority in the Jammu region of the state, forced Muslims to flee to Pakistan between October and November 1947. The displacement quickly devolved into the killing of hundreds of thousands of Muslims by mobs and paramilitaries. Soon enough, Muslims, who had previously composed 60 percent of the population of Jammu, were a minority in the region. What is striking—and alarming—about Stanton's framework is how normal and seemingly innocuous many of the early stages of genocide are. Muslims in Jammu were initially told that they were being "evacuated." Only later, once they were rounded up and put on buses, or attempted to cross the border, were they killed. If you are in a country in the early stages of ethnic cleansing, you might not even notice the dangerous path your country is on.

The first two stages are known as "classification" and "symbolization." This is when an identity group in power begins to highlight differences among a country's citizens, categorizing them by groups—as Belgian colonizers in Rwanda did when they created identity cards for the previously indistinguishable Tutsis and Hutus—and then adopting certain markers for themselves or others (as the Nazis did when they appropriated swastikas and forced Jews to wear yellow stars of David on their clothing). Already, the United States has moved through both of these stages. Consider our deep ideological divide: We have classified ourselves by race, geography, and beliefs. Members of America's far-right faction have appropriated symbols—think of the now ubiquitous Confederate flag, the orange hats of the Proud Boys, or even the Hawaiian shirts flaunted by extremists in Charlottesville or at the Capitol. And members of both parties have proposed issuing national ID cards that would be synced to a government database. Stage three is "discrimination," which is when a dominant group denies or suppresses the rights of others by means of law or custom—as the Buddhist majority did in Myanmar, stripping the Rohingya of voting rights, jobs, and citizenship. Stage four, or "dehumanization," easily follows: Those in power use public discourse to turn regular citizens against the targeted minority, denigrating them as criminals (as Serbs did with Bosniaks) or subhuman (as when Hutus called Tutsis "cockroaches").

The United States has already passed through these stages, too. Racial discrimination has long been a fact of American life. Research has shown that Blacks are half as likely as whites to get a callback when applying for a job, even when their qualifications are exactly the same. Another experiment showed that legislators are much more likely to respond to and act on an email from a white-sounding name than from an identical email with a Black-sounding name. Black families get fewer loans to buy homes than whites and are redlined into poorer neighborhoods. And the recent wave of voting restriction laws in Georgia, Alabama, Wisconsin, Florida, and likely Texas, have been designed specifically to target and reduce minority turnout at elections. Trump—as well as the Republican lawmakers and conservative media figures who abetted him—ushered us into the dehumanization stage, embracing abuse in public discourse by calling immigrants rapists, animals, and killers and even denigrating his Black former White House aide, Omarosa Manigault Newman, as a "dog." In May 2018, Trump said about undocumented immigrants, at a White House meeting: "You wouldn't believe how bad these people are. These aren't people—these are animals."

"Organization," the fifth stage, comes next. This is where a dominant group begins to assemble an army or militia and formulate plans to eradicate other groups. In Bosnia, a plan to exterminate Muslims was drawn up by Radovan Karadžić, the former supreme commander of the Bosnian Serb Army, as early as the 1980s. Karadžić envisioned a secret police force that would train Serbs to form local paramilitary groups, utilizing weapons caches stored in strategic locations throughout Croatia and Bosnia. In stage six, "polarization," the dominant group escalates the propaganda, further demonizing and separating the target group. Often, interaction between groups is discouraged or prohibited, and moderate members of the dominant group—those who resist or protest these efforts—are imprisoned or killed. The relentless hate-filled radio broadcasts disseminated by Hutu extremists in the months leading up to the Rwandan genocide were a clear example of this.

This is where the United States is today: solidly in stage five, perhaps entering stage six. Militias, which exploded under Obama, have been increasingly organizing, training, and arming themselves. Stewart Rhodes, an army veteran and Yale Law School graduate, founded the Oath Keepers in 2009, and has been talking about civil war ever since. When seventeen-year-old Kyle Rittenhouse allegedly killed two people at protests in Kenosha, Wisconsin, Rhodes called him "a Hero, a Patriot." And after a Trump supporter was killed in Portland, Oregon, he tweeted, "The first shot has been fired brother. Civil war is here, right now." Extremists in the Republican Party, as well as their followers, are increasingly choosing to amplify polarizing propaganda over the airwaves and the internet. Marjorie Taylor Greene, a recently elected Republican member of Congress from Georgia, has repeatedly endorsed using violence against Democrats, saying that "the only way you get your freedoms back is it's earned with the price of blood." Moderates who resist or refuse to espouse these views, such as South Carolina Republican representative Tom Rice and Wyoming representative Liz Cheney, have been censured by the GOP, or have even had their lives threatened, as happened to Peter Meijer, a Republican representative from Michigan after he voted to impeach Donald Trump.

AMERICA'S EXTREMISTS TODAY subscribe to an idea known as accelerationism: the apocalyptic belief that modern society is irredeemable and that its end must be hastened, so that a new order can be brought into being. In a way, it's their language for pushing the country up the insurgency scale and perhaps also toward ethnic cleansing. Adherents believe that they are not making enough progress through regular means—rallies, election of right-wing politicians—and as a result must precipitate the change through violence. As the terrorism expert JJ MacNab has explained, they are looking for any excuse, from COVID lockdowns to protests for racial justice, to incite conflict. The hope is that this will set off a chain reaction of violence, which will, in turn, cause moderate citizens—their eyes now open to government oppression and social injustice—to join their cause. MacNab even sees a possibility of far-right extremists joining with the far left: "Some of the groups that are traditionally left-wing extremist, I think, have realized that they are in the same boat. They are equally unhappy. They feel disenfranchised. They do not have any control over their lives, the government, or anything else. This is their way of acting out."

Atomwaffen Division (AWD) was the first accelerationist group to gain notoriety, in part because of a documentary film released by ProPublica and PBS's *Frontline* in 2018. Founded two years earlier on Iron March, a fascist web forum linked to Russian nationalist Aliser Mukhitdinov, Atomwaffen, which means "nuclear weapons" in German, is a neo-Nazi, anti-Semitic, fascist, and national-socialist group whose members believe that widespread violence will cause a race war and allow them to rebuild society into a white utopia.

Experts estimate that AWD has between fifty and one hundred members, all of whom are young white men. James Mason's book is mandatory for new recruits, and AWD message boards feature countless references to *The Turner Diaries*. Despite its small size, the group is one of the most violent alt-right groups in the United States. It's been linked to multiple killings and attacks in the United States. (When former AWD member Devon Arthurs was arrested for killing his two roommates in Florida in 2017, he left a shrine to *The Turner Diaries* above their bodies.) The group is currently located in Texas, where they gather at "hate camps" to train members. It has also traveled to Europe to train with other far-right groups. In 2019 and 2020, the FBI arrested members across the country, and James Mason declared the organization dead. (Mason, though idolized by the group, is not a member.) In the summer of 2020, however, reports of new AWD cells spread across news platforms. In August 2020, the group rebranded and changed its name to the National Socialist Order (NSO), creating a new leadership structure.

Members of AWD were among those who participated in the Unite the Right rally in Charlottesville, yelling "You will not replace us!" as they marched with torches. Soon after the rally, the hashtag #ReadSiege spread like wildfire on Twitter. Some in the group found Charlottesville—and the subsequent arrests, deplatforming, and bad press—to be disheartening, proof that Mason had been right all along: They would not be successful if they stayed within the bounds of the law. As one former AWD member later told investigative journalist A. C. Thompson (who made the ProPublica documentary), Charlottesville sparked the group's shift toward violence, because members felt their efforts had been ineffectual. "Huge rallies don't work," he explained. "All that happens is people get arrested, people lose jobs, and you get put on some FBI watch list." The answer, he continued, was to go underground, and to pursue a form of cell-style terrorism known as "leaderless resistance."

The term "leaderless resistance" originated in the 1950s with a former CIA officer named Ulius Amoss, who was analyzing ways to protect CIA-supported resistance cells in Eastern Europe. The concept was picked up by Louis Beam, a soldier in the Vietnam War who, after returning to the United States, became a Ku Klux Klan member. In 1983, Beam published an essay advocating leaderless resistance as the best way for white nationalists to continue their struggle against the far more powerful U.S. government. Beam believed that the movement could survive only if it became decentralized. As J. M. Berger recounts, Beam envisioned a collection of small, independent groups, and even lone actors, who would loosely coordinate their activities based on shared information distributed via leaflets and newspapers. Beam felt it was important to keep the numbers small, because the FBI would find it impossible to identify, infiltrate, and investigate so many individuals and tiny, disparate groups. "A thousand small phantom cells . . . is an intelligence nightmare for a government," he wrote.

It turned out to be difficult for small, disconnected cells to communicate and recruit primarily through printed leaflets in a pre-internet age. But this changed with social media. Suddenly, groups could not only coordinate—via 4chan, Twitter, Facebook, YouTube, and Telegram—but they could also attract thousands of new members. Two groups on the forefront of this internet revolution have been al-Qaeda and the Islamic State; al-Qaeda even created an online magazine called *Inspire,* which contained step-by-step instructions for carrying out terrorist attacks. Both terrorist groups have embraced the idea of leaderless resistance. Al-Qaeda's decentralized strategy has come to be called "leaderless jihad."

In the United States, perhaps the best example of a leaderless resistance movement is the Boogaloo Bois. A loose affiliation of different types of far-right groups—pro-gun, radical right, anarchical—it coalesced first on 4chan and then later on Instagram, Reddit, and Facebook. The Boogaloo movement has no leadership structure, no local chapters, and no manifesto, or even a fully articulated ideology—at least not yet—and its ultimate goals differ depending on which

Facebook or Telegram group you are following. Members, however, are unified in their desire to drive America to civil war in order to change the status quo. Most of the members are young white men who believe that a revolution in America is imminent and necessary. They call this showdown Civil War 2: Electric Boogaloo, after a 1984 breakdancing movie called *Breakin' 2: Electric Boogaloo*. (The movie is the basis for a longstanding internet joke about sequels, and the floral Hawaiian shirts that members have adopted as a uniform came about after references to "boogaloo" got contorted into "big luau.") Subscribers to the movement urge people to be "boogaloo ready" or to "bring on the boogaloo." Adam Fox, one of the men behind the plot to kidnap Governor Whitmer, talked about Boogaloo as "the battle that would erupt if the government tried to take away Second Amendment rights." Another man charged in the Whitmer plot, Joseph Morrison, the leader of the Wolverine Watchmen, referred to himself as "Boogaloo Bunyan" on social media.

It's not clear exactly how the Boogaloo Bois plan to achieve their goals. Some individuals simply want to create chaos. Others see civil war as necessary to counter government overreach, especially related to guns. Others want to kill immigrants. What is clear, however, is that they can turn out in force. The first time most Americans heard anything about the Boogaloo movement was in January 2020, when a bunch of white men wearing Hawaiian shirts and carrying assault rifles showed up at a massive pro-gun rally in Richmond, Virginia. The Hawaiian shirts caught people's attention; there were too many of them for it to be a coincidence. The movement then grew rapidly during the COVID pandemic as some people reacted to what they saw as tyrannical moves by government officials to strip Americans of their liberties. Men with Hawaiian shirts started showing up in greater numbers at anti-lockdown protests across the United States. In the spring of 2020, one watchdog group identified 125 "boogaloo" Facebook groups. According to the report, more than half of the groups had been established between February and April 2020, as mask mandates and shutdowns took hold in the country. By that summer, there were more than ten thousand adherents.

On Facebook, Boogaloo members share military playbooks and instruction manuals for developing homemade explosives. One group even compiled a document detailing government supply lines so that weapons and ammunition could be pilfered if necessary, and a hit list of potential government officials to target or assassinate. The group's bible is the *Yeetalonian,* a 133-page document covering the steps to war and a how-to guide for winning public sympathy and support through propaganda. Boogaloo Bois have engaged in violence at rallies, killed law enforcement officers, and orchestrated larger plots against the government. (The Wolverine Watchmen militia group involved in the Whitmer kidnapping plot includes Boogaloo supporters. And three men arrested in Las Vegas for trying to incite violence at protests are also part of the movement.)

In May 2020, Facebook banned the use of "boogaloo" and similar terms when used together with mentions of weapons or calls to action. It then changed its recommendation algorithms, removed hundreds of accounts and groups associated with the movement, and banned Boogaloo content on its platforms. But members have flocked to other social media networks such as Gab and Telegram, which are encrypted. This means that it will become only more difficult to curb their reach and influence.

And yet, if there's another civil war, these will be its sol-diers. There are hundreds of far-right groups in America today that believe the country needs a major conflict to right itself. Their names may change—the Proud Boys, the Three Percenters, and the Oath Keepers are the biggest at the moment—but they agree on similar goals. Most want the federal government out of their lives. They want fewer laws and restrictions on their freedom. An increasing number of them want white Christian men in charge. And all of them believe that violence is the way to make their vision a reality.

THE RAPIDLY EVOLVING, ever-more-diffuse nature of homegrown extremist groups can make them difficult to penetrate and hard to predict. But a look at how terrorists have prepared for, and executed, battle in other democracies can help us imagine how a civil war might unfold here. Just as there are multiple large datasets examining the myriad fac-tors leading to civil war, so, too, are there datasets examining the many dimensions of organized terror campaigns. Hun-dreds of studies have looked at who tends to engage in terror, when they tend to do so, and how effective it is in achieving a rebel group's goals. Though these studies cover terrorism in general—not specifically the homegrown variety—they can help us identify common tactics and strategies.

There are a number of strategies that insurgents tend to use against powerful democracies. One is essentially a war of attrition, involving a steady stream of attacks against both people and public infrastructure: federal buildings, markets, schools, courthouses, transportation systems, and electrical grids. This sort of campaign is designed to inflict pain on citizens until they plead for relief and demand that the government give in to the terrorists' demands. Hamas employed this strategy for years, detonating bombs on buses in Jerusalem, Nablus, and Beersheba; launching suicide attacks on cafés in Tel Aviv; booby-trapping cars on busy streets in Haifa; and bombing medical clinics, shopping malls, and security checkpoints. Al-Qaeda's attack on the United States on 9/11 was also part of a war of attrition; it came after a series of attacks on other U.S. targets, including two U.S. embassies in Africa and the USS *Cole*. The strategy succeeded: It convinced the United States to pull its soldiers out of Saudi Arabia, a key goal of al-Qaeda's.

If the demands of far-right groups in America are ignored, they could resort to the same strategy. A classic war of attrition campaign would target high-value buildings, infrastructure, and people—anything that could inflict financial or psychological pain on the U.S. population. This would include not only churches and subway systems but places like Federal Reserve buildings, state capitols, or monuments in Washington, D.C. It would also target citizens who are likely to vote for liberal candidates, such as immigrants or those who live in cities or swing states. Violent extremists would continue to target these sites and individuals until those in power offered the terrorists the concessions they wanted, or voters replaced existing politicians with ones who were more sympathetic to the extremists' cause.

Another strategy is intimidation. If you cannot topple the central government, then you can use violence to goad the population directly into submission. Targeted violence can be used to intimidate agents of the federal government—law enforcement personnel, civil servants, members of Congress, and the judiciary—convincing them not to enforce existing rules. That's one of the things that death threats to Republican members of Congress such as Peter Meijer are designed to do. Violent extremists can target and kill liberal politicians who have voted in favor of gun control, judges who have ruled in favor of abortion rights, or police officers who protect immigrants' civil liberties. But they can also target moderate Republicans who do not toe the extremists' line. Militias become a form of vigilantism designed to prevent the implementation of social change. Mexican drug cartels pursued this strategy against the judges and police officers who refused to be bribed into turning a blind eye to the lucrative drug trade. Once headless bodies began appearing in the streets of Ciudad Juárez and Tijuana, government agents became much more hesitant to enforce the law, and drug cartels and their leaders had freer reign.

We've already seen this kind of strategy in the United States. Intimidation was the preferred tactic of the Ku Klux Klan, which responded to the federal government's expansion of civil rights by turning to violence and murder to suppress the Black vote, win control of state legislatures, and enforce white supremacy in the South. Intimidation has also been the tactic of anti-abortion terrorists, when they target Planned Parenthood clinics or the doctors who perform abortions. If the government won't outlaw abortions, then these extremists turn to violence to prevent women from having the procedures and doctors from performing them. This same thinking animated Patrick Crusius, the accused El Paso shooter. In his manifesto, he wrote that the massacre was meant to serve as an "incentive" for Hispanics to leave the country.

In a country flush with guns, legal militias, and open-carry laws, politicians and citizens have good reason to be afraid. This is even more true in rural areas, where the reach of the federal government is weaker, and where overlapping jurisdictions between the federal, state, and local governments leave citizens uncertain about who is really in charge. One of America's unique attributes is its decentralized federal structure, but this also leaves it vulnerable to rogue elements taking control of a region—even gaining the support of local law enforcement. State-level militias are legal in twenty-two states, and during the pandemic, they frequently positioned themselves as defenders of small businesses that insisted on staying open despite government-mandated shutdowns. In Kenosha, Wisconsin, a call from former city council member Kevin Mathewson for armed citizens to protect the city in the wake of Black Lives Matter protests brought hundreds of men to town. After Kyle Rittenhouse was accused of killing two protesters and wounding another, his lawyer argued that his involvement in the militia was necessary. "He was in Kenosha as part of his right and duty to protect his community where the state and local government had totally failed in their most basic responsibility to provide law and order."

Another terror strategy is known as "outbidding." This tactic is used when one militant group competes with other groups to cement its dominance. Hamas embraced suicide bombing in part to signal that it was more committed to the Palestinian cause than its main competitor, Fatah. The Islamic State, which was late to enter the civil war in Syria, switched to brutal kidnappings and killings in part to differentiate itself from a rival group, Jabhat al-Nusra. Rebel groups that embrace an extreme ideology and methods often do better in war than more moderate groups. This is because they often attract a more dedicated fighting force and more determined supporters. Extremist groups also tend to wield greater psychological power by offering greater recompense: Honor, martyr status, and glory in the afterlife, and an extreme ideology weeds out those who are less committed to a cause, reducing the problem of poor performance, side switching, or betrayal.

We have not yet seen the outbidding strategy take hold in the United States, but it's easy to imagine it as right-wing groups proliferate. What ISIS did in Iraq and Syria provides a blueprint: The group invested heavily in internet propaganda, advertising its military strength and publicizing both the brutal acts it was willing to commit and the public services it was willing to provide to local populations. When it entered a town, it quickly targeted leaders of the opposition. If this was to occur in the United States, you would see one extreme group, such as Atomwaffen, escalating to ever-more brutal acts of violence, to prove that it was stronger, more capable, and more dedicated to the cause than other groups.

A final terror strategy is "spoiling." Terrorists wield this tactic when they fear that more moderate groups—those that would put aside violence in exchange for, say, concessions from the government on immigration—will compromise and subvert the larger goal of establishing a new ethno-state. This strategy usually comes into play when relations between more moderate insurgent groups and the government are improving, and a peace agreement seems imminent. Terrorists know that most citizens will not support ongoing violence once a deal is in place. When Iranian radicals kidnapped fifty-two Americans in Tehran in 1979, it wasn't because relations between the United States and Iran were worsening, but because there were signs of rapprochement: Three days earlier, Mehdi Bazargan, Iran's relatively moderate prime minister, and Zbigniew Brzezinski, the U.S. national security adviser, had appeared in a photograph together shaking hands. The radicals knew that reconciliation between the two countries would be disastrous for them, so they did whatever they could to prevent it. Arab-Israeli peace negotiations, and talks between Protestants and Catholics in Northern Ireland, have also been "spoiled" in this way.

In the United States, one could imagine the Proud Boys, the Three Percenters, and the Oath Keepers eventually forming an alliance. (Rebel groups in civil wars frequently join forces, if only temporarily.) The new unified group might then decide to sign a peace deal with the federal government, guaranteeing no future gun control legislation and a significant reduction in immigration—or any set of terms that would be acceptable to a majority of the group's supporters. By definition, the most radical anti-government and white supremacist groups would be left out of this deal because no compromise would help them achieve their ultimate goal: the establishment of a white ethno-state. Their only recourse would be to try to scuttle the deal. And the best way to accomplish that would be to trigger a civil war.

To do this, they would likely need foreign support. The Provisional IRA survived in large part because of substantial financial backing from Irish Americans living in the United States. The Contra rebels in Nicaragua were able to continue fighting only because the United States funneled money their way. Rebels in the Donbas region of Ukraine depended on material assistance and manpower from neighboring Russia. And Hezbollah has succeeded largely thanks to sponsorship by Syria, Iran, and Lebanon. Here in the United States, terrorist groups could be aided by America's enemies (China, Russia, and Iran), as well as by sympathetic white supremacist groups in other white-majority countries (Canada, Ukraine, the United Kingdom). Thanks to the internet, this would be easy to facilitate. China and Russia could supply money and materials to far-right groups with little trouble. Ukraine could supply training and combat experience. And rural Canada could provide a safe haven from which groups could escape the U.S. government's reach. The Rise Above Movement (RAM), a white supremacist group based in California, has traveled to Ukraine for training with Azov Battalion. As Tim Hume reports in *Vice,* Azov has handed out pamphlets at neo-Nazi concerts in Europe, created propaganda videos, and headlined far-right conferences in Scandinavia. They've sold the war in Ukraine as a way for far-right groups to gain combat experience, which they can then use to train their own militants. As intelligence analyst Mollie Saltskog told Hume, "You have a global network of violent white supremacists now who can easily keep in touch on different platforms and go back home, spread that propaganda, conduct training—or move on to the next fight."

THE STEPS TOWARD ethnic cleansing are often so gradual as to feel imperceptible. But according to "The Ten Stages of Genocide," there's a noticeable shift that takes place with stage seven. Known as the "preparation" stage, this is when a dominant group forms an army. Leaders also indoctrinate the populace with fear of becoming the victim, claiming that "if we don't kill them, they will kill us." It's after this indoctrination that a country can explode quickly into stages eight and nine—"persecution" and "extermination"—and then the final stage, "denial," which is when perpetrators deny having committed their crimes. Turkey still refuses to acknowledge the Armenian genocide one hundred years after the fact.

Stage seven is significant, in other words, because it's when the logic of genocide develops as a means of self-defense. It's common to think that ethnic cleansing is driven by hate. There is hate, yes, but the real fuel is fear—fear that you are threatened and vulnerable. Violence entrepreneurs tap into this anxiety, exploiting the survival instinct that cues you to destroy your enemy before he can destroy you. During the Nuremberg trials, Hermann Göring was interviewed by a young American psychologist, Gustave Gilbert, who told Göring that he didn't think the average person wanted to be dragged into war. Göring responded: "Why, of course, the people don't want war. Why would some poor slob on a farm want to risk his life in a war when the best that he can get out of it is to come back to his farm in one piece? . . . It is always a simple matter to drag the people along. . . . All you have to do is tell them they are being attacked and denounce the pacifists for lack of patriotism, and [for] exposing the country to greater danger."

This existential fear leads to a domestic arms race, in which one group is made to feel insecure and, in an attempt to feel more secure, forms militias and purchases weapons, which in turn makes the rival group feel insecure, and so it, too, forms militias and purchases weapons—which then triggers the original side to arm itself even more. Both sides believe they are taking defensive measures, but the effect is to create ever more insecurity, which can spiral into war. Average Serbs in Bosnia did not want war. Neither did average Hutus in Rwanda. Their leaders, however, needed average citizens to fight on their behalf to secure power. Their solution? To tell their followers that they would soon be attacked, prompting many to jump into action. The organizers of the genocide in Rwanda used newspapers and then state radio to spread false ideas: that Tutsis were newcomers who had no claim to the land, that they were perpetuating Hutu impoverishment, and that Hutus had a right to protect themselves. A report by Human Rights Watch concluded that "it was particularly the last idea—that [the] Hutu were threatened and had to defend themselves—that proved most successful in mobilizing attacks on Tutsis from 1990 through the 1994 genocide."

An armed population increases the likelihood of this kind of security dilemma. U.S. gun sales hit an all-time high in 2020, with seventeen million firearms sold between January and October. Buyers were primarily conservatives, who tend to buy guns in response to Democratic electoral gains (16.6 million firearms were sold in 2016, driven by the candidacy of Hillary Clinton, who advocated strong gun control legislation). But it is also the greatest number of guns sold in any single year in America's history, according to the chief economist of Small Arms Analytics. Many sales were to first-time buyers, data suggests, and researchers at the University of California, Davis, found that new gun owners were driven predominantly by fears of lawlessness and government instability. According to Kareem Shaya, a Second Amendment advocate, "The common thread is just uncertainty, a feeling of, hey, if nobody else is going to be able to take care of me, push comes to shove, I want to be able to take care of myself."

Whether or not the United States will find itself in a security dilemma depends on whether those on the left— liberals, minorities, city dwellers—decide they should also arm themselves. There's some evidence that this is already starting to happen: The loose affiliation of left-wing activists known as antifa, who define themselves in opposition to fascism, nationalism, and racism, have grown more active in the past few years. In the spring of 2017, for example, antifa launched hammers, pipes, and homemade explosives at alt-right protesters in California; two years later, the police killed an antifa member before he could detonate a propane tank at a U.S. Immigration and Customs Enforcement facility in Washington.

A broader movement among the left appears to be growing. In 2019, only 8 percent of terrorist incidents were perpetrated by left-wing groups; in 2020, it was 20 percent. Armed groups, such as the Socialist Rifle Association—which is dedicated "to providing working class people the information they need to be effectively armed for self and community defense"—and the Not Fucking Around Coalition (NFAC), a Black nationalist militia group that supports self-policing and firearms training in Black communities, have made appearances in Louisville, Kentucky, in the wake of Breonna Taylor's killing, and in Stone Mountain, Georgia, to protest the nation's largest Confederate monument. The Redneck Revolt, which stands "for organized defense of our communities," was founded in 2009 and re-formed in the summer of 2016. Members have shown up at protests to protect minorities and at gun shows, flea markets, state fairs, and NASCAR races to try to counter recruitment into white supremacist groups.

Even as they arm themselves, however, it won't be left-wing groups that instigate the ultimate clash. This is in part because their members, who are often ethnic minorities, have historically experienced repression; Black militias have not been tolerated in the same way as white militias. The left-wing movement, with its loose association of subgroups, is also more diverse, including everyone from anarchists, radical environmentalists, and animal rights activists to anti-globalists, anti-capitalists, and gun rights advocates, which makes coordination more difficult. Most critically, however, left-wing groups simply have less to lose in a changing world, and less to gain from violence. The coalition of minorities who support the Democratic Party, and the extremists who would fight on their behalf, know that time is on their side: as long as the system isn't heavily rigged against them, they are the future majority.

Still, the specter of left-wing radicals flexing their muscle will be what right-wing extremists invoke—to stoke fear and, ultimately, justify their own violence. It will be the evidence they use to gain even more support for their movement. Trump already set the example when he and his national security team insisted that the main domestic terror threat in the United States came from antifa, devoting resources to eradicating leftist groups while ignoring those on the far right. That the left is violent and filled with terrorists is a useful narrative of fear—it creates a common enemy and supports the idea of self-defense.

A country does not need a large percentage of the population to be involved for violent ethnic cleansing to occur. Small numbers of heavily armed citizens—together with help from law enforcement and the military—are often enough to move to stage nine, the "extermination" phase. In fact, Dartmouth's Benjamin Valentino found that a remarkably small number of people can organize and mobilize to commit mass genocide. You just need the rest of the population to remain passive, which can easily be accomplished through intimidation. In Bosnia, for example, Višegrad's violence was perpetrated by one man, Milan Lukić, and fifteen well-armed buddies, including his brother and cousin. Most citizens did not join in the fighting.

The United States is not on the verge of genocide. But if militias were to rapidly expand, and violence entrepreneurs were able to work citizens into a frenzy over the need for self-defense, stage seven could be on the horizon. If militias become more brazen, and a sense of insecurity grows, right-wing terrorism in the United States could accomplish a more immediate objective: It could shift the country even more willingly toward authoritarianism. Sustained campaigns of terror typically move citizens ideologically to the right, in favor of law-and-order candidates; this often brings even more conservative politicians to power. This is what happened in Israel during the second intifada. Terror shifted the Israeli public to the right, in support of a far-right pro-security agenda. Something similar happened in the United States after 9/11; a large study found that the attacks, though unleashed by foreign terrorists, caused citizens to become more active in politics, more involved in the military, and more likely to change their affiliation from independent to Republican.

There is evidence that Americans would, in fact, support a more authoritarian government. The number of people who have a negative view of democracy has grown from 9 percent in 1995 to 14 percent today. Meanwhile, a recent study by two Yale political scientists found that only 3.5 percent of Americans—Republican or Democrat—would refuse to vote for their preferred candidate if he or she did or said something anti-democratic, like shutting down polling stations. Faith in government has plummeted: From 1964 to

2019, the share of Americans who trust those in Washington to do "what is right" tumbled from 77 percent to 17 percent. Americans are also losing faith in one another: The percentage of Americans who don't have confidence in the electorate to make good political decisions has grown from 35 percent in 1997 to 59 percent today. Perhaps even more troubling, those who would view "army rule" as a good thing has risen, from just 7 percent in 1995 to 18 percent today.

America was lucky that its first modern autocratic president was neither smart nor politically experienced. Other ambitious, more effective Republicans—Tom Cotton, Josh Hawley—have taken note and will seek to do better. They will try to adopt Trump's eighty-eight million passionate followers, knowing that the Republican Party will bend to the will of these voters. Or new politicians will rise and play by their own new rules. How far will these leaders go? How far will we let them?

CHAPTER 8

PREVENTING A CIVIL WAR

When I was a college student, in the mid-1980s, my classmates and I were asked to identify where in the world civil war was most likely to break out. Without hesitation, we knew exactly: South Africa. The country's system of apartheid, which enforced segregation among government-defined ethnic groups—white, Black, and mixed race—was under increasing stress as the majority Black population pushed back against restrictions, and the dominant white minority responded with violence. In 1976, the government had fired into crowds of Black schoolchildren, killing at least 176—an incident that caused international outrage. But rather than reform, the apartheid regime had pursued a policy of "total onslaught" against Black citizens, declaring a state of emergency in 1985 that allowed for indiscriminate arrests, police killings, and torture.

South Africa had all the risk factors associated with civil war: The country was an anocracy in 1988 and had been for decades, scoring just +4 on the polity scale. There was a minority government that excluded people from power based on race, and white citizens saw themselves as the country's rightful heirs. They understood that any move to majority rule would mean a loss in their political status. Similar conditions had existed in Rhodesia, a country just north of South Africa, and a brutal civil war had occurred there.

But then something happened that brought South Africa back from the brink. In 1986, in response to the escalating oppression by the apartheid government, South Africa's most important trading partners—the United States, the European Community, and Japan—imposed economic sanctions. South Africa was already suffering a recession, and in 1989, when F. W. de Klerk became president, replacing the inflexible P. W. Botha, he made an important calculus: to focus on his country's survival. Though a member of the ruling National Party, de Klerk was also a pragmatist. If the economy collapsed, so would white wealth. Three out of four South Africans were Black; if he continued to insist on white rule, the ensuing civil war would be, for whites, unwinnable. Instead, de Klerk lifted the twenty-nine-year ban on the African National Congress and other Black liberation parties, restored freedom of the press, and released political prisoners, including ANC leader Nelson Mandela.

South Africa was closer to civil war in 1989 than the United States is today. The apartheid state that white South Africans created to suppress Blacks was far more repressive than the pseudo-apartheid state the United States had until 1965. It was illegal for Black South Africans to marry white people, to establish their own businesses in white parts of town, or to access beaches, hospitals, and parks that were marked "white only." Also, South Africa's history as an anocracy was much deeper than that of contemporary America, having lasted for decades. The United States was only briefly in the middle zone. South Africa also had two major groups that considered themselves sons of the soil: both

Blacks and whites claimed a historical stake to the land. In the United States, only one group (besides the marginalized and relatively small population of Indigenous peoples) makes that claim. The threat of bloody conflict in late-1980s South Africa dwarfs the danger in America today, and yet South Africa avoided war.

South Africa reminds us of the power of leaders—business leaders, political leaders, opposition leaders. Leaders can compromise in the face of danger, or they can choose to fight. Botha chose to fight. De Klerk and Mandela chose to work together. Mandela and other Black leaders could have rejected terms that allowed whites to retain significant political and economic power. De Klerk could have refused to give Blacks full civil rights and majority control of the government. Botha hadn't been willing to do what de Klerk did. The same is true of President Assad in Syria. He chose not to compromise with the majority Sunnis despite the enormous costs of remaining firm. Ulster Protestants didn't compromise with Irish Catholics. Maliki didn't compromise with Iraq's Sunnis. Mandela, who had originally been in favor of violent resistance, could have advocated ethnic violence—he could have been an ethnic entrepreneur, tapping the anger and resentment of his Black countrymen to seek full control of South Africa through civil war. But instead he preached healing, unity, and peace. It was the leaders in charge who spared South Africa more conflict and bloodshed.

In 1993, both de Klerk and Mandela received the Nobel Peace Prize. Critics have argued that de Klerk did not deserve the award; he had been part of the system that had oppressed Black South Africans for decades and had compromised only to survive. It was Mandela, they argue, who saved the country. This is only partly true. Mandela certainly had the moral high ground; most leaders who had spent twenty-seven years in a prison cell would have wanted to exact revenge, especially with such an overwhelming demographic advantage. But de Klerk's actions were no less critical. Had South Africa's new leader refused to negotiate in 1990, had he not agreed to significant political reforms, Black South Africans would have eventually rebelled with or without Mandela. This is what we saw in Syria in 2011, when Assad chose to start bombing his people. This is what we saw in Northern Ireland in the late 1960s and early '70s, when the British government sent troops rather than mediators. De Klerk made a different decision.

Violence often springs from a sense of injustice, inequality, and insecurity—and a sense that those grievances and fears will not be addressed by the current system. But systems can change. No one thought that white South Africans would reform a system designed specifically to cement their dominance. But when the costs of maintaining that dominance became too high, and business leaders who were hurt by sanctions insisted on reform, they dismantled it. If South Africa could reform, so can the United States.

I wish I could take all the facts and figures that experts have collected over the past half century and tell you exactly what will happen to our country. But even with the best data, we cannot predict the future. All we can do is try, along with our fellow citizens, to shape it in a positive, peaceful way. Political scientists have spent decades studying the forces behind civil wars and the dynamics of terrorism; these insights can be used not just to anticipate war but to thwart it. We know why democracies decline. We know why factions emerge and the conditions under which they thrive. We know the early warning signs and the tactics of violent extremists. Groups like the Proud Boys have a playbook. But there is no reason why we, the people of the United States, cannot choose to carve out our future; we, too, have a playbook.

CIVIL WARS ARE RARE—in any given year, less than 4 percent of countries that meet the conditions for war actually descend into armed conflict—but where they do happen, they tend to repeat themselves. Between 1945 and 1996, over a third of civil wars were followed by a second conflict. Since 2003, with the exception of conflicts in Libya and Syria, every civil war has been a sequel—a repeat of a previous war. Leaders of these movements (or their modern incarnations) will go underground or disappear, waiting for a moment when grievances are reignited or the government is once again weak. Then they will begin to build a new movement. Even if the original leaders and soldiers are long dead, old fault lines often haven't been repaired, and the myths and stories live on. Ethnic groups, especially those in decline, often fight a second civil war because the conditions that drove their original grievances either haven't been addressed or have worsened. The next generation of fighters has lived with the loss, and witnessed the further downgrading of their people. They are determined to take back what they believe is rightfully theirs. Croats and Serbs have fought multiple times throughout history. So have the Sunni and Shia in Iraq. And the war between the Moros and the Philippine government has gone through several iterations as various groups have disappeared, only to reemerge in new forms. Ethiopia, Myanmar, and India have experienced multiple civil wars. Experts call it "the conflict trap," and while it's of course bad for the combatants, it's good for outside observers. Countries like China and the United States, which have each experienced only one civil war, can learn from others' mistakes.

Back in 2014, I was commissioned by the World Bank to study the conflict trap. I looked at all civil wars between 1945 and 2009, and what I found was this: Most countries that were able to avoid a second civil war shared an ability to strengthen the quality of their governance. They doubled down on democracy and moved up the polity scale. Mozambique did this after its civil war ended in 1992, when the country moved from one-party rule to multiparty elections. In the wake of a conflict that ended in 2003, Liberia increased institutional restraints on presidential power and pushed for more judicial independence. Countries that created more transparent and participatory political environments and limited the power of their executive branch were less susceptible to repeat episodes of violence.

Improving the quality of a country's governance was significantly more important than improving its economy. In another large study commissioned by the World Bank, James Fearon considered the economic question. When a rich country had a worse government than experts would expect given its prosperity, he found that it faced "a significantly greater risk of civil war outbreak in subsequent years." So a wealthy country like the United States is more likely to experience a civil war when its government becomes less effective and more corrupt, even if its per-capita income doesn't change.

Until this study, we knew that anocracy left a country at higher risk of civil war, but we didn't know exactly why. What was it about anocracies that made them particularly vulnerable? Or to put it another way, which features of democracy were more or less important? Fearon found that "all good things tend to go together" but that three features stood out: "the rule of law" (the equal and impartial application of legal procedure); "voice and accountability" (the extent to which citizens are able to participate in selecting their government, as well as freedom of expression, freedom of association, and a free media); and "government effectiveness" (the quality of public services and the quality and independence of the civil service). These three features reflect the degree to which a government serves its people and the degree to which its political institutions are strong, legitimate, and accountable. Improvements in governance tend to reduce the subsequent risk of war.

The quality of American governance has been declining since 2016, according to the Polity Scale and since 2015 according to V-Dem's scale. One of the most obvious ways has been in accountability. Free elections are the central mechanism of accountability in a democracy, but unlike many other countries, America lacks an independent and centralized election management system. According to the political scientist Pippa Norris, an elections expert and the founding director of Harvard University's Electoral Integrity Project, almost every new democracy going through a transition sets up a central independent election management system to protect the integrity of elections. This helps to build trust in the electoral process. Uruguay, Costa Rica, and South Korea all did this when they created their democracies. Large federal democracies such as Australia, Canada, India, and Nigeria have also managed their elections this way. Canada's election system is run by Elections Canada, and all voters follow the same procedures no matter where they live.

An independent and centralized election management

system establishes a standard procedure for designing and printing ballots and tabulating votes accurately and securely, untainted by partisan politics. It can handle legal disputes without the involvement of politicized courts. In a 2019 report, the Electoral Integrity Project examined countries' electoral laws and processes and found that the quality of U.S. elections from 2012 to 2018 was "lower than any other long-established democracies and affluent societies." The United States received the same score as Mexico and Panama, and a much lower score than Costa Rica, Uruguay, and Chile. This is the reason why it is easier to spread claims about voter fraud in the United States, and why Americans are more likely to question the results.

The right to vote has also been increasingly politicized, with Republicans repeatedly stacking the deck against minorities. Strengthening the Voting Rights Act would go a long way toward eliminating voter suppression and deepening people's trust in the system. Another important reform is automatic voter registration (AVR), where anyone who interacts with the Department of Motor Vehicles is automatically registered to vote unless they opt out. In states that have already adopted AVR, including California, Oregon, and Washington, the measure has led to major increases in voter turnout. It is the single easiest thing that we could do to make our government more participatory and, therefore, more democratic. These measures won't assuage the far right—their vision of a white Christian nation depends on disenfranchising minorities—but shoring up the system as a whole could earn the support of moderate Americans and deepen their trust in the legitimacy of their leaders.

America might also take inspiration from the small wave of democratic rejuvenation that is occurring, even as democracy retreats worldwide. Canada and Scandinavia are leading the way. Canada focused on reaffirming voting rights after the center-left Liberal Party won a majority of votes in 2015. The 2018 Elections Modernization Act eliminated voter identification requirements, restricted political party and independent campaign spending and donations, expanded voting rights to include all Canadians abroad (even those who have lived outside the country for more than five years and are not planning to return), improved voter privacy, gave the commissioner of Canada elections more investigatory power, banned foreign donations, and required online platforms such as Google and Facebook to "create a registry of digital political advertisements" so that citizens could see who was trying to influence elections. In 2020, Canada received one of the highest freedom and democracy scores in the Freedom House Report.

In our country, gerrymandering—the practice of redrawing congressional districts to favor one party—tends to bring more extreme candidates to the forefront, since getting through primaries requires appealing to more extreme voters in those districts. These voters turn out in higher numbers because they tend to be more passionate about the outcome. Only federal lawmakers—America's own de Klerks—have the power to institute a national reform of this system. Doing so would weaken the influence of extremist voters in both parties and greatly increase the potential for bipartisanship.

The U.S. government could also increase bipartisanship—and help avert conflict—by reexamining the electoral college system, which is, in its own way, a form of political gerrymandering. The American system is structured to exacerbate the urban-rural divide by giving small states disproportionate power in the Senate. Since 2000, two presidents have lost the popular vote but won the election after electoral college victories. Switching to a system where the popular vote determines who is president would prevent that, and also make it virtually impossible to win without appealing across racial lines. Want to know how to undercut destructive ethnic factions in the United States? Make each citizen's vote count equally rather than giving preferential treatment to the white, rural vote.

This type of reform, however, is unlikely. Eliminating the electoral college through a constitutional amendment would require supermajority support, and this will be hard to achieve, since jettisoning the current system will put the Republican party at a disadvantage. But Congress could work to resolve another factor in Americans' loss of faith in democracy: the idea that government serves special interests more than voters. Thanks to the Supreme Court's 2010 ruling in *Citizens United v. Federal Election Commission,* individual donors can contribute unlimited amounts of cash to tilt the political scale in favor of candidates aligned with their own, rather than the country's, best interests. The handful of individuals who donate billions of dollars to float dubious campaigns also tend to be far more ideologically extreme than the average American citizen. To prevent this, the federal government should close fundraising loopholes for candidates and officeholders, as Canada and other countries have done, and reinstate campaign finance rules.

All of these electoral problems damage the perceived legitimacy of the government, weaken America's democracy, and worsen governance. They could also move the country back into the anocracy zone. Today, Americans are distrustful of their government. They believe, quite rightly, that their democratic institutions often don't serve the people's interests. The solution is not to abandon democracy but rather to improve it. America needs to reform its government to make it more transparent, more accountable to voters, and more equitable and inclusive of all citizens. Rather than manipulate institutions to serve a narrower and narrower group of citizens and corporate interests, the United States needs to reverse course, amplifying citizens' voices, increasing government accountability, improving public services, and eradicating corruption. We need to make sure that all Americans are allowed to vote, that all votes count, and that, in turn, those votes influence which policies are enacted in Washington. Americans are going to regain trust in their government only when it becomes clear that it is serving them rather than lobbyists, billionaires, and a declining group of rural voters.

Americans must be educated about the key levers of power in our democracy and the ways in which they can be manipulated. According to community organizer Eric Liu, "too many people are profoundly—and willfully—illiterate [about] power: what it is, what forms it takes, who has it, who doesn't, why that is, how it is exercised." And if Americans remain ignorant about how power operates in American politics, then people with nefarious purposes will step in and take it away from them. A 2016 survey led by the Annenberg Public Policy Center found that one in four Americans could not name the three branches of government. This is why civic education, which has been declining for decades, must be reinstated. It teaches America's youth how our democracy works, and the values, habits, and norms that are necessary to maintain it. A group of six former U.S. education secretaries, both Democrat and Republican, recently made the case for revamping civics through a project called the Roadmap to Educating for American Democracy. They pointed out that we spend 1,000 times more per student on STEM education than we do on history and civics. The roadmap "cultivates civil disagreement and reflective patriotism"—an urgent task now that our democratic institutions are so vulnerable and precarious. A twenty-first-century civics curriculum would not only create a stronger electorate to balance the power of elites, but also lead to greater faith and trust in the system. "Our democracy," according to Liu, "works only if enough of us believe democracy works."

MOST PEOPLE DON'T realize they are on the path to civil war until the violence is a feature of everyday life. Noor in Baghdad, Berina and Daris Kovac in Sarajevo, and Mikhail Minakov and Anton Melnyk in Ukraine—all confess that they didn't see war coming until it was too late. By the time they grasped that something had changed, militias were operating in the streets and extremist leaders were hungry for war.

And these leaders, of course, have an incentive to keep the average citizen distracted from the work of the militias. At first, at least, they operate not by upending normal life but by reshaping it gradually, protecting their larger aims against possible countermeasures. This is a historical pattern. Milton Mayer, an American journalist who traveled to Germany in 1951, asked ordinary citizens about daily life in the years Hitler rose to power. One man, a baker, repeated a common refrain: "One had no time to think. There was so much going on." Another German, a philologist, recounted that people could no more see it "developing from day to day than a farmer in his field sees the corn growing. One day it is over his head."

Our own psychological biases often prevent us from recognizing internal threats. It is much easier to blame outsiders for a heinous act than our own fellow citizens. Law enforcement officials, for example, are more likely to minimize the danger posed by individuals living in communities they know—most often, white communities—than by those they are less familiar with. It is no surprise that we tend to regard foreign terrorists as part of a larger movement while domestic terrorism is thought of as rare and isolated. In fact, unlike in other countries, such as Canada, the United States designates only foreign (not domestic) groups as terrorist organizations. There is no law that criminalizes domestic terrorism—none of the Capitol insurgents could be arrested on these grounds. Many Americans just don't want to believe that our biggest threat comes from within.

Politicians on both the left and the right have also been reluctant to discuss America's domestic terror problem, for political reasons: They either actively benefit from the support of extremists or worry about the political cost of turning on them. This collective blindness, willful or not, has put us in a precarious position. We are more prepared, as a country, to counter foreign enemies such as al-Qaeda than we are to disarm the warriors in our midst, even though the latter are currently more virulent and dangerous. If we are to avert civil war, we must devote the same resources to finding and neutralizing homegrown combatants as we do to foreign ones.

Already, we are behind. The United States has been slow to identify far-right infiltration of our security services, a threat that is common in the buildup to civil war. A 2009 report from the Department of Homeland Security observed that "right-wing extremism" was on the rise. The team behind the report, led by Daryl Johnson, had begun to scour extremist websites and message boards in 2007 and were surprised by what they found: bomb-making manuals, weapons training, and hundreds of militia-recruitment videos (on YouTube). Johnson's report suggested that veterans might be especially susceptible to recruitment, based on a 2008 FBI assessment that found that more than two hundred individuals with military experience had joined white-supremacist organizations since the 9/11 attacks. The report, however, led to an outcry among congressional Republicans and veterans groups, and the DHS was pressured to withdraw it.

But Johnson was on to something. Though the networks of the armed services and law enforcement are vast, and white supremacist sympathies are far from dominant, there is nevertheless some overlap. An FBI report written in 2006, "White Supremacist Infiltration of Law Enforcement," detailed the influence of white nationalism on police forces. "Having personnel within law enforcement agencies," the report said, "has historically been and will continue to be a desired asset for white supremacist groups seeking to anticipate law enforcement interest in and actions against them." A follow-up report, in 2015, found that right-wing and anti-government "domestic terrorists" appeared to be using contacts in law enforcement to access intelligence and avoid detection.

Indeed, the recruitment of former fighters appears to strengthen a movement. Janet Lewis, a civil war expert from George Washington University, found that almost all the rebel groups that were able to grow and endure in Uganda did so, in part, because they were able to enlist former soldiers and police officers to their cause. Ex-military and those in law enforcement offer a ready-made band of individuals with the training and experience to be effective soldiers. The 2009 Department of Homeland Security report also identified this phenomenon and concluded that "rightwing extremists [in the United States] will attempt to recruit and radicalize returning veterans in order to exploit their skills and knowledge."

If Obama was slow to respond to the threat of domestic terrorism, whether from outside or within government agencies, Trump simply ignored it. Instead, he continued the government's policy, since 9/11, of focusing aggressively on Islamic terrorism. When he was pressed on domestic terror, he repeatedly portrayed left-wing militants as the real danger. FBI director Christopher Wray highlighted the threat posed by right-wing groups, and Trump's response was to publicly criticize him. The muddled reaction by law enforcement to the attacks on the Capitol revealed the widespread failure to grasp the true menace—and reach—of extremism in America. After the attack, Wray told the Senate Judiciary Committee that arrests of white supremacists had almost tripled over the course of the last three years. He warned them that domestic terrorism was "metastasizing across the country."

Stopping this cancer must be a priority. The decline in militias after the Oklahoma City bombing was in large part the result of an aggressive counterterrorism strategy supported by both Democratic and Republican administrations. The immense scale of the bombing led to real change within the FBI: In less than a year, the number of Joint Terrorism Task Forces (JTTFs) doubled—these are units that draw on the expertise of various agencies and levels of law enforcement— and there was an increase in hazardous-device training programs for local, federal, and state police officers. In 1996, the Antiterrorism and Effective Death Penalty Act was passed, leading to the hiring of hundreds more investigators by the FBI. In 1997, various of the new JTTFs were responsible for preventing domestic terrorism acts by the KKK and other white supremacist groups. After the Oklahoma City bombing, the FBI enlisted more than 1,400 investigators to sift through three tons of evidence to find the bomber Timothy McVeigh without any digital photographs. Deputy Attorney General Merrick B. Garland was the man put in charge of the investigation, and as the Biden administration's new attorney general, he will also oversee the investigation of the Capitol attack. In this way, he will help shape the American response to domestic terror over the next decade.

WHAT SHOULD AMERICA'S response look like? If we know what terrorists are after, and how they are likely to pursue their goals, we can formulate our own counterstrategy, drawing on the experiences of other countries around the world. In the same way that extremists wield common tactics to destabilize democracies, so too are there field-tested methods of undermining, and disabling, their efforts.

The best way to neutralize a budding insurgency is to reform a degraded government: bolster the rule of law, give all citizens equal access to the vote, and improve the quality of government services. In the words of David Kilcullen— former special adviser for counterinsurgency in George W. Bush's administration and chief counterterrorism strategist for the U.S. State Department—the most important thing governments can do is to "remedy grievances and fix problems of governance that create the conditions that extremists exploit." If America does not change its current course, dangers loom.

In the case of the United States, the federal government should renew its commitment to providing for its most vulnerable citizens, white, Black, or brown. We need to undo fifty years of declining social services, invest in safety nets and human capital across racial and religious lines, and prioritize high-quality early education, universal healthcare, and a higher minimum wage. Right now many working-class and middle-class Americans live their lives "one small step from catastrophe," and that makes them ready recruits for militants. Investing in real political reform and economic security would make it much harder for white nationalists to gain sympathizers and would prevent the rise of a new generation of far-right extremists.

This is how most governments respond when faced with the possibility of insurgency—they institute the reforms necessary to avoid war—and it usually works. The Provisional IRA actively pursued a war of attrition against Great Britain, demanding fairer treatment, and they continued to launch terrorist attacks until Westminster eventually agreed to reform. The U.S. government shouldn't indulge extremists— the creation of a white ethno-state would be disastrous for the country—nor should it exempt them from federal laws, but it could address grievances that affect a broad range of citizens, improving living standards and increasing social mobility after decades of decline. As Robert A. Johnson, head of the Institute for New Economic Thinking, put it: If America put "much more money and energy . . . into public school systems, parks and recreation, the arts, and healthcare, it could take an awful lot of sting out of society. We've largely dismantled those things."

Governments that work to show they're effective receive an added benefit. Not only do they make it harder for extremists to radicalize moderates, they also undercut the ability of extremists to step in and compete with the state to offer services. Hamas's popularity was built on the benefits it provided to Palestinians who were being neglected by the Israeli government, not on the attacks it launched against Israeli civilians. On some level, the support of the population comes down to who can provide the best services and the most protection. Today, U.S. lawmakers could, for example, reform existing immigration laws, laying out a path to citizenship and reducing the number of illegal immigrants, while ensuring that *all* citizens—white, Black, and brown—have affordable housing, the opportunity to go to college, and access to effective addiction treatment. The government should obviously take a zero-tolerance stance on hate, and punish domestic terrorism, but it could weaken support for extremism by addressing the legitimate grievances that many citizens have.

There are times, however, when the demands of insurgents would be dangerous for democracy, leaving a government little choice but to engage in targeted retaliation. President Lincoln was correct to refuse to negotiate with Confederate states over slavery. In these cases, governments should arrest, prosecute, and seize the assets of insurgents, making it harder for them to operate. Governments should also pursue a strategy called "leadership decapitation," which involves imprisoning the leader or leaders of a terrorist group to hasten its collapse. Sometimes there is legal recourse. Following the Unite the Right rally at Charlottesville, a team from Georgetown Law School sued the right-wing demonstrators, citing an archaic state law prohibiting the gathering of "unauthorized militias." Most of the groups that participated in the rally are now barred from ever returning to the city in an armed group of two or more.

In the United States, lawsuits have been particularly effective against the Ku Klux Klan. In 1980, a group of three Klansmen went on a shooting spree in a Black neighborhood in Chattanooga. They burned a cross on the train tracks and then, using a shotgun loaded with birdshot, injured four Black women who were two blocks away. Flying glass injured a fifth. The women sued and were awarded $535,000. More important, the judge issued an injunction against the Klan, preventing it from engaging in violence in Chattanooga. That means that if members of the Klan in Chattanooga were to violate the order they would be criminally liable. In another case, in 1981, a man named Michael Donald was walking into a store in Mobile, Alabama, when he was abducted by two members of the United Klans of America who were seeking retribution for the acquittal of a Black man in the shooting of a white police officer. Donald was beaten, had his throat slit, and was hanged; he was nineteen years old. The Southern Poverty Law Center sued the United Klans of America, then one of the largest KKK groups, on behalf of Michael's mother, Beulah Mae Donald, using the Civil Rights Act of 1870 as the basis. Ms. Donald was awarded $7 million in damages for the loss of her son. This bankrupted the group, leaving Ms. Donald the owner of their headquarters.

Governments can also undermine extremists' attempts to intimidate. Intimidation works only because the local population doesn't believe that the government can take care of them or protect them from violence. The best way to counter this is not only by reestablishing people's trust in the legitimacy of government, but also by ensuring adequate law enforcement and justice. This signals that the government is capable of protecting the population and identifying and punishing the perpetrators of crimes. It also discourages citizens from seeking protection from the extremists, which is often the first step in switching moderates' allegiance. If citizens in rural Nevada or Oregon know that the federal government is in charge, as opposed to a far-right sheriff, they might be less apt to support a militia. This strategy, however, could also backfire, particularly in the West, where people are more likely to be fearful of federal encroachment on their land or freedom. In this case, the government could enlist federal agents who are from the area, or it could shore up local security forces that are viewed as legitimate by local citizens. This could go a long way toward building trust and acceptance of government even in places skeptical of government overreach.

What about outbidding? Local citizens will gravitate to the group they believe is more likely to deliver security and success. *If you make sure my family is safe, and I believe you will give me a good job, I'll support you.* Governments can undercut support for extremists by reducing grievances, providing benefits for all citizens, and supplying hard evidence that playing within the system is more fruitful than defecting. The U.S. government, with its enormous wealth and institutional capacity, has the ability to outbid any insurgent group. If people feel that the government is on their side, they won't need the insurgents. Delivering basic services can help the United States break out of the cycle of loss of hope and loss of faith in government.

What happens when insurgents want to prevent a compromise with the government? Moderate lawmakers and citizens have to believe that extremists can't thwart a deal or impede reform by issuing death threats or threatening other violent action. Here in the United States, a deal would likely take the form of gun control legislation or immigration reform, and members of Congress would need to feel safe enough to publicly support such measures. Northern Ireland's peace deal, the Belfast Agreement, succeeded, in part, because it required the passage of a popular referendum, which then revealed overwhelming Catholic and Protestant support for the deal. Governments can prevent extremists from holding legislation hostage by advertising public support for reform, and by identifying and punishing those who threaten or resort to violence in an effort to stop it.

WE LIVE IN deeply partisan times, and it is common to hear polarization described as the root of our problems. Liberals have become more liberal, conservatives have become more conservative, and there is little chance of the two sides meeting in the middle. Polarization, many pundits have argued, is tearing America apart.

But political polarization does not increase the likelihood of civil war. What increases the likelihood of civil war is factionalization—when citizens form groups based on ethnic, religious, or geographic distinctions—and a country's political parties become predatory, cutting out rivals and enacting policies that primarily benefit them and their constituents. And nothing abets and accelerates factionalization as much as social media. After January 6, people kept asking me: What should we do? Do we need better policing? Better domestic terror laws? Does the FBI need to aggressively infiltrate far-right militias? My first answer was always the same. Take away the social media bullhorn and you turn down the volume on bullies, conspiracy theorists, bots, trolls, disinformation machines, hate-mongers, and enemies of democracy. America's collective anger would drop almost immediately, as it did when Donald Trump could no longer reach every American twenty times a day, every day. (As the journalist Matthew Yglesias noted on Twitter: "It's kinda weird that deplatforming Trump just like completely worked with no visible downside whatsoever.") Curbing the dissemination of hate and disinformation would greatly reduce the risk of civil war.

A central driver to factionalism has always been conspiracy theories. If you want to incite people to action, give them an "other" to target. Emphasize a behind-the-scenes plot designed to hurt their group. Convince them that an enemy is steering the country to their disadvantage. This is exactly what slaveholders in the South did in the years before the Civil War. They portrayed abolitionists as an existential threat to their way of life. Online platforms have made conspiracies more virulent, more powerful. Modern conspiracy theorists like Alex Jones of Infowars have painted immigrants and Jews as an existential threat. As Voltaire once said, "Those who can make you believe absurdities can make you commit atrocities."

This kind of paranoia has always been part of the fabric of American life. But a new conspiracy theory took hold during the Trump era: QAnon, a fringe movement claiming that a secret cabal of prominent pedophilic Democrats are plotting to take down Trump. A December 2020 poll found that fully 17 percent of all Americans—*almost one in five*— agree with the statement "A group of Satan-worshiping elites who run a child sex ring are trying to control our politics." Perhaps even more destructive, QAnon followers have joined with millions of other Trump supporters to spread the Big Lie—the idea that the 2020 election was stolen and that Democrats are intent on cheating to preserve power. In the weeks after the chaos of January 6, 2021, Facebook, YouTube, and Twitter cracked down on QAnon, removing accounts and pages associated with the group.

It doesn't have to be this way. America is where the social media industry was born, and it's home to the five major tech companies that control most of the information that is spread on social media. The U.S. government regulates all kinds of industries—from utilities and drug companies to food processing plants—to promote the common good. For the sake of democracy and societal cohesion, social media platforms should be added to the list. The impact would be global. Indeed, events in Charlottesville and elsewhere have inspired far-right movements around the world. The Capitol insurrection brought to light how U.S.-based movements are part of a global network of extremism. As pro-Trump supporters marched from the White House to the Capitol, alt-right propagandists in Berlin cheered them on. In Tokyo, meanwhile, demonstrators rallied under Rising Sun flags. Regulating social media would likely strengthen liberal democracies around the world.

It would also minimize factionalism by inhibiting foreign meddlers. Foreign governments have long sought to influence the outcome of civil wars. The United States sent billions of dollars to Chiang Kai-shek to try to help him defeat Mao's communist rebels. European countries sent supplies to the Confederacy during our own Civil War. The United States fought proxy battles with the Soviet Union in civil wars in Nicaragua, El Salvador, Guatemala, Peru, Angola, Cambodia, Vietnam, and Laos.

But now any country, any group, and any individual can use the internet to destabilize an adversary. Rivals of the United States are deeply invested in stoking civil conflict, through support for a preferred group or by inciting both sides. Vladimir Putin, an ex-KGB officer, has long understood the power of disinformation. Others have caught on. The Empirical Studies of Conflict Project—together with a team of scholars at Princeton—found that Russia, together with China, Iran, and Saudi Arabia, used clandestine social media campaigns fifty-three times between 2013 and 2018 to try to influence the internal politics of another country. Most of the campaigns examined by the Princeton team (65 percent) aimed to denigrate a public figure, usually a politician, in order to get his or her opponent elected. (Between 2012 and 2017, for example, seven of the ten most-read online pieces about Angela Merkel were fabricated, according to BuzzFeed.) The United States was the main target of these attacks but not the only one. Great Britain, Germany, Australia, and others were also targeted. Almost all the attacks were aimed at democracies.

Social media has created the perfect conditions for factionalism by making it easy for outsiders to sow distrust and division. In 2016, a Facebook account called Blacktivist, supposedly run by Baltimore-based Black Lives Matter organizers, shared videos of police brutality and information on upcoming rallies. It also hawked "Blacktivist" merchandise with T-shirts emblazoned with "Young, Gifted, and Black." The page had received 360,000 likes—even more than the official BLM page. CNN later reported that Blacktivist was one of more than 470 accounts linked to a Kremlin effort to infiltrate the Black Lives Matter movement. The larger goal, experts believe, was to inflame racial, regional, and religious tensions here in the United States.

The threat is as serious as a foreign power hiring mercenaries to fight on U.S. soil. America is a technological and military giant, but the internet and social media have left our democracy vulnerable to potent attacks. It used to be that if you wanted to aid a radical movement in another country you would drop leaflets from planes, distribute books and newspapers, send advisers to instruct soldiers, and smuggle arms and ammunition across borders. Now all you have to do is dominate the narrative on social media, and watch factionalism take root.

The United States is supposed to be a model of democracy, a beacon of freedom, but we have allowed money and extremism to infiltrate our politics. We can strengthen our democratic institutions and our society: We did this with the New Deal, when our government put people back to work, lifted many Americans out of poverty, and restored Americans' faith in their economic system, reviving a sense of hope. We did it in the civil rights era, when citizens demanded equal rights and freedoms for African Americans, and the government responded, satisfying a desire for equity and justice.

And we can do it again, by reclaiming and mediating our public discourse so we can get off the path of self-segregating, predatory factionalism and restore hope in the long-term health of our country. We are already seeing this at the local level, where groups of citizens in every state are forming small organizations to try to restore civic values. One such group is Citizen University, started by Eric Liu, the son of

Chinese immigrants, and Jená Cane, the granddaughter of a family who owned slaves and fought for the Confederacy. Both have dedicated their lives to rebuilding America's civil society, one block, one neighborhood, one town at a time. "We want to put an end to the myth," Cane said, "that we're a rugged, individualistic society, when the truth is that throughout our history, when disaster strikes, when a community needs rebuilding, when people are in need, Americans come together to help one another. That's who we really are."

One of the programs run by Citizen University is called Civic Saturday. Jen Boynton, a reporter, attended a Civic Saturday in Athens, Tennessee, in 2019. Almost seventy people attended the event in a dilapidated downtown park. What she found was the civic version of a church service: local citizens coming together to worship the Constitution and build their faith in our democracy. Instead of opening with a prayer, they opened with the Pledge of Allegiance. Instead of singing a hymn, they read a poem from an American author. Instead of reading a Bible passage, they read the Declaration of Independence. The first Civic Saturday was held in 2016 in Seattle, and Liu and Cane (who happen to be married) hoped—prayed—that people would show up. They came in droves; more than two hundred crowded into the bookstore that was hosting the first event. Five months later, eight hundred people came. What people are hungry for, said Liu, is community. Today, Civic Saturdays are being held in over thirty cities and towns around the country, both red and blue, from Indianapolis, Phoenix, and Kansas City to Southern Pines, North Carolina. "The great majority of people in America," said Liu, "want to be part of a healthy version of us and not the January 6th version."

And then there is EmbraceRace, a small nonprofit based in Amherst, Massachusetts. It was founded in 2016 by two parents of mixed-race children whose goal is to help other parents raise kids in a world where race is appreciated and embraced. BriteHeart is another nonpartisan group based in Tennessee that is dedicated to strengthening civic participation. According to Kate Tucker, who helps lead the group, "We don't know if Tennessee is a red state. We do know it's a non-voting state." Living Room Conversations and Braver Angels both pair people from the left and the right in order to begin to rehumanize "the other."

There are so many organizations like this emerging around the country, as Americans have begun to realize how fragile our democracy is and take action to preserve it. It is at the local level—in churches, voluntary associations, and grassroots groups—that we can once again come together and relearn the power of citizenship and community. Our shared history and ideals can inspire and guide us, reviving our national pride in a system that is truly of the people, for the people, and by the people.

LAST SUMMER, in the lead-up to the 2020 election, my husband, Zoli, and I found ourselves asking a question neither of us had ever contemplated before: Were we nearing the time when we would have to leave our country?

My mother immigrated to the United States from a tiny town in Switzerland where women in her home canton did not get the right to vote until 1991. Her life on a small dairy farm had been hard, and there was no possibility of college. She moved to New York City in 1958 and fell in love with baseball, business, and the friendliness and ease of Americans. She never wanted to go back. My father journeyed to New York from a small town in Bavaria where he had lived through World War II. He started a small business and built it into a success. "Only in America," he says, "could this have happened."

Zoli, who came from Canada to attend college in America, has his own immigrant story. His father fled to Canada in 1956 from Hungary, after the Russians moved in and cracked down on student protesters. Between us, Zoli and I have many passports: Swiss, Canadian, Hungarian, German. But the United States is home. The most joyous holiday at our house in San Diego is Thanksgiving. It embodies everything we are grateful for: friends, family, food. America has given our family the gift to pursue our dreams. The gift to be ourselves. The gift to feel safe and free and to prosper.

This is where we want to live. But in November, after the election, Zoli and I began to actively discuss a plan B. Joe Biden had won, but Trump and many Republicans were doing everything they could to overturn the results. When the attack on the Capitol took place, on January 6, it seemed that America might be at a turning point. I knew from my research what happened to people who waited too long to leave combat zones. Daris was lucky enough to survive the siege of Sarajevo. Many of his neighbors were not.

Over the Christmas holidays, Zoli renewed our passports. We considered whether it made sense to apply for Hungarian citizenship for our daughter, Lina. In the end, we decided on Canada, because we could drive there in less than a day if necessary. Switzerland would be the backup. We were used to making emergency plans while traveling to conflict-prone countries: "If a coup happens in Zimbabwe while we are there, what do we do?" But now, suddenly, we were charting an escape route from our own beloved country. It seemed unfathomable.

The founding fathers could have created any political system they wanted. They could have anointed George Washington king, established an aristocracy, divided America's rich land, and made themselves lords. But they were determined to create a democracy. The idea of such a system existed—in the narrow model provided by the ancient Greeks, and in the writings of Hume, Locke, Rousseau, and other political philosophers—but the reality did not. No country had ever attempted democracy on this scale, over such a large territory, where so many people would rule themselves. Madison, Hamilton, and John Jay tried to anticipate all the challenges the new nation would face: state versus federal power; how to prevent the tyranny of the majority; the threat of destructive factions. They knew that such a country would be raucous, unwieldy, and prone to conflict. And yet they persisted, believing a better, freer world was possible.

Of course, from another perspective—shared by millions—the dream was a nightmare. America was created to serve white men with property. The founders themselves were slave owners and did not believe that slaves deserved rights and freedoms. In fact, they did not even consider the enslaved to be full human beings. They also did not believe that white workers who didn't own land could hold public office. And they did not believe women had any say in any of these matters. They were broad-minded, but only by the standards of their era. And even if they had been visionary enough to reify the idea that all men and women were created equal, it would have been impossible for them to anticipate the many changes America would face. Industrialization. Megacities. Cars. They had no way to predict the country's future wealth and military power, or the changes wrought by globalization. The internet? Climate change? Trips to Mars? These are things they could not have fathomed.

America faces a monumental challenge: to create a truly multiethnic democracy, one that can survive and thrive as global migration continues to mold the country's demographics and identity. The world has changed dramatically since the late 1700s. Democracy is no longer just for white men who own farms. It now includes women; rural, urban, and suburban families; people who were born here and people who risked their lives to come here; white, Black, brown, mixed race, and everything in between. We need them all: Countries with low birth rates that try to stop immigration will slowly die because their populations will dwindle. Our democracy will have to protect the rights of small groups while also forging a unifying national identity. We will need to show the world that a transition to multiethnic democracy can be done peacefully and with no decline in prosperity.

The United States will be the first Western democracy where white citizens lose their majority status. This is projected to happen in 2045, but other countries are likely to follow. Far-right parties in wealthy western countries have issued ominous warnings about the end of white dominance, seeking to stoke hatred by emphasizing the great costs— economic, social, moral—of such transformation.

But that's a myth, the latest in a long line of fables spun by people who see power as a zero-sum proposition. Many American cities have already proven it wrong. In Birmingham and Memphis—and other cities that have transitioned from a white to a Black majority—Black mayors have been elected and won the support of white voters. Whites who had worried that Black leadership would lead to Black retribution and white economic decline realized that their fear had been misplaced. Their lives continued much as before, while the lives of Black residents improved. People learned that having a multiethnic party in power was not a threat to their well-being. A new peaceful equilibrium was reached.

California is another successful example. Since becoming minority-white in 1998 (Texas followed in 2004), the state has seen its economy grow by 200 percent. Unemployment has dropped by almost 3 percent. GDP per capita in the state has increased by 52.5 percent. I moved to California in 1996. I live forty miles north of the Mexican border and teach on a campus that is only 21 percent white. Every day I see a vision of a more promising future: eager students, hardworking immigrants.

California's transition met fierce resistance. In 1994, the state passed Proposition 187, the so-called Save Our State measure, prohibiting undocumented immigrants from receiving public services like healthcare and education. The referendum made the state the first in the modern era to approve major legislation aimed at deterring immigration and punishing the undocumented. Governor Pete Wilson, a Republican, handily won reelection by campaigning in favor of Prop 187, running ads showing grainy footage of immigrants crossing the border en masse. He was California's version of an ethnic entrepreneur. His play to white fear, which included harsher criminal justice policies, was a winning strategy. The greater the minority population—the greater the threat to white supremacy—the greater the white backlash.

But all of that began to change when California became a majority-minority state. As the minority population amassed enough support to wield political power, the state began to embrace its diversity, feeling its way toward policies that benefited not just white citizens but also Black citizens and immigrants—including laws that provided in-state tuition and driver's licenses for the undocumented. Large-scale increases in education spending and major reductions in prison populations followed, improving the welfare and well-being of all residents. In less than three decades, the state shed its reputation for anti-immigrant activism to become a forward-thinking model for policies on immigration and inclusion. California still has many challenges: It has a quarter of the nation's homeless residents, and ranks fourth highest in terms of income inequality. There has also been a number of recent attacks on elderly Asian residents. It is by no means a utopia. But the state's journey from racial fear to broad racial acceptance shows what's possible.

To fulfill the promise of a truly multiethnic democracy, the nation must navigate deep peril. We need to shore up our democracy, stay out of the anocracy zone, and rein in social media, which will help reduce factionalism. This will give us a chance to avoid a second civil war. If we can do that, we might be in a position to tackle another looming threat: climate change. A warming planet will increase the number and severity of natural disasters, endangering our coastal cities, and causing heat waves, wildfires, hurricanes, and droughts. It will also certainly increase migration from the global south to the wealthier, white north. In the absence of a strong and effective government response, it will tear at our social fabric. My students know about these challenges, and they are inspired and emboldened to do something about them. They are the new face of the American dream. When I get depressed, I think of them. There is no better place to be than a classroom filled with a bunch of first-generation students determined to change the world.

Zoli and I renewed our passports last December, but we have no intention of leaving. We love this country too much to walk away. If America leads the way for the rest of the world, then California leads the way for the rest of America, and we want to be here to help with the transition. America, I have to believe, is not at the end of its history. It is at the beginning of a remarkable new era, when we will have the chance to live up to our founding motto—E Pluribus Unum—where out of many, we will become one.

ACKNOWLEDGMENTS

When I started to write this book in 2018, I didn't tell many people it was about a possible second civil war in America. Those I did tell tended to look at me with concern. In their minds, another civil war was never going to happen in the United States, and thinking otherwise was an exercise in fearmongering—perhaps even irresponsible. Was I really going to go down this misguided path?

I wish they had been right. By the time the manuscript was almost complete, thousands of Americans were storming the U.S. Capitol and the President of the United States was demanding a fight should he be removed from office. Suddenly the manuscript seemed prophetic.

Writing a book is a lonely, uncertain experience. It is an act of faith: faith that one has the ability to do justice to the subject, that one's vision is clear and dispassionate, and that it will find an audience. But it is also a collaborative process. From the start, I have been blessed with friends, colleagues, and strangers who have given generously of their time. They answered endless questions, checked my work, and pointed me in new and promising directions; I would not have been able to write this particular book without their gracious help.

I owe an enormous debt to Amanda Cook, my editor at Penguin Random House, who was my biggest advocate. She embraced the project from the start and gently coaxed me to write the book that she, and the world, would want to read. Thank you also to Gareth Cook—my book whisperer— who taught me how to construct a tight narrative and tell stories that were both rich and absorbing. He was relentless but kind, demanding but generous, uncompromising but enthusiastic. This would have been a very different book without him.

Many strands of research needed to come together to craft these chapters, and I needed help from a community of scholars to do so. Monty Marshall answered a hundred emails about the PITF and Polity data with unshakable good cheer. He gave me an enormous amount of free information and for that I am deeply grateful. Richard English answered my questions on Northern Ireland's Troubles and made sure I got my facts straight. Lars-Erik Cederman, Simon Hug, and Kristian Gleditsch happily engaged with my detailed inquiries about ethnic civil wars, explaining the nuances of different statistical findings. Jim Fearon, David Laitin, and Jesse Driscoll read the manuscript and served as my "canaries" in the coal mine; if it didn't pass their sniff test it was unlikely to pass the test of other civil war experts. Thank you also to Judybeth Tropp, Chris Parker, Steph Haggard, Rose McDermott, Paul Frymer, Ken Pollack, Zachary Steinert-Threlkeld, Gregoire Phillips, Nico Ravanilla, Isaac Pelt, Jacob Glashof, Seth G. Jones, and Jonathan Moller, all of whom rapidly responded to questions related to particular parts of the book. Thanks to my students in my civil war class at UC San Diego in the winter of 2020 who helped me work through the big ideas that formed the structure of the book. Finally, thank you to Marin Strmecki and the Smith-Richardson Foundation for financial support, and to my dean, Peter Cowhey, and Nancy Gilson at GPS, who ensured that I had time to write during what turned out to be two challenging years.

I had the great good fortune to interview a set of extraordinary people. I thank Noor, Berina and Daris Marcov, Mikhail Minakov, Anton Melnyk, Jonathan Powell, Lukas Pietrzak, Jená Cane, and Eric Liu for sharing their personal and sometimes painful stories with me. I also thank James Fearon, David Laitin, Monty Marshall, Erica Chenoweth, Christian Davenport, and Jay Ulfelder for sharing their expert knowledge of both violent and nonviolent conflict as well as their thoughts on America's current situation. I learned much from each of them.

Autumn Brewington is not only a dear friend but an extraordinary editor. She read the very earliest parts of the manuscript with characteristic enthusiasm, propelling me forward while gently steering me away from writing like an academic. I was lucky to have a team of RAs helping me throughout the process. Thank you to Summer Bales, Ama Debrah, Wendy Wagner, and Wakako Maekawa. An even bigger thanks to Natalie Boyer, who was my indispensable finder-of-all-facts no matter how obscure. She had the gift to synthesize enormous amounts of difficult material into simple summaries which were then easy for me to use. Hilary McClellen swooped in at the end of the process to fact-check the entire book. Her stream of excited emails made this final punctilious phase surprisingly pleasurable.

Writing also requires the love and support of good

friends. Thank you to Lindi Nicol, Ronan Brown, Emilie Hafner-Burton, Angela Amoroso, Shannon Delaney, Amy Mueller, Tim Burke, Casey Burke, Jeannie Chufo, Nindy Leroy, Donn Van Winkle, Chris Parker, Mary Braunwarth, Ernie Villanueva, Giselle Brown, Camryn Delaney, Lina and Christian Waage, Marie and Faheem Hasnain, Colette and Glynn Bolitho, Laura and Ethan Boyer, Emma and John Spence and the Hajnal/Licharz/McGrath clans for always checking in on me even at my most grumpy.

But the greatest debt I owe to my family. My daughter, Lina, has lived her whole life in the shadow of my study of civil wars. She has endured trips to former conflict zones and seen things that most young kids don't see. On a particularly difficult trip to northern Laos (age 7), she turned to me with tears in her eyes and said: "Why can't we go someplace normal like Hawaii or Mammoth—like everyone else? No one goes to Laos, Mommy!" But most of all she has had to share her mother with a computer screen during a time when we both would rather have been dancing, or cooking, or doing anything else together. She is my greatest joy and source of pride. I love her twice as much and four times more.

And then there is Zoli. When I first signed my book contract, I turned to Zoli and said, "I can't do this without you." Without complaining, he took care of everything—everything—in our life so that all I had to do was write. Not only that, but at the end of the day he was waiting for me with big, open arms, a glass of wine, and all the love and adoration I could ask for. He has been my number one supporter, my best friend and confidante, my inspiration for how to live an honorable and compassionate life, and the person who makes everything better. He is the best human being I know.

NOTES

INTRODUCTION

ix **Adam Fox flipped over the carpet** "GR Vac Shop Owner Picking Up the Pieces After Business and Home Raided," Fox 17, October 9, 2020; Aaron C. Davis et al., "Alleged Michigan Plotters Attended Multiple Anti-Lockdown Protests, Photos and Videos Show," *The Washington Post,* November 1, 2020; "Accused Leader of Plot to Kidnap Michigan Governor Was Struggling Financially, Living in Basement Storage Space," *The Washington Post,* October 9, 2020.

ix **It had hit Detroit and Grand Rapids** "Governor Whitmer Signs 'Stay Home, Stay Safe' Executive Order," Office of Governor Gretchen Whitmer, March 23, 2020; "Stay-Home Order Violators Face $500 Fines; Jail Possible," *The Detroit News,* March 23, 2020.

x **join hundreds of protesters** Matt Zapotosky, Devlin Barrett, and Abigail Hauslohner, "FBI Charges Six Who It Says Plotted to Kidnap Michigan Gov. Gretchen Whitmer, as Seven More Who Wanted to Ignite Civil War Face State Charges," *The Washington Post,* October 8, 2020.

x **"We are in a war for the hearts"** Davis et al., "Alleged Michigan Plotters Attended Multiple Anti-lockdown Protests, Photos and Videos Show," *The Washington Post,* November 1, 2020.

x **That June, he livestreamed a video** "Michigan Kidnapping

Plot, Like So Many Other Extremist Crimes, Foreshadowed on Social Media," *The Washington Post,* October 8, 2020.

x **Soon afterward, he reached out over Facebook** Zapotosky, Barrett, and Hauslohner, "FBI Charges Six Who It Says Plotted to Kidnap Michigan Gov. Gretchen Whitmer"; Gus Burns, Roberto Acosta, and John Tunison, "The Ties That Bind the Men Behind the Plot to Kidnap Gov. Whitmer," *MLive,* October 20, 2020.

xi **they settled on a different plan** "Northern Michigan Town Grapples with Plot to Kidnap Gov. Whitmer from Local Vacation Home," *MLive,* October 9, 2020; Nicholas Bogel-Burroughs, Shaila Dewan, and Kathleen Gray, "F.B.I. Says Michigan Anti-Government Group Plotted to Kidnap Gov. Gretchen Whitmer," *The New York Times,* October 8, 2020.

xi **That August and September, the men spied** Bogel-Burroughs, Dewan, and Gray, "F.B.I. Says Michigan Anti-Government Group Plotted to Kidnap Gov. Gretchen Whitmer"; Burns, Acosta, and Tunison, "Ties That Bind the Men Behind the Plot to Kidnap Gov. Whitmer."

xi **The fourteen men, including Fox** "Michigan Charges 8th Man in Alleged Domestic Terrorism Plot to Kidnap Gov. Whitmer," NPR, October 15, 2020.

xii **President Donald Trump criticized Whitmer** "Trump Criticizes Whitmer After FBI Foiled Plot to Kidnap Michigan Governor," *MLive,* October 8, 2020.

xii **"I knew he was in a militia"** "What We Know About the Alleged Plot to Kidnap Michigan's Governor," *The New York Times,* October 9, 2020.

xii **"I just wanna make the world glow"** Bogel-Burroughs, Dewan, and Gray, "F.B.I. Says Michigan Anti-Government Group Plotted to Kidnap Gov. Gretchen Whitmer."

xiii **In 2010, an article published** Jack A. Goldstone et al., "A Global Model for Forecasting Political Instability," *American Journal of Political Science* 54 (January 2010): 190–208.

xiii **Written by a team of academics** The original name of the group was the State Failure Task Force.

xv   **Michigan also has a strong anti-government culture**
"Antigovernment Movement," Southern Poverty Law Center,
https://www.splcenter.org/fighting-hate/extremist-files/ideol
ogy/antigovernment.

xv   **Free Syrian Army—was a mix of hundreds** "Defected
Soldiers Formed Free Syrian Army," NPR, July 20, 2012; Emile
Hokayem, *Syria's Uprising and the Fracturing of the Levant* (Abing-
don, Oxfordshire: Routledge, 2017).

xvii   **Since 2008, over 70 percent of extremist-related deaths**
"U.S. Law Enforcement Failed to See the Threat of White Na-
tionalism. Now They Don't Know How to Stop It," *The New
York Times,* November 3, 2018.

xvii   **Their growth may have felt imperceptible** Janet I. Lewis,
*How Insurgency Begins: Rebel Group Formation in Uganda and Be-
yond* (Cambridge: Cambridge University Press, 2020), 31–36.

xvii   **It took three years for Mexico's Zapatista to grow** Ibid.

xix   **"And then suddenly," Kovac told me** Author interview
with Berina Kovac, July 16, 2020. Berina Kovac is a pseudonym.

CHAPTER 1: THE DANGER OF ANOCRACY

3   **"It was like a movie"** Author interview with Noor, July 1,
2020. Noor is a pseudonym.

5   **"We thought we would breathe freedom"** "15 Years After
U.S. Invasion, Some Iraqis are Nostalgic For Saddam Hussein
Era," *NPR*, April 30, 2018.

6   **In an effort to bring rapid democracy** "Fateful Choice on
Iraq Army Bypassed Debate," *The New York Times,* March 17,
2008; "Report Cites Americans for Purging Baath Party Members," *The New York Times,* July 6, 2020.

6   **Suddenly, before a new government could be formed**
"Debate Lingering on Decision to Dissolve the Iraqi Military,"
The New York Times, October 21, 2004; James P. Pfiffner, "U.S.
Blunders in Iraq: De-Baathification and Disbanding the Army,"
Intelligence and National Security 25 (February 2010): 76–85;
Thomas E. Ricks, *Fiasco: The American Military Adventure in Iraq*
(New York: Penguin, 2006).

7 **Nascent insurgent organizations began to form** Daniel Byman, "An Autopsy of the Iraq Debacle: Policy Failure or Bridge Too Far?," *Security Studies* 17 (December 2008): 599–643.

7 **"We were on top of the system"** Ibid.

7 **fighting escalated in April 2004** "The Struggle for Iraq: The Occupation; Troops Hold Fire for Negotiations at 3 Iraqi Cities," *The New York Times,* April 12, 2004.

8 **"Saudi Arabia supported the Sunni militias"** Author interview with Noor, July 1, 2020.

8 **the animals were either starving to death** "Author Describes Rescue of Baghdad's Zoo Animals," NPR, March 7, 2007.

9 **But by 1948, world leaders had embraced** "Human Rights Declaration Adopted by U.N. Assembly," *The New York Times,* December 11, 1948; UN General Assembly, Resolution 217 A (III), Universal Declaration of Human Rights, A/RES/3/217A (December 10, 1948).

9 **Today, almost 60 percent** "Despite Global Concerns About Democracy, More Than Half of Countries Are Democratic," Pew Research Center, May 14, 2019, citing the Polity5 Project, Center for Systemic Peace.

9 **"a free Iraq at the heart"** "Remarks by the President at the 20th Anniversary of the National Endowment for Democracy," United States Chamber of Commerce, November 6, 2003.

10 **But given a choice between** "Globally, Broad Support for Representative and Direct Democracy," Pew Research Center, October 16, 2017.

10 **Since 1946, right after World War II ended** Samuel P. Huntington, "How Countries Democratize," *Political Science Quarterly* 106 (Winter 1991–92): 579–616.

10 **Civil wars rose alongside democracies** "Armed Conflict by Region 1946–2019," Uppsala Conflict Data Program, 20.1 Data (UCDP 20.1 data); "Global Trends in Governance, 1800–2018," Polity5 Project, Center for Systemic Peace.

10 **In 1870, almost no countries were experiencing civil war** A. C. Lopez and D.D.P. Johnson, "The Determinants of War in

International Relations," *Journal of Economic Behavior and Organization,* 2017.

11 **In 2019, we reached a new peak** UCDP 20.1 data.

11 **It turns out that one of the best predictors** This sentence is a quote by Barbara F. Walter from Sean Illing, "Is America's Political Violence Problem Getting Worse? I Asked 7 Experts," *Vox,* October 30, 2018.

11 **It is in this middle zone that most civil wars occur** Havard Hegre et al., "Toward a Democratic Civil Peace? Democracy, Political Change, and Civil War, 1816–1992," *American Political Science Review,* March 2001; Kristian Skrede Gledtisch, *All International Politics Is Local: The Diffusion of Conflict, Integration, and Democratization* (Ann Arbor: University of Michigan Press, 2002); Zachary M. Jones and Yonatan Lupu, "Is There More Violence in the Middle?" *American Journal of Political Science,* 2018.

11 **Experts call countries in this middle zone** Monty G. Marshall and Ted Robert Gurr, *Peace and Conflict 2003: A Global Survey of Armed Conflicts, Self-Determination Movements, and Democracy* (College Park, Md.: Center for International Development and Conflict Management, University of Maryland, 2003).

12 **The same was true of Spain in the 1930s** Note that Spain's First Republic had a democratic election in 1873.

12 **The dataset is useful** Boese, Vanessa A. 2019. "How (not) to Measure Democracy," *International Area Studies Review.* 22(2): 95–127; Vaccaro, Andrea. 2021, "Comparing Measures of Democracy: Statistical Properties, Convergence, and Interchangeability," *European Political Science.*

13 **Fareed Zakaria calls these types of governments** Fareed Zakaria, *The Future of Freedom: Illiberal Democracy at Home and Abroad* (New York: W.W. Norton, 2003).

14 **The CIA first discovered the relationship** Daniel C. Esty et al., "State Failure Task Force Report: Phase II Findings," *Environmental Change and Security Project Report* 5, Summer 1999.

14 **Anocracies, particularly those with more democratic** Ibid.

15 **When I asked Noor about the transition** Author interview with Noor, July 1, 2020.

15 **Former rebel leaders in Uganda** Lewis, *How Insurgency Begins,* Chapter 6.

16 **Though a reformist named Zviad Gamsakhurdia** "Gamsakhurdia Wins Presidential Election," UPI, May 27, 1991; "Tbilisi Battle Ends as President Flees," *The Washington Post,* January 7, 1992; "In Crushing Blow to Georgia, City Falls to Secessionists," *The New York Times,* September 28, 1993.

17 **This happened in Indonesia** "The Fall of Suharto: The Overview; Suharto, Besieged, Steps Down After 32-Year Rule in Indonesia," *The New York Times,* May 21, 1998.

17 **Within weeks of entering office** "New Leader Vows Early Elections for Indonesians," *The New York Times,* May 26, 1998; "Indonesia Changed, But Who Deserves the Credit?" *The New York Times,* June 13, 1999.

17 **the Christian Ambonese, an ethnic group in the province of Maluku** For a more in-depth history on the revolt, see especially Richard Chauvel, *Nationalists, Soldiers and Separatists: The Ambonese Islands from Colonialism to Revolt, 1880–1950* (Leiden, Netherlands: KITLV Press, 1990).

17 **"then there is no reason Aceh"** Quote by Kautsar, an activist in Aceh, from Slobodan Lekic, "The Legacy of East Timor: Other Indonesian Provinces Feel Stirrings of Separatism," *Montreal Gazette,* November 7, 1999.

18 **Rapid regime change—a six-point or more** Patrick M. Regan and Sam R. Bell, "Changing Lanes or Stuck in the Middle: Why Are Anocracies More Prone to Civil Wars?" *Political Research Quarterly* 63, no. 4 (December 2010): 747–59.

18 **Ethiopia's recent political violence** "Abiy Ahmed: Ethiopia's Prime Minister," BBC, October 11, 2019; "In Ethiopian Leader's New Cabinet, Half the Ministers Are Women," *The Washington Post,* October 16, 2018.

18 **"beyond our wildest dreams"** Interview with author, February 1, 2019.

18 **"such a remarkable level of democratic opening"** "Ethi-

opia: Thousands Protest After Deadly Ethnic Violence," Al Jazeera, September 17, 2018.

18 **Today, a full-scale civil war** "Why Is Ethiopia at War With Itself?," *The New York Times,* July 2, 2021.

19 **Mexico weathered democratization relatively peacefully** Roderic Ai Camp, "Democratizing Mexican Politics, 1982–2012," in *Oxford Research Encyclopedia of Latin American History,* ed. William H. Beezley (New York: Oxford University Press, 2015).

19 **Even once-safe liberal democracies** "Polity5 Annual Time-Series, 1946–2018," Center for Systemic Peace.

19 **We've seen this in Poland** "Democracy in Poland Is in Mortal Danger," *The Atlantic,* October 9, 2019.

20 **The government controls the media** Zach Beauchamp, "It Happened There: How Democracy Died in Hungary," *Vox,* September 13, 2018.

20 **Orbán and his party may have won** Beauchamp, "It Happened There."

20 **According to the V-Dem Institute** "Autocratization Turns Viral: Democracy Report 2021," V-Dem Institute, March 2021.

20 **Democratic countries that veer into anocracy** Steven Levitsky and Daniel Ziblatt, *How Democracies Die* (New York: Crown, 2018).

20 **There are three widely used** Boese, Vanessa A. 2019: "How (not) to Measure Democracy," *International Area Studies Review,* 22(2): 95–127; Vaccaro, Andrea. 2021: "Comparing Measures of Democracy: Statistical Properties, Convergence, and Interchangeability," European Political Science.

22 **For a decaying democracy** "Polity5 Annual Time-Series, 1946–2018," Center for Systemic Peace.

22 **Annual Likelihood of Armed Conflict** The numbers on the y axis represent the probability that a civil war begins in a particular country in any given year, depending on its polity score. An anocracy with a polity score of +1, for example, is more than six times more likely to experience a civil war than a full democracy with a polity score of +10.

23 **One cautionary tale is Ukraine** "Ukraine Protests After Ya-
    nukovych EU Deal Rejection," BBC, November 30, 2013;
    "Pro-European Businessman Claims Victory in Ukraine Presi-
    dential Vote," *The New York Times,* May 25, 2014.

24 **"We had dreams of a new life"** Author interview with
    Anton Melnyk, June 30, 2020. Anton Melnyk is a pseudonym.

24 **Within weeks of Yanukovych's ouster** "Russians Find Few
    Barriers to Joining Ukraine Battle," *The New York Times,* June 9,
    2014.

24 **The decline of democracy in Ukraine** "Why Ukraine's
    Government, Which Just Collapsed, Is Such a Mess," *Vox,*
    July 25, 2014.

25 **When he showed up in Kyiv on March 3** Author interview
    with Mikhail Minakov, July 1, 2020.

25 **By April 6, after weeks of protests** "Pro-Russia Protesters
    Seize Ukraine Buildings, Kiev Blames Putin," Reuters, April 6,
    2014; "Ukraine: President Calls Emergency Meeting Over
    Protests," BBC, April 7, 2014.

26 **The love affair with democratization** "Autocratization
    Turns Viral: Democracy Report 2021," V-Dem Institute, March
    2021.

26 **Some democracies that have crossed into anocracy**
    "How Venezuela Went from a Rich Democracy to a Dictator-
    ship on the Brink of Collapse," *Vox,* September 19, 2017.

26 **have resisted civil war by resorting to straight-up repres-
    sion** Christian Davenport, "State Repression and Political
    Order," Annual Review of Political Science, June 15, 2007.

27 **People began asking whether you** Author interview with
    Noor, July 1, 2020.

CHAPTER 2: THE RISE OF FACTIONS

28 **The men in military uniform inched the casket** "Thou-
    sands Join Ceremonies for Tito's Return to Belgrade," *The
    Washington Post,* May 6, 1980; "Leaders Gathering for Tito's
    Funeral," *The New York Times,* May 7, 1980.

29 **"the most frightful mix-up of races"** This passage was

quoted in Robert D. Kaplan, *Balkan Ghosts: A Journey Through History* (New York: St. Martin's Press, 1993), 52.

30 **"One-third we will kill"** Alex N. Dragnich, *Serbs and Croats: The Struggle in Yugoslavia* (New York: Harcourt Brace, 1992), 102.

30 **Each ethnic group would have a geographic home base** Vesna Pesic, "Serbian Nationalism and the Origins of the Yugoslav Crisis," United States Institute of Peace, April 1996.

30 **Tensions broke out almost immediately** Misha Glenny, *The Balkans: Nationalism, War, and the Great Powers, 1804–2012* (Toronto: House of Anansi Press, 2012); Anton Logoreci, "Riots and Trials in Kosovo," *Index on Censorship* 11 (1982): 23–40; "Yugoslavia Destroyed Its Own Economy," *The Wall Street Journal,* April 28, 1999.

31 **Serbs viewed Kosovo as their cherished homeland** Monica Duffy Toft, *The Geography of Ethnic Violence: Identity, Interests, and the Indivisibility of Territory* (Princeton, N.J.: Princeton University Press, 2003).

32 **Instead, that June, on the six hundredth anniversary** "1 Million Serbs Cheer Their Nationalist Leader in Kosovo," Associated Press, June 28, 1989; Paul R. Bartrop, *Modern Genocide: A Documentary and Reference Guide* (Santa Barbara, Calif.: ABC-CLIO, 2019), 64.

33 **the world would come to know the term "ethnic cleansing"** "On Language: Ethnic Cleansing," *The New York Times,* March 14, 1993.

34 **In the first five years after World War II** James D. Fearon and David D. Laitin, "Sons of the Soil, Migrants, and Civil War," *World Development* 39, no. 2 (February 2011): 199–211.

34 **they focused on ethnicity as a potential cause** Donald L. Horowitz, *Ethnic Groups in Conflict* (Berkeley: University of California Press, 234).

34 **But the dawn of datasets cast doubt on this theory** Paul Collier and Anke Hoeffler, "Greed and Grievance in Civil War," *Oxford Economic Papers* 56 (October 2004): 563–95; James D. Fearon and David D. Laitin, "Ethnicity, Insurgency,

and Civil War," *American Political Science Review* 97, no. 1 (February 2003): 75–90.

35 **"We studied every situation of factionalism"** Author interview with Monty Marshall, September 22, 2020.

39 **found that once these types of political parties** Andreas Wimmer, *Waves of War: Nationalism, State Formation, and Ethnic Exclusion in the Modern World* (Cambridge: Cambridge University Press, 2013), 5.

39 **And if a country was an anocracy** "Political Instability Task Force: New Findings," Wilson Center, February 5, 2004.

39 **War is even more likely** Joshua R. Gubler and Joel Sawat Selway, "Horizontal Inequality, Crosscutting Cleavages, and Civil War," *Journal of Conflict Resolution* 56 (April 2012): 206–32.

39 **Experts have found that the most volatile countries** Tanja Ellingsen, "Colorful Community or Ethnic Witches' Brew? Multiethnicity and Domestic Conflict During and After the Cold War," *Journal of Conflict Resolution* 44, no. 2: 228–49; Collier and Hoeffler, "Greed and Grievance in Civil War"; Joan Esteban and Gerald Schneider, "Polarization and Conflict: Theoretical and Empirical Issues," *Journal of Peace Research,* March 2008.

42 **Perhaps there is no greater picture of the deep divide** "Croatian Cityscape: Stray Dogs, Rows of Wounded, Piles of Dead," *The New York Times,* November 21, 1991.

43 **"We kept telling jokes at [the Serbs'] expense"** Zlatko Dizdarević, *Sarajevo: A War Journal* (New York: Fromm International, 1993), 112.

43 **citizens exposed to its broadcast** Stefano DellaVigna et al., "Cross-Border Media and Nationalism: Evidence from Serbian Radio in Croatia," *American Economic Journal: Applied Economics* 6 (July 2014): 103–32.

43 **By the time Vukovar finally fell** "Murder of the City," *The New York Review,* May 27, 1993; "A War on Civilians: The Struggle for Land in Bosnia Is Waged Mainly by Serbs With Help from Belgrade," *The New York Times,* July 18, 1992.

44 **Experts have a term for these individuals: ethnic entre-preneurs** V. P. Gagnon Jr., "Ethnic Nationalism and International Conflict: The Case of Serbia," *International Security* 19, no. 3 (Winter 1994–95), 130–66; V. P. Gagnon, Jr., *The Myth of Ethnic War: Serbia and Croatia in the 1990s* (Ithaca, N.Y.: Cornell University Press, 2006).

45 **"gambling for resurrection"—an aggressive** George W. Downs and David M. Rocke, "Conflict, Agency, and Gambling for Resurrection: The Principal-Agent Problem Goes to War," *American Journal of Political Science*. May 1994; Rui De Figueiredo and Barry Weingast, "The Rationality of Fear: Political Opportunism and Ethnic Conflict," in *Civil Wars, Insecurity, and Intervention,* ed. Barbara F. Walter and Jack Snyder (New York: Columbia University Press) 1999, 261–302.

45 **This is how, at a 1992 rally** "Cockroaches" was a term used in the Hutu revolution in 1959 to refer to Tutsi rebels "scurrying" at night across borders. I thank James Fearon for this reference. "Trial of Ex-Quebec Resident on Genocide Charges Stirs Ethnic Tensions in Rwanda," *National Post,* November 17, 2013.

45 **In 2012, Sudanese president Omar al-Bashir** "Sudan President Seeks to 'Liberate' South Sudan," BBC, April 19, 2012.

46 **After purging disloyal journalists** "Media Controls Leave Serbians in the Dark," *The Washington Post,* October 18, 1998.

46 **"dark, genocidal urges of the Croats"** Misha Glenny, *The Fall of Yugoslavia: The Third Balkan War* (London: Penguin Books), 1996, 66.

48 **The republic had the highest percentage of people** Ibid., 161.

48 **Sarajevo had hosted the Winter Olympics** "And Now, Dovidjenja, Sarajevo," *The New York Times,* February 21, 1984.

48 **"I was sure that what happened in Croatia"** Author interview with Berina Kovac, July 16, 2020.

48 **"We are culturally very, very close"** Author interview with Daris Kovac, July 16, 2020. Daris Kovac is a pseudonym.

49 **"The facts started to get twisted"** Ibid.

49 **In 1991, the Serbian Pale TV company** "For Sarajevo Serbs, Grief Upon Grief," *The New York Times,* April 26, 1995.

49 **Newscasters mocked Muslim prayers** Kemal Kurspahić, *Prime Time Crime: Balkan Media in War and Peace* (Washington, D.C.: Institute of Peace Press, 2003), 102–3.

49 **"At weddings in Bosnia"** Author interview with Berina Kovac, July 16, 2020.

50 **In the rhetoric of Milošević and Karadžić** Roger D. Petersen, *Understanding Ethnic Violence: Fear, Hatred, and Resentment in Twentieth-Century Eastern Europe* (Cambridge: Cambridge University Press, 2002), 238.

50 **agreed to divide Bosnia into two parts** "Serbs, Croats Met Secretly to Split Bosnia," *Los Angeles Times,* May 9, 1992.

50 **"We are bound to the Serbs"** Tom Gallagher, *The Balkans After the Cold War: From Tyranny to Tragedy* (London: Routledge), 2003.

51 **more than 1,500 Muslim men, women, and children** "The Warlord of Visegrad," *The Guardian,* August 10, 2005.

51 **At the start of the war, 63 percent** "Serb Forces Overwhelm Key Town," *The Washington Post,* April 15, 1992; "War Is Over—Now Serbs and Bosniaks Fight to Win Control of a Brutal History," *The Guardian,* March 23, 2014.

51 **"We see their fires when they cook"** Author interview with Berina Kovac, July 16, 2020.

52 **granting key government positions to extremists** "Firebrand Hindu Cleric Ascends India's Political Ladder," *The New York Times,* July 12, 2017.

53 **Modi went on to put extremists in charge** "India Is Changing Some Cities' Names, and Muslims Fear Their Heritage Is Being Erased," NPR, April 23, 2019; "India's New Textbooks Are Promoting the Prime Minister's Favorite Policies, Critics Allege," *The Washington Post,* July 1, 2018.

53 **In 2019, he rescinded special status** "India Revokes Kashmir's Special Status, Raising Fears of Unrest," *The New York Times,* August 5, 2019; "India Says the Path to Citizenship Will Get Easier, But Muslims See a Hindu Plot," *The Wall Street Journal,* December 11, 2019.

54 **Though the economy has not improved** "India Has to Create More Jobs. Modi May Need Some Help from State Governments," CNBC, June 6, 2019.

54 **This pattern is repeating itself in democracies** "Jair Bolsonaro: Brazil's Firebrand Leader Dubbed the Trump of the Tropics," BBC, December 31, 2018; "How Jair Bolsonaro Entranced Brazil's Minorities—While Also Insulting Them," *The Washington Post,* October 24, 2018.

55 **"We called him a crazy psychiatrist"** Author interview with Berina Kovac, July 16, 2020.

55 **"I didn't know at the time"** Author interview with Daris Kovac, July 16, 2020.

56 **five months before the genocide** "Serbia Arrests Seven Over 1995 Srebrenica Massacre," BBC, March 18, 1995.

56 **"I couldn't believe it"** Author interview with Daris Kovac, July 16, 2020.

56 **In October 1990, the CIA issued a report** "A Bloody Failure in the Balkans," *The Washington Post,* February 8, 1993; "Yugoslavia Transformed: National Intelligence Estimate," Director of Central Intelligence, National Foreign Intelligence Board, October 18, 1990.

CHAPTER 3: THE DARK CONSEQUENCES
OF LOSING STATUS

58 **To Muslims, he was a World War II hero** There are multiple accounts of Matalam's life, some of them conflicting, and none of them completely reliable.

58 **Matalam was born at the turn of the twentieth century** Thomas M. McKenna, *Muslim Rulers and Rebels: Everyday Politics and Armed Separatism in the Southern Philippines* (Berkeley: University of California Press), 1998.

59 **Catholics increasingly began to migrate to Mindanao** Ibid.

59 **Many Muslims were physically thrown off land** Thomas M. McKenna, "The Origins of the Muslim Separatist Movement in the Philippines," Asia Society, https://asiasociety.org/origins -muslim-separatist-movement-philippines.

60   **Matalam's loss of political stature** McKenna, *Muslim Rulers and Rebels,* 146.

60   **"Once our religion is no more"** Anabelle Ragsag, *Ethnic Boundary-Making at the Margins of Conflict in the Philippines: Everyday Identity Politics in Mindanao* (Singapore: Springer, 2020).

60   **Matalam's manifesto, however, caused a spiral** McKenna, *Muslim Rulers and Rebels,* 146.

61   **But the creation of the MIM** Ibid., 147–50.

61   **It was the classic "security dilemma,"** John J. Herz, "Idealist Internationalism and the Security Dilemma," *World Politics* 2, no. 2 (January 1950): 157–80; Robert Jervis, "Cooperation Under the Security Dilemma," *World Politics* 30, no. 2 (January 1978): 167–214; Barry R. Posen, "The Security Dilemma and Ethnic Conflict," *Survival* 35, no. 1 (Spring 1993), 27–41.

61   **But what really tempted all-out conflict** "Mass Arrests and Curfew Announced in Philippines," *The New York Times,* September 24, 1972.

61   **A few days before the weapons deadline** McKenna, *Muslim Rulers and Rebels,* 157; Ruben G. Domingo, "The Muslim Secessionist Movement in the Philippines: Issues and Prospects" (thesis, Naval Postgraduate School, June 1995).

62   **leading to the deaths** "Philippines-Mindanao (1971 – First Conflict Deaths)," Project Ploughshares, https://ploughshares .ca/pl_armedconflict/philippines-mindanao-1971-first -combat-deaths/#:~:text=Total%3A%20At%20least%20100 %2C63%20people,by%20the%2040%2Dyear%20conflict.

63   **Over the past three decades, scholars have zeroed in** For excellent research on this subject, see Lars-Erik Cederman, Andreas Wimmer, and Brian Min, "Why Do Ethnic Groups Rebel? New Data and Analysis," *World Politics* 62 (2010): 87–119; Halvard Buhaug, Lars-Erik Cederman, and Jan K. Rød, "Disaggregating Ethno-Nationalist Civil Wars: A Dyadic Test of Exclusion Theory," *International Organization* 62 (2008): 531–51.

63   **But the most powerful determinant of violence** Petersen, *Understanding Ethnic Violence,* 2002.

65 **"immediately caused a reaction among Tamils"** Fearon and Laitin, "Sons of the Soil, Migrants, and Civil War," 199–211.

65 **psychologists Daniel Kahneman and Amos Tversky demonstrated** Daniel Kahneman and Amos Tversky, "Prospect Theory: An Analysis of Decision Under Risk," *Econometrica* 47 (1979): 263–91.

67 **Thousands of Georgians and Abkhazians were killed,** "Georgia/Abkhazia: Violations of the Laws of War and Russia's Role in the Conflict," *Human Rights Watch* 7, no. 7 (March 1995), https://www.hrw.org/reports/1995/Georgia2 .htm#P117_4464; Jared Ferrie, "Can They Ever Go Home? The Forgotten Victims of Georgia's Civil War," *New Humanitarian,* May 27, 2019, https://www.thenewhumanitarian.org/news -feature/2019/05/27/Abkhazia-georgia-civil-war-forgotten -victims.

67 **what experts call "sons of the soil"** This term was coined by Myron Weiner, a political scientist at MIT, and then developed by David Laitin. Myron Weiner, *Sons of the Soil: Migration and Ethnic Conflict in India* (Princeton, N.J.: Princeton University Press), 1978; Fearon and Laitin, "Sons of the Soil, Migrants, and Civil War."

67 **In one study of civil wars since 1800** David D. Laitin, "Immigrant Communities and Civil War," *International Migration Review* 43 (2009): 35–59.

68 **In 1965, Indigenous Papuans formed the Free Papua Movement** R. G. Crocombe, *Asia in the Pacific Islands: Replacing the West* (Suva, Fiji: IPS Publications), 2007.

68 **Native speakers of a country's official language** David D. Laitin, "Language Games," *Comparative Politics* 20, no. 3 (April 1988): 289–302.

69 **"numbers are an indicator"** Horowitz, *Ethnic Groups in Conflict,* 194.

69 **The first migrants were brought in by the British** "The Economic Basis of Assam's Linguistic Politics and Anti-Immigrant Movements," *The Wire,* September 27, 2018.

69 **But migration continued even after India** "Ethnic and Religious Conflicts in India," *Cultural Survival Quarterly*, September 1983.

70 **The Assamese responded by organizing** Myron Weiner, "The Political Demography of Assam's Anti-Immigrant Movement," *Population and Development Review* 9 (June 1983): 279–92.

71 **The surge in new voters** Ibid.

71 **"For the Assamese, the towns"** Ibid.

72 **In 1979, student leaders from Assam's** Ibid.

72 **The government ignored these demands, leading to the formation of an even more radical group** Sandhya Goswami, *Assam Politics in Post-Congress Era: 1985 and Beyond* (New Delhi: SAGE Publications), 2020.

72 **The leaders of the AASU** Ibid.

73 **demanding that all immigrants** Sanjib Baruah, "Immigration, Ethnic Conflict, and Political Turmoil—Assam, 1979–1985," *Asian Survey* 26 (November 1986): 1184–206.

73 **"last struggle for survival"** Baruah, "Immigration, Ethnic Conflict, and Political Turmoil."

73 **"We will give blood, not country"** Manash Firaq Bhattacharjee, "We Foreigners: What It Means to Be Bengali in India's Assam," Al Jazeera, February 26, 2020.

74 **Violence reached its peak** "Nellie Massacre—How Xenophobia, Politics Caused Assam's Genocide," *Quint,* February 18, 2020; Makiko Kimura, *The Nellie Massacre of 1983: Agency of Rioters* (New Delhi: SAGE Publications), 2013.

74 **Using machetes, spears, and homemade guns** Weiner, "Political Demography of Assam's Anti-Immigrant Movement."

74 **"Not only is there no apparent"** James D. Fearon, "Governance and Civil War Onset," World Development Report 2011 Background Paper, August 31, 2010.

75 **The citizens living in the Donbas** Tim Judah, *In Wartime: Stories from Ukraine* (New York: Crown), 2016.

75 **They were both politically excluded** Lars-Erik Cederman, Kristian Skrede Gleditsch, and Halvard Buhaug, *Inequality, Grievances, and Civil War* (Cambridge: Cambridge University Press, 2013); Ted Robert Gurr, "Why Minorities Rebel: A Global Analysis of Communal Mobilization and Conflict Since 1945," *International Political Science Review,* 1993; F. Stewart, "Social Exclusion and Conflict: Analysis and Policy Implications" (report prepared for the UK Department for International Development, London, 2004).

75 **"Loggers came to despoil our beautiful hills"** Federico V. Magdalena, "Population Growth and Changing Ecosystems in Mindanao," *Philippine Quarterly of Culture and Society* 25 (1997): 5–30.

76 **By 2050, the World Bank predicts** Kanta Kumari Rigaud et al., "Groundswell: Preparing for Internal Climate Migration," World Bank, 2018.

76 **The Syrian war is an early example** Colin P. Kelley et al., "Climate Change in the Fertile Crescent and Implications of the Recent Syrian Drought," *Proceedings of the National Academy of Sciences* 112 (March 17, 2015): 3241–46.

77 **found that armed conflict was more likely** Carl-Friedrich Schleussner et al., "Armed-Conflict Risks Enhanced by Climate-Related Disasters in Ethnically Fractionalized Countries," *Proceedings of the National Academy of Sciences* 113 (August 16, 2016), 9216–21.

CHAPTER 4: WHEN HOPE DIES

79 **designed to exclude Irish Catholics** James Waller, *A Troubled Sleep: Risk and Resilience in Contemporary Northern Ireland* (New York: Oxford University Press, 2021).

79 **The councils also controlled government jobs** Peter Taylor, *The Provos: The IRA and Sinn Fein* (London: Bloomsbury, 2014), 44.

79 **"It was basically designed"** Ibid., 50.

82 **"Catholics were convinced"** Eamonn Mallie and Patrick Bishop, *The Provisional IRA* (London: Corgi, 1987).

83 **All attempts to change the system** Gerry Adams, *Before the Dawn: An Autobiography* (Dublin: Brandon, 1996), 51.

84 **It's when a group looks** This conclusion is based on my read of qualitative case studies as well as interviews with the political leaders of rebel groups.

85 **"People were in a hopeless"** Richard English, *Armed Struggle: The History of the IRA* (New York: Oxford University Press, 2003), 121.

85 **Sunnis living in these new "misery belts"** Sam Dagher, *Assad or We Burn the Country: How One Family's Lust for Power Destroyed Syria* (New York: Little, Brown, 2019), 158.

87 **"We were only chanting in the streets"** Wendy Pearlman, *We Crossed a Bridge and It Trembled: Voices from Syria* (New York: Custom House, 2017), 145.

88 **But Assad's response removed any doubt** "Assad Blames Conspirators for Syrian Protests," *The Guardian,* March 30, 2011.

88 **"We couldn't believe what we were hearing"** Pearlman, *We Crossed a Bridge,* 100.

88 **"the one that sent Syria"** David W. Lesch, "Anatomy of an Uprising: Bashar al-Assad's Fateful Choices That Launched the Civil War," in *The Arab Spring: The Hope and Reality of the Uprisings,* ed. Mark L. Haas and David W. Lesch (Boulder, Colo.: Westview Press, 2017).

89 **The result? "People exploded"** Mary Elizabeth King, *A Quiet Revolution: The First Palestinian Intifada and Nonviolent Resistance* (New York: Nation Books, 2007), 2–4, 205.

89 **violence tends to escalate** Paul Collier et al., "Post-Conflict Risks," *Journal of Peace Research* 45 (July 2008): 461–78; Lars-Erik Cederman et al., "Elections and Ethnic Civil War," *Comparative Political Studies* 46 (March 2013): 387–417.

89 **This is why civil wars** Ibid.

90 **"Irish people for hundreds of years"** Interview with Brendan Hughes, "Behind the Mask: The IRA and Sinn Fein," *Frontline,* October 21, 1997.

91 **Since 2010, protests have surged** Thomas S. Szayna et al., "Conflict Trends and Conflict Drivers: An Empirical Assessment of Historical Conflict Patterns and Future Conflict" (Santa Monica, Calif.: RAND Corporation, 2017); Erica Chenoweth, *Civil Resistance: What Everyone Needs to Know* (New York: Oxford University Press, 2021).

91 **In 2019 alone, political protests** Global Protest Tracker, Carnegie Endowment for International Peace, 2020.

92 **In the 1990s, peaceful protests** Chenoweth, *Civil Resistance*.

92 **"Something has really shifted"** "From Chile to Lebanon, Protests Flare Over Wallet Issues," *The New York Times,* October 23, 2019.

93 **In a study of global conflict** Cederman et al., "Elections and Ethnic Civil War."

94 **Elections give people hope** Adam Przeworski, *Democracy and the Market: Political and Economic Reforms in Eastern Europe and Latin America* (Cambridge: Cambridge University Press), 1991.

94 **One study revealed that all** Marta Reynal-Querol, "Political Systems, Stability and Civil Wars," *Defence and Peace Economics* 13 (February 2002): 465–83.

96 **Once elections take place** Cederman et al., "Elections and Ethnic Civil War."

97 **In the American Civil War** Maury Klein, *Days of Defiance: Sumter, Secession, and the Coming of the Civil War* (New York: Alfred A. Knopf, 1997).

97 **Multiple studies have found** Fearon, "Governance and Civil War Onset"; Jason Lyall and Isaiah Wilson, "Rage Against the Machines: Explaining Outcomes in Counterinsurgency Wars," *International Organization* 63 (2009): 67–106; Luke N. Condra and Jacob N. Shapiro, "Who Takes the Blame? The Strategic Effects of Collateral Damage," *American Journal of Political Science* 56 (January 2012): 167–87; Mark Irving Lichbach, "Deterrence or Escalation? The Puzzle of Aggregate Studies of Repression and Dissent," *Journal of Conflict Resolution* 31 (June 1987): 266–97.

97 **"If I ever write a book"** Pearlman, *We Crossed a Bridge*, 66.

98 **Hamas has stored weapons** "Israel Says That Hamas Uses Civilian Shields, Reviving Debate," *The New York Times*, July 23, 2014.

98 **Carlos Marighella, a Brazilian Marxist** Carlos Marighella, "Minimanual of the Urban Guerilla," *Survival: Global Politics and Strategy* 13 (1971): 95–100; David B. Carter, "Provocation and the Strategy of Terrorist and Guerrilla Attacks," *International Organization* 70 (January 2016): 133–73.

98 **"were our best recruiting agents"** English, *Armed Struggle*, 122.

98 **"Nothing radicalizes a people faster"** Paddy Woodworth, "Why Do They Kill? The Basque Conflict in Spain," *World Policy Journal* 18 (2001): 1–12.

98 **violent conflict entrepreneurs** Chenoweth, *Civil Resistance*.

99 **In a study of self-determination movements** Barbara F. Walter, *Reputation and Civil War: Why Separatist Conflicts Are So Violent* (Cambridge: Cambridge University Press, 2009).

100 **Studies have shown that governments** Stefan Lindemann and Andreas Wimmer, "Repression and Refuge: Why Only Some Politically Excluded Ethnic Groups Rebel," *Journal of Peace Research* 55 (May 2018): 305–19; Stathis N. Kalyvas, *The Logic of Violence in Civil War* (New York: Cambridge University Press, 2006).

100 **"really had no idea what was going on"** Author interview with Jonathan Powell, July 2011.

CHAPTER 5: THE ACCELERANT

103 **"Burma for the Burmans"** Matthew Bowser, "Origins of an Atrocity: Tracing the Roots of Islamophobia in Myanmar," *AHA Today*, June 25, 2018.

103 **Ever since then, Indian Muslims** Ibid.

103 **When rebel groups tried to resist** Afroza Anwary, "Atrocities Against the Rohingya Community of Myanmar," *Indian Journal of Asian Affairs* 31 (2018): 93.

104 **In 2012, a group of Buddhist ultranationalists** Christina Fink, "Dangerous Speech, Anti-Muslim Violence, and Facebook in Myanmar," *Journal of International Affairs* 71 (2018): 43–52.

104 **The posts, which went viral** Steve Stecklow, "Why Facebook Is Losing the War on Hate Speech in Myanmar," Reuters, August 15, 2018.

104 **Myanmar's military leaders were using it to post** Paul Mozur, "A Genocide Incited on Facebook, with Posts from Myanmar's Military," *The New York Times,* October 15, 2018.

105 **world began to hear reports** Peter Shadbolt, "Rights Group Accuses Myanmar of 'Ethnic Cleansing,'" CNN, April 22, 2013.

105 **In the years that followed** "Facebook Bans Rohingya Group's Posts as Minority Faces 'Ethnic Cleansing,'" *The Guardian,* September 20, 2017.

106 **Violence began to escalate** "Myanmar's Killing Fields," *Frontline,* May 8, 2018; "Myanmar Rohingya: What You Need to Know About the Crisis," BBC, January 23, 2020; Mohshin Habib et al., *Forced Migration of Rohingya: An Untold Experience* (Ottawa: Ontario International Development Agency, 2018); "Rohingya Crisis: Villages Destroyed for Government Facilities," BBC, September 10, 2019.

106 **"women and children raped or sexually assaulted"** For excellent in-depth analysis of rape as a tactic of civil war, see Dara Kay Cohen, *Rape During Civil War* (Ithaca: Cornell University Press, 2016).

106 **"We know very well"** Information Committee post, Facebook, September 5, 2017; "Rohingya Crisis: Aung San Suu Kyi Breaks Silence on Myanmar Violence," NBC News, September 6, 2017.

106 **Every year since 2010** This is based on V-Dem's measure of liberal electoral democracy, which reached a record high in 2011; 2012 was the high on the measure of participatory democracy. Not only was the net decline in democracy larger than the improvements, but continuously more countries declined on the liberal democracy index than countries that gained; Mi-

chael Coppedge et al., "V-Dem Codebook v10," Varieties of Democracy (V-Dem) Project.

107 **the one glaring exception to this trend** "Autocratization Surges—Resistance Grows, Democracy Report 2020," V-Dem Institute, March 2020.

107 **Africa was an outlier in another way** "Individuals Using the Internet (% of Population)," World Bank, 2016.

108 **In Ethiopia, for example, longstanding tensions** "Ethiopia Violence: Facebook to Blame, Says Runner Gebrselassie," BBC, November 2, 2019.

108 **"a rapid increase in access"** "Hate Speech on Facebook Is Pushing Ethiopia Dangerously Close to a Genocide," *Vice,* September 14, 2020.

108 **It's not likely to be a coincidence** "Autocratization Turns Viral, Democracy Report 2021," V-Dem Institute, March 2021.

109 **By 2013, 23 percent of Americans** "State of the News Media 2013: Pew Research Center's Project for Excellence in Journalism," *Journalist's Resource,* March 18, 2013; "News Use Across Social Media Platforms 2016," Pew Research Center, May 26, 2016.

109 **"The problem of misinformation"** "Social Media in 2020: A Year of Misinformation and Disinformation," *The Wall Street Journal,* December 11, 2020.

110 **The problem is social media's business model** See Tristan Harris's website for the Center for Humane Technology, which makes this argument.

110 **When William J. Brady and his colleagues** William J. Brady, et al., "Emotion Shapes the Diffusion of Moralized Content in Social Networks," *Proceedings of the National Academy of Sciences* 114 (July 2017): 7313–18.

110 **Another study by the Pew Research Center** "Critical Posts Get More Likes, Comments, and Shares Than Other Posts," Pew Research Center, February 21, 2017.

111 **"If I'm YouTube"** "The Making of a YouTube Radical," *The New York Times,* June 8, 2019.

111 **These recommendation engines** "What's New About Con-

spiracy Theories?," *The New Yorker,* April 15, 2019; Eli Pariser, *The Filter Bubble: How the New Personalized Web Is Changing What We Read and How We Think* (New York: Penguin, 2012); Eytan Bakshy et al., "Political Science: Exposure to Ideologically Diverse News and Opinion on Facebook," *Science* 348 (June 5, 2015): 1130–32.

111 **Walter Quattrociocchi, a computer scientist** Peter Pomerantsev, *This Is Not Propaganda: Adventures in the War Against Reality* (New York: PublicAffairs, 2019), 125.

111 **YouTube is "a radicalization pipeline"** Manoel Horta Ribeiro et al., "Auditing Radicalization Pathways on YouTube," Proceedings of the 2020 Conference on Fairness, Accountability, and Transparency (January 2020), 131–41.

112 **Wirathu found an eager audience** "He Incited Massacre, But Insulting Aung San Suu Kyi Was the Last Straw," *The New York Times,* May 29, 2019.

112 **In 2018, Facebook finally admitted** "Facebook Admits It Was Used to Incite Violence in Myanmar," *The New York Times,* November 6, 2018.

112 **Most activists and human rights groups felt** Jen Kirby, "Mark Zuckerberg on Facebook Role in Ethnic Cleansing in Myanmar: 'It's a Real Issue,'" *Vox,* April 2, 2018; Matthew Smith, "Facebook Wanted to Be a Force for Good in Myanmar. Now It Is Rejecting a Request to Help with a Genocide Investigation," *Time,* August 18, 2020; Anthony Kuhn, "Activists in Myanmar Say Facebook Needs to Do More to Quell Hate Speech, NPR, June 14, 2018.

112 **blocked from Facebook turned to Twitter** Stecklow, "Why Facebook Is Losing the War on Hate Speech in Myanmar."

112 **"There is no Rohingya"** Ibid.; "Myanmar's Coup and Violence, Explained," *The New York Times,* April 24, 2021.

113 **"though Facebook barred Myanmar's military"** "Facebook Takes a Side, Barring Myanmar Military After Coup," *The New York Times,* March 3, 2021.

113 **Facebook's dominance over Myanmar's national conversation** "Myanmar President Htin Kyaw Resigns," BBC, March 21, 2018.

114   **One of the local leaders of the protest** "Why a Protest Leader in Myanmar Is Reluctantly Giving Up Nonviolence and Preparing for Combat," *Mother Jones,* March 31, 2021.

114   **"prime Facebook country"** "What Happens When the Government Uses Facebook as a Weapon?," *Bloomberg Businessweek,* December 7, 2017.

114   **At the start of Duterte's campaign** Ibid.

115   **The strategy worked** "Official Count: Duterte Is New President, Robredo Is Vice President," CNN, May 17, 2016.

115   **Exit polls showed** " 'I Held Back Tears': Young Filipinos Vote in Divisive Midterm Election," *Vice,* May 13, 2019.

115   **his campaign budget was much smaller** Sean Williams, "Rodrigo Duterte's Army of Online Trolls," *The New Republic,* January 4, 2017.

116   **disinformation campaigns influenced elections** Sanja Kelly et al., "Freedom on the Net 2017: Manipulating Social Media to Undermine Democracy," Freedom House, 2017.

116   **"Government agents in Venezuela"** Ibid.

117   **a poll of Brazilian voters** Fadi Quran, "The Bully's Pulpit," podcast, Center for Humane Technology, June 22, 2020, https://www.humanetech.com/podcast/20-the-bullys-pulpit.

117   **Bolsonaro used what little money** "Jair Bolsonaro, Brazil's President, Is a Master of Social Media," *Economist,* March 14, 2019.

117   **His early YouTube videos** "Ministra Das Mulheres Confessa Que É Gay," YouTube, February 28, 2013.

117   **Like other populist leaders** "In Brazil, a President Under Fire Lashes Out at Investigators," *The New York Times,* May 29, 2020.

118   **As Bolsonaro faced greater scrutiny** Ricardo F. Mendonça and Renato Duarte Caetano, "Populism as Parody: The Visual Self-Presentation of Jair Bolsonaro on Instagram," *International Journal of Press/Politics* 26 (January 2021): 210–35.

118   **Duterte has hired hundreds** In September 2020, Facebook

suspended 155 of these accounts after they were revealed to be part of a Chinese-based network of purchased accounts. In addition to these, fake accounts made by police and government officials were also taken down. An avid supporter of China, the Philippines president has used Chinese internet scams to raise his popularity in his own country. Furious at the takedown of accounts, Duterte reprimanded Facebook with harsh remarks, but continues to rely on the company for his base of support. See also "Facebook Removes Chinese Accounts Active in Philippines and U.S. Politics," Reuters, September 22, 2020.

118 **20 percent are in fact bots** Williams, "Rodrigo Duterte's Army of Online Trolls."

119 **The fact that Sweden** "The Global Machine Behind the Rise of Far-Right Nationalism," *The New York Times,* August 10, 2019.

120 **More than a million Swedes viewed these sites weekly** Amy Watson, "Sweden: Usage of Digital News Sources, 2020," *Statista,* April 28, 2021.

120 **the party gained seats** "Swedish Far-Right Wins First Seats in Parliament," BBC, September 20, 2010.

121 **restore "the national home"** Danielle Lee Tomson, "The Rise of Sweden Democrats: Islam, Populism and the End of Swedish Exceptionalism," Brookings Institution, March 26, 2020.

121 **Ethnic entrepreneurs use it to craft** Angry Foreigner, YouTube channel, https://www.youtube.com/channel/UC8kf0zcr Jkz7muZg2C_J-XQ, accessed April 26, 2021.

121 **Another Swedish YouTuber** Lennart Matikainen, YouTube channel, https://www.youtube.com/channel/UCMkVJrQM6 YRUymwGamEJNNA, accessed April 26, 2021.

122 **Modi had the third-highest number** "PM Modi Crosses 60 Million Followers on Twitter," *Times of India,* July 19, 2020.

122 **TV presenter Arnab Goswami** "Indian News Channel Fined in UK for Hate Speech About Pakistan," *The Guardian,* December 23, 2020.

122   **famous yogi Baba Ramdev** "The Billionaire Yogi Behind Modi's Rise," *The New York Times,* July 26, 2018.

122   **In Brazil, YouTuber Nando Moura** "How YouTube Radicalized Brazil," *The New York Times,* August 11, 2019.

122   **In the United Kingdom, YouTuber** "How Far-Right Extremists Rebrand to Evade Facebook's Ban," *National Observer,* May 10, 2019.

123   **Le Pen has fifteen permanent staffers** "Marine Le Pen's Internet Army," *Politico,* February 3, 2017.

123   **Despite losing the 2017 runoff** "Marine Le Pen Defeated But France's Far Right Is Far from Finished," *The Guardian,* May 7, 2017; "Marine Le Pen's Financial Scandal Continues," *The Atlantic,* June 30, 2017; "Far-Right Wins French Vote in EU Election, But Macron Limits Damage," Reuters, May 26, 2019.

123   **"Right-wing populism is always"** "Why the Right Wing Has a Massive Advantage on Facebook," *Politico,* September 26, 2020.

124   **It was easy for Shane Bauer** "Undercover with a Border Militia," *Mother Jones,* November/December 2016.

125   **They can now easily share information** Vera Mironova, *From Freedom Fighters to Jihadists: Human Resources of Non-State Armed Groups* (New York: Oxford University Press, 2019).

125   **"sprawling online arms bazaars"** "Facebook Groups Act as Weapons Bazaars for Militias," *The New York Times,* April 6, 2016.

126   **"hundreds of thousands of new"** "The Strategy of Violent White Supremacy Is Evolving," *The Atlantic,* August 7, 2019.

126   **Since 2018, the number of white nationalist groups** "The Year in Hate and Extremism 2020: Hate Groups Became More Difficult to Track Amid COVID and Migration to Online Networks," Southern Poverty Law Center, February 1, 2021.

126   **"The media people are more important"** "Inside the Surreal World of the Islamic State's Propaganda Machine," *The Washington Post,* November 20, 2015.

127 **"The first thing I did"** Mironova, *From Freedom Fighters to Jihadists*, 8.

127 **"people who are more likely"** "To Russia with Likes (Part 2)," *Your Undivided Attention* podcast, episode 6, August 1, 2019.

CHAPTER 6: HOW CLOSE ARE WE?

129 **Wearing winter coats and MAGA hats** "How a Presidential Rally Turned into a Capitol Rampage," *The New York Times*, January 12, 2021; "Trump's Full Speech at D.C. Rally on January 6," *The Wall Street Journal*, February 7, 2021.

130 **Grassroots groups, along with Republican** "77 Days: Trump's Campaign to Subvert the Election," *The New York Times*, January 31, 2021.

130 **tweeting on December 19** "'Be There. Will Be Wild!': Trump All But Circled the Date," *The New York Times*, January 6, 2021.

130 **On January 4, at a rally** "President Trump Remarks at Georgia U.S. Senate Campaign Event," C-SPAN, January 4, 2021.

130 **"Today is not the end!"** "Former President Donald Trump's January 6 Speech," CNN, February 8, 2021.

131 **At a rally the night before, pastor Greg Locke** Katherine Stewart, "The Roots of Josh Hawley's Rage," *The New York Times*, January 11, 2021.

131 **Many came armed for battle** "Arrested Capitol Rioters Had Guns and Bombs, Everyday Careers and Olympic Medals," Reuters, January 14, 2021.

132 **he would cover their legal fees** "Trump Urges Crowd to 'Knock the Crap Out of' Anyone with Tomatoes," *Politico*, February 1, 2016.

132 **when a rally in Las Vegas** "Trump on Protester: 'I'd Like to Punch Him in the Face,'" *Politico*, February 23, 2016.

132 **by hinting that gun owners** "Trump Says Maybe '2nd Amendment People' Can Stop Clinton's Supreme Court Picks," ABC News, August 9, 2016.

132 **The presidency had emboldened him** "Man Charged After White Nationalist Rally in Charlottesville Ends in Deadly Violence," *The New York Times,* August 12, 2017.

132 **"liberate Michigan" by going to the state's capitol** "Trump Tweets 'Liberate' Michigan, Two Other States with Dem Governors," *The Detroit News,* April 17, 2020; "Trump Tweets Support for Michigan Protesters, Some of Whom Were Armed, as 2020 Stress Mounts," CNN, May 1, 2020.

132 **"If you don't fight like hell"** "Former President Donald Trump's January 6 Speech," CNN, February 8, 2021.

133 **"Mike Pence didn't have"** "Inside the Remarkable Rift Between Donald Trump and Mike Pence," *The Washington Post,* January 11, 2021.

134 **At around three P.M., Trump tweeted: "No violence!"** Courtney Subramanian, "A Minute-by-Minute Timeline of Trump's Day as the Capitol Siege Unfolded on Jan. 6," *USA Today,* February 11, 2021.

134 **"It was a landslide election"** Ibid.

134 **"Remember this day forever!"** "Deleted Tweets from Donald J. Trump, R-Fla.," ProPublica, January 8, 2021.

135 **The first condition—how close we are to anocracy** "Polity5 Annual Time-Series, 1946–2018," Center for Systemic Peace.

135 **"mostly for its limited political competitiveness"** The Polity scale, unlike V-Dem, does not take suffrage into account in its democracy score.

137 **as presidential historian** Arthur M. Schlesinger, Jr., *The Imperial Presidency* (New York: Houghton Mifflin, 1973); "America Is Living James Madison's Nightmare," *The Atlantic,* October 2018.

137 **"We're supposed to be in a system"** "Clash Between Trump and House Democrats Poses Threat to Constitutional Order," *The New York Times,* May 7, 2019.

138 **"LIBERATE MICHIGAN! LIBERATE MINNESOTA!"** "Trump Accelerates the Unrest," *Axios,* April 17, 2020.

138 **He then wielded it for his own purposes** "Forceful Removal of Protesters From Outside White House Spurs Debate," *The Wall Street Journal,* June 2, 2020.

138 **"If a city or state refuses"** "Trump's Full June 1 Address at the Rose Garden," *The Washington Post,* June 1, 2020.

138 **The United States became an anocracy** "Polity5 Annual Time-Series, 1946–2018," Center for Systemic Peace; "Mapped: The World's Oldest Democracies," World Economic Forum, August 8, 2019.

139 **Though Trump and the Republican Party filed** "Elections Results Under Attack: Here Are the Facts," *The Washington Post,* March 11, 2021; "Fact Check: Courts Have Dismissed Multiple Lawsuits of Alleged Electoral Fraud Presented by Trump Campaign," Reuters, February 15, 2021; "By the Numbers: President Donald Trump's Failed Efforts to Overturn the Election," *USA Today,* January 6, 2021.

139 **Republican state officials** "Arizona Governor Becomes Latest Trump Target After Certifying Biden's Win," NBC News, December 2, 2020; "Trump Pressured Georgia Secretary of State to 'Find' Votes," *The Wall Street Journal,* January 4, 2021.

139 **Secretary of Defense Mark Esper** "Trump Fires Mark Esper, Defense Secretary Who Opposed Use of Troops on U.S. Streets," *The New York Times,* November 9, 2020.

139 **the ten living former defense secretaries** "Opinion: All 10 Living Former Defense Secretaries: Involving the Military in Election Disputes Would Cross into Dangerous Territory," *The Washington Post,* January 3, 2021.

139 **FBI immediately launched investigations** "Conspiracy Charges Filed Over Capitol Riot," *The Wall Street Journal,* January 19, 2021.

140 **That's not quite as fast** Goldstone et al., "A Global Model for Forecasting Political Instability."

140 **"A drop of five points"** Author interview with Monty Marshall, September 22, 2020.

140 **the democratic decay in the United States** Anna Lührmann and Matthew Wilson, "One-Third of the World's Popu-

lation Lives in a Declining Democracy. That Includes the United States," *The Washington Post,* July 4, 2018.

140 **country standing on this threshold** Fearon, "Governance and Civil War Onset"; Barbara F. Walter, "Why Bad Governance Leads to Repeat Civil War," *Journal of Conflict Resolution* 59 (October 2015): 1242–72.

141 **"adverse to the rights"** "*The Federalist* Number 10," November 22, 1787, *Founders Online,* National Archives.

141 **Today, the best predictor** And race is aligning with religion, especially a particular right-wing religion. Evangelical Christians are the strongest supporters of the Republican Party. In 2020, eight in ten white evangelicals voted for Trump. On the other side is a mixed bag of atheists, agnostics, Jews, and Muslims. They line up overwhelmingly in favor of the Democratic Party. Biden won the support of 72 percent of atheists and agnostics, 68 percent of Jewish voters, and 64 percent of Muslims. Elana Schor and David Crary, "AP VoteCast: Trump Wins White Evangelicals, Catholics Split," Associated Press, November 6, 2020.

141 **Two-thirds or more of Black, Latino** Zoltan L. Hajnal, *Dangerously Divided: How Race and Class Shape Winning and Losing in American Politics* (Cambridge: Cambridge University Press, 2020).

142 **In fact, as late as 2007** Ibid.

142 **win all of the Deep South's electoral votes** "South Reverses Voting Patterns; Goldwater Makes Inroads, But More Electoral Votes Go to the President," *The New York Times,* November 4, 1964.

142 **"If Goldwater wins his fight"** "What Republicans Must Do to Regain the Negro Vote," *Ebony,* April 1962.

143 **White evangelicals now represent** "In Changing U.S. Electorate, Race and Education Remain Stark Dividing Lines," Pew Research Center, June 2, 2020.

145 **by 2010, *The Alex Jones Show*** "Alex Jones," Southern Poverty Law Center, https://www.splcenter.org/fighting-hate/extremist -files/individual/alex-jones, accessed April 27, 2021.

145 **retweeted a video of a retiree** "Trump Retweets Video of Apparent Supporter Saying 'White Power,'" NPR, June 28, 2020.

145 **It's exactly what Tudjman did** Gordana Uzelak, "Franjo Tudjman's Nationalist Ideology," *East European Quarterly* 31 (1997): 449–72.

146 **No Republican president in the past fifty years** "Religion and Right-Wing Politics: How Evangelicals Reshaped Elections," *The New York Times,* October 28, 2018; "Ronald Reagan's Long-Hidden Racist Conversation with Richard Nixon," *The Atlantic,* July 30, 2019.

146 **even withhold food and drink from people waiting in lengthy voting lines** Tim Carman, "New Limits on Food and Water at Georgia's Polls Could Hinder Black and Low-Income Voters, Advocates Say," *The Washington Post,* April 9, 2021.

146 **In 2016, the United States dropped to a 3** Author correspondence with Monty Marshall, December 14, 2020. See also Polity Change File for 2016.

146 **this level of political factionalism** "Why Reconstruction Matters," *The New York Times,* March 28, 2015.

147 **The same is happening today** "'The Civil War Lies on Us Like a Sleeping Dragon': America's Deadly Divide—and Why It Has Returned," *The Guardian,* August 20, 2017.

147 **In a 2019 survey** Pippa Norris, "Measuring Populism Worldwide," *Party Politics* 26 (November 2020): 697–717.

147 **a poll of attendees revealed** "Trump Wins CPAC Straw Poll, but Only 68 Percent Want Him to Run Again," New York Times, February 28, 2021; "Trump Wins CPAC Straw Poll on the 2024 Presidential Primary, with 55 Percent Support," *Vox,* March 1, 2021.

147 **Ted Cruz went on Fox News's** "Cruz Says Supreme Court 'Better Forum' for Election Disputes Amid Electoral College Objection Push," Fox News, January 3, 2021.

147 **On January 6, as Trump supporters** "The 147 Republicans Who Voted to Overturn Election Results," *The New York Times,* January 7, 2021.

148 **His victory was clear evidence** For an excellent account of how white Americans became increasingly reactionary as a result of a loss of status, see Matt A. Barreto and Christopher S. Parker, *Change They Can't Believe In: The Tea Party and Reactionary Politics in Contemporary America* (Princeton, N.J.: Princeton University Press, 2013).

148 **The seismic change reflected** "Census: Minority Babies Are Now Majority in United States," *The Washington Post,* May 17, 2012.

149 **The census, according to Andrew Cherlin** "Census: Minority Babies Are Now Majority in United States," *The Washington Post,* May 17, 2012.

149 **In 2015, Lin-Manuel Miranda** "All About the Hamiltons," *The New Yorker,* February 2, 2015.

149 **the quality of life for the white working class** William Emmons et al., "Why Is the White Working Class in Decline?," *On the Economy* blog, Federal Reserve Bank of St. Louis, May 20, 2019.

151 **"Their pain is our pain"** "Full Text: 2017 Donald Trump Inauguration Speech Transcript," *Politico,* January 20, 2017.

152 **This included a focus on the perils** "Down the Breitbart Hole," *The New York Times,* August 16, 2017; "Who Is Mike Cernovich? A Guide," *The New York Times,* April 5, 2017.

152 **found that self-identified conservatives** Andrew Guess et al., "Less Than You Think: Prevalence and Predictors of Fake News Dissemination on Facebook," *Science Advances* 5 (January 9, 2019).

152 **Researchers at the University of Oxford** Samantha Bradshaw and Philip N. Howard, "The Global Disinformation Order: 2019 Global Inventory of Organised Social Media Manipulation" (working paper, Project on Computational Propaganda, 2019).

152 **This pattern was present in the most recent** "Stranger Than Fiction," *Your Undivided Attention* podcast, episode 14, March 30, 2020.

153 **best predictor of voters who switched** Diana C. Mutz,

"Status Threat, Not Economic Hardship, Explains the 2016 Presidential Vote, *Proceedings of the National Academy of Sciences* 115 (May 2018): E4330–39.

153   **best way to predict Republican support** Justin Gest, *The New Minority: White Working Class Politics in an Age of Immigration and Inequality* (Oxford: Oxford University Press, 2016).

153   **experimentally triggering threats** Rachel Wetts and Robb Willer, "Privilege on the Precipice: Perceived Racial Status Threats Lead White Americans to Oppose Welfare Programs," *Social Forces* 97 (December 2018): 793–822.

153   **Almost everyone who scored highest** "Racial Prejudice, Not Populism or Authoritarianism, Predicts Support for Trump Over Clinton," *The Washington Post,* May 26, 2016.

153   **Republicans with high racial resentment** "Trump Is the First Modern Republican to Win the Nomination Based on Racial Prejudice," *The Washington Post,* August 1, 2016.

153   **Perhaps most convincing are studies** Ilyana Kuziemko and Ebonya Washington, "Why Did the Democrats Lose the South? Bringing New Data to an Old Debate," *American Economic Review* 108 (2018): 2830–67; Rory McVeigh et al., "Political Polarization as a Social Movement Outcome: 1960s Klan Activism and Its Enduring Impact on Political Realignment in Southern Counties, 1960 to 2000," *American Sociological Review* 79 (December 2014): 1144–71.

154   **created the racial resentment scale** Donald R. Kinder and Lynn M. Sanders, *Divided by Color: Racial Politics and Democratic Ideals* (Chicago: University of Chicago Press, 1996.

154   **In the 2016 American National Election Study** Zoltan Hajnal, Vince Hutchings, and Taeku Lee, *Racial and Ethnic Politics in the United States* (Cambridge: Cambridge University Press, forthcoming). Source of underlying data is the "Times Series Study," American National Election Study, 2016.

154   **it's not the desperately poor** Francis Fukuyama, *Identity: The Demand for Dignity and the Politics of Resentment* (New York: Farrar, Straus and Giroux, 2018); Petersen, *Understanding Ethnic Violence,* 2002.

155 **In a poll conducted days after** "About Half of Republicans Don't Think Joe Biden Should Be Sworn in as President," *Vox,* January 11, 2021.

155 **Polls also revealed that 45 percent** "Most Voters Say the Events at the U.S. Capitol Are a Threat to Democracy," You-Gov, January 6, 2021.

155 **And more than six months after the election** "53% of Republicans View Trump as True U.S. President," *Reuters,* May 24, 2021.

156 **feel "somewhat justified" in using violence** "Feelings of Political Violence Rise," Statista, January 7, 2021; "Americans Increasingly Believe Violence Is Justified if the Other Side Wins," *Politico,* October 1, 2020.

156 **Another recent survey found that 20 percent of Republicans** Nathan P. Kalmoe and Lilliana Mason, "Lethal Mass Partisanship: Prevalence, Correlates, and Electoral Contingencies" (paper presented at the American Political Science Association Conference, 2018).

156 **"pass through similar stages"** "Guide to the Analysis of Insurgency," Central Intelligence Agency, 2012.

157 **The number of militias** "Active 'Patriot' Groups in the United States in 2011," Southern Poverty Law Center, March 8, 2012; "The Second Wave: Return of the Militias," Southern Poverty Law Center, August 1, 2009.

157 **Today, less than a quarter** Seth G. Jones, Catrina Doxsee, Grace Hwang, and Jared Thompson, "The Military, Police, and the Rise of Terrorism in the United States," *CSIS: CSIS Briefs,* April 2021.

157 **About 65 percent of far-right extremists** "Profiles of Individual Radicalization in the United States (PIRUS)" (research brief, National Consortium for the Study of Terrorism and the Responses to Terrorism, May 2020).

157 **Two of the most high-profile militias** "Oath Keepers," Southern Poverty Law Center, https://www.splcenter.org/fighting-hate/extremist-files/group/oath-keepers, accessed April 28, 2021.

157 **According to JJ MacNab** "One-on-One with JJ MacNab," *Intelligence Unclassified* podcast, episode 22, State of New Jersey Office of Homeland Security and Preparedness, June 6, 2016.

158 **The second stage of insurgency** CIA, "Guide to the Analysis of Insurgency."

158 **the number of right-wing terrorist attacks** "The War Comes Home: The Evolution of Domestic Terrorism in the United States," Center for Strategic and International Studies (CSIS), October 22, 2020; "The Rise of Far-Right Extremism in the United States," CSIS, November 7, 2018.

159 **The open insurgency stage** CIA, "Guide to the Analysis of Insurgency."

160 **At least 14 percent of those arrested** "The Capitol Siege: The Arrested and Their Stories," NPR, April 23, 2021.

160 **As Tim Alberta, chief political correspondent for *Politico*, tweeted** Tim Alberta (@TimAlberta)," Twitter, January 10, 2021.

CHAPTER 7: WHAT A WAR WOULD LOOK LIKE

161 **On the morning of Tuesday, November 14, 2028** Experts disagree on how a civil war would start in the United States. Some believe it will never happen; others think it could happen much sooner. This opening is my attempt to dramatize what the early stages of conflict could look like, but it is by no means a scientific prediction. There are literally millions of possible scenarios.

167 **stationed west of the Mississippi** Clayton R. Newell, *The Regular Army Before the Civil War, 1845–1860* (Washington, D.C.: Center of Military History, United States Army, 2014).

168 **And, increasingly, domestic terror campaigns are aimed** Robert A. Pape, *Dying to Win: The Strategic Logic of Suicide Terrorism*, (New York: Random House, 2005).

169 **"bible of the racist right"** "*The Turner Diaries,* Other Racist Novels, Inspire Extremist Violence," Southern Poverty Law Center, October 14, 2004.

169 **"heady heroic narrative"** Aja Romano, "How a Dystopian

Neo-Nazi Novel Helped Fuel Decades of White Supremacist Terrorism," *Vox,* January 28. 2021.

170 **the influence of the book** "How 'The Turner Diaries' Incites White Supremacists," *The New York Times,* January 12, 2021; " 'The Turner Diaries' Didn't Just Inspire the Capitol Attack. It Warns Us What Might Be Next," *Los Angeles Times,* January 8, 2021.

170 **wrote a series of newsletters** "Influential Neo-Nazi Eats at Soup Kitchens, Lives in Government Housing," NBC News, November 26, 2019; "Atomwaffen and the SIEGE Parallax: How One Neo-Nazi's Life's Work Is Fueling a Younger Generation," Southern Poverty Law Center, February 22, 2018.

170 **As reported by ProPublica** "Inside Atomwaffen as It Celebrates a Member for Allegedly Killing a Gay Jewish College Student," ProPublica, February 23, 2018.

170 **"If I were asked by anyone"** "Accelerationism: The Obscure Idea Inspiring White Supremacist Killers Around the World," *Vox,* November 18, 2019.

171 **Amazon is the biggest distributor** "The Hate Store: Amazon's Self-Publishing Arm Is a Haven for White Supremacists," ProPublica, April 7, 2020.

171 **civil wars involve some type of ethnic cleansing** "As Global Democracy Retreats, Ethnic Cleansing Is on the Rise," Freedom House, February 25, 2019.

171 **"You came here from there"** "Stratton Town Report Cover Draws Attention for All the Wrong Reasons," *VTDigger,* February 24, 2021; Ellen Barry (@EllenBarryNYT), "Holy Moly, Stratton, Vermont's annual report," Twitter, February 23, 2021.

172 **argues that countries go through eight steps** Gregory Stanton, "The Ten Steps of Genocide," Genocide Watch, 1996.

173 **members of both parties have proposed** "Dems Spark Alarm with Call for National ID Card," *The Hill,* April 30, 2010.

173 **Stage three is "discrimination"** "The Ten Steps of Genocide," Genocide Watch.

173 **Research has shown that Blacks are half as likely** Marianne Bertrand and Sendhil Mullainathan, "Are Emily and Greg More Employable than Lakisha and Jamal?" *American Economic Review* 94 (2004): 991–1013.

173 **showed that legislators are much more likely** Daniel M. Butler and David E. Broockman, "Do Politicians Racially Discriminate Against Constituents? A Field Experiment on State Legislators," *American Journal of Political Science* 55 (2011): 463–77.

173 **Black families get fewer loans** "A Troubling Tale of a Black Man Trying to Refinance His Mortgage," CNBC, August 19, 2020; Peter Christensen and Christopher Timmins, "Sorting or Steering: Experimental Evidence on the Economic Effects of Housing Discrimination" (NBER working paper, 2020).

174 **embracing abuse in public discourse** "Trump Used Words Like 'Invasion' and 'Killer' to Discuss Immigrants at Rallies 500 Times," *USA Today,* August 8, 2019; "Trump Calls Omarosa Manigault Newman 'That Dog' in His Latest Insult," *The New York Times,* August 14, 2019.

174 **"You wouldn't believe how bad"** "Trump Ramps Up Rhetoric on Undocumented Immigrants: 'These Aren't People. These Are Animals,'" *USA Today,* May 16, 2018.

174 **In Bosnia, a plan to exterminate Muslims** "What Are the 10 Stages of Genocide?," Al Jazeera, July 10, 2020.

174 **increasingly organizing, training, and arming themselves** "A Pro-Trump Militant Group Has Recruited Thousands of Police, Soldiers, and Veterans," *The Atlantic,* November 2020.

175 **"the only way you get your freedoms"** "A Guide to Rep. Marjorie Taylor Greene's Conspiracy Theories and Toxic Rhetoric," *Media Matters,* February 2, 2021.

175 **Moderates who resist or refuse** "South Carolina GOP Censures SC-07 Representative Tom Rice After 'Disappointing' Vote to Impeach Trump," Fox News, January 30, 2021; "Wyoming GOP Censures Liz Cheney for Voting to Impeach Trump," NPR, February 6, 2021; "GOP Rep. Meijer Receiving Threats After 'Vote of Conscience' to Impeach Trump," *The Detroit News,* January 14, 2021.

175   **they are looking for any excuse** "The Boogaloo Bois Pre-
      pare for Civil War," *The Atlantic,* January 15, 2021; "Atom-
      waffen Division," Anti-Defamation League, 2021.

176   **MacNab even sees a possibility of far-right extremists
      joining** "One-on-One with JJ MacNab," *Intelligence Unclassified*
      podcast.

176   **the first accelerationist group** "Documenting Hate: New
      American Nazis," *Frontline,* November 20, 2018.

176   **Despite its small size, the group** "What Is Atomwaffen? A
      Neo-Nazi Group, Linked to Multiple Murders," *The New York
      Times,* February 12, 2018; "An Atomwaffen Member Sketched
      a Map to Take the Neo-Nazis Down. What Path Officials Took
      Is a Mystery," ProPublica, November 20, 2018.

177   **In August 2020, the group rebranded** "Neo-Nazi Terror
      Group Atomwaffen Division Re-Emerges Under New Name,"
      Vice, August 5, 2020.

177   **Members of AWD were among** "He's a Proud Neo-Nazi,
      Charlottesville Attacker—and a U.S. Marine," ProPublica,
      May 11, 2018.

177   **"Huge rallies don't work"** "Documenting Hate: New
      American Nazis," *Frontline.*

177   **The term "leaderless resistance"** Max Taylor, Donald Hol-
      brook, and P. M. Currie, *Extreme Right Wing Political Violence
      and Terrorism* (London: Bloomsbury, 2013).

178   **As J. M. Berger recounts** J. M. Berger, "The Strategy of
      Violent White Supremacy Is Evolving," *The Atlantic,* August 7,
      2019.

178   **Two groups on the forefront** Ibid.

178   **the best example of a leaderless resistance** "Facebook's
      Boogaloo Problem: A Record of Failure," Tech Transparency
      Project, August 12, 2020; "The Boogaloo: Extremists' New
      Slang Term for a Coming Civil War," Anti-Defamation League,
      November 26, 2019; "The Boogaloo Tipping Point," *The At-
      lantic,* July 4, 2020; "Who Are the Boogaloo Bois? A Man Who
      Shot Up a Minneapolis Police Precinct Was Associated with the

Extremist Movement, According to Unsealed Documents," *Insider,* October 26, 2020.

179 **They call this showdown Civil War 2** "Why the Extremist 'Boogaloo Boys' Wear Hawaiian Shirts," *The Wall Street Journal,* June 8, 2020.

179 **be "boogaloo ready"** "Boogaloo: Extremists' New Slang Term for a Coming Civil War," ADL.

179 **"the battle that would erupt"** "Boss: Kidnapping Plot Suspect Was 'On Edge' Recently," WOOD-TV, October 8, 2020.

179 **referred to himself as "Boogaloo Bunyan"** "FBI Charges Six Who It Says Plotted to Kidnap Michigan Gov. Gretchen Whitmer, as Seven More Who Wanted to Ignite Civil War Face State Charges," *The Washington Post,* October 8, 2020.

179 **The first time most Americans heard** "Boogaloo: Extremists' New Slang Term for a Coming Civil War," ADL.

180 **In the spring of 2020, one watchdog group** "Extremists Are Using Facebook to Organize for Civil War Amid Coronavirus," Tech Transparency Project, April 22, 2020.

180 **On Facebook, Boogaloo members** Ibid.

180 **One group even compiled a document detailing** Ibid.

180 **Boogaloo Bois have engaged in violence** "3 Men Tied to 'Boogaloo' Movement Plotted to Terrorize Las Vegas Protests, Officials Say," ABC7, June 4, 2020.

180 **In May 2020, Facebook banned the use** "Facebook Bans Large Segment of Boogaloo Movement," *The Wall Street Journal,* June 20, 2020.

183 **Intimidation was the preferred tactic** David Zucchino, *Wilmington's Lie: The Murderous Coup of 1898 and the Rise of White Supremacy* (New York: Grove Atlantic, 2020).

183 **the massacre was meant to serve as an "incentive"** "What's Inside the Hate-Filled Manifesto Linked to the Alleged El Paso Shooter," *The Washington Post,* August 4, 2019.

184 **militias are legal in twenty-two states** "The Private Militias Providing 'Security' for Anti-Lockdown Protests, Explained," *Vox,* May 11, 2020.

184 **"He was in Kenosha as part"** "Where Protesters Go, Armed
      Militias, Vigilantes Likely to Follow with Little to Stop Them,"
      NBC News, September 1, 2020.

184 **Rebel groups that embrace** Barbara F. Walter, "The Extrem-
      ist's Advantage in Civil Wars," *International Security* 42 (2017):
      7–39.

185 **When it entered a town** Barbara F. Walter and Gregoire
      Philipps, "Who Uses Internet Propaganda in Civil War?"
      (forthcoming).

185 **because there were signs of rapprochement** Andrew H.
      Kydd and Barbara F. Walter, "The Strategies of Terrorism," *In-
      ternational Security* 31 (2006): 49–80.

186 **Rebels in the Donbas region** Sergiy Kudelia, *Dismantling the
      State from Below: Intervention, Collaborationism, and Resistance in
      the Armed Conflict in Donbas* (forthcoming).

187 **"You have a global network of violent"** Tim Hume, "Far-
      Right Extremists Have Been Using Ukraine's War as a Training
      Ground. They're Returning Home," *Vice,* July 31, 2019.

188 **There is hate, yes, but the real fuel is fear** According to
      David Kilcullen, "The strongest indicator that shit is about to
      get extremely bad is not hate. There's always hate. It's fear";
      Matthew Gault, "Is the U.S. Already in a New Civil War," *Vice,*
      October 27, 2020.

188 **"Why, of course, the people don't want war"** G. M. Gil-
      bert, *Nuremberg Diary* (New York: Farrar, Straus, 1947), 278.

189 **"it was particularly the last idea"** Human Rights Watch,
      "The Rwandan Genocide: How It Was Prepared" (briefing
      paper, April 2006).

189 **U.S. gun sales hit an all-time high** "Americans Have
      Bought Record 17m Guns in Year of Unrest, Analysis Finds,"
      The Guardian, October 30, 2020.

189 **"The common thread is just uncertainty"** Ibid.

190 **In 2019, only 8 percent of terrorist incidents** "The War
      Comes Home: The Evolution of Domestic Terrorism in the
      United States," CSIS, October 22, 2020; "In America, Far-

Right Terrorist Plots Have Outnumbered Far-Left Ones in 2020," *The Economist,* October 27, 2020.

190 **"to providing working class people"** Wikipedia, s.v. "Socialist Rifle Association." Note that the quote came from the group's original website, which is now no longer operational. See also https://www.facebook.com/SocialistRifle/about/.

190 **supports self-policing and firearms training** "'If You Attack Us, We Will Kill You': The Not Fucking Around Coalition Wants to Protect Black Americans," *Vice,* October 28, 2020.

190 **The Redneck Revolt, which stands** "What Is Redneck Revolt? These Left-wing Activists Protect Minorities with Guns," *Newsweek,* December 27, 2017.

191 **Valentino found that a remarkably small number** Benjamin A. Valentino, *Final Solutions: Mass Killing and Genocide in the 20th Century* (Ithaca, N.Y.: Cornell University Press, 2013).

192 **Terror shifted the Israeli public to the right** C. Berrebi and E. Klor, "Are Voters Sensitive to Terrorism? Direct Evidence from the Israeli Electorate," *American Political Science Review* 102, no. 3 (2008): 279–301; Anna Getmansky and Thomas Zeitzoff, "Terrorism and Voting: The Effect of Rocket Threat on Voting in Israeli Elections," *American Political Science Review* 108, no. 3 (2014): 588–604.

192 **a large study found that the attacks** Eitan D. Hersch, "Long-Term Effect of September 11 on the Political Behavior of Victims' Families and Neighbors," *Proceedings of the National Academy of Sciences* 52 (December 24, 2013): 20959–63.

192 **a negative view of democracy** Roberto Stefan Foa and Yascha Mounk, "The Democratic Disconnect," *Journal of Democracy* 27 (2016): 5–17.

192 **a recent study by two Yale political scientists** Matthew H. Graham and Milan W. Svolik, "Democracy in America? Partisanship, Polarization, and the Robustness of Support for Democracy in the United States," *American Political Science Review* 114 (2020): 392–409.

192 **Faith in government has plummeted** "Public Trust in Government: 1958–2019," Pew Research Center, April 11, 2019.

193 **Americans are also losing faith in one another** "Little Public Support for Reductions in Federal Spending," Pew Research Center, April 11, 2019.

193 **those who would view "army rule"** "Follow the Leader: Exploring American Support for Democracy and Authoritarianism," Democracy Fund Voter Study Group, March 2018.

CHAPTER 8: PREVENTING A CIVIL WAR

194 **we knew exactly: South Africa** Barbara F. Walter, "In Memoriam: Nelson Mandela," *Political Violence @ A Glance,* December 6, 2013.

198 **Civil wars are rare** Readers should note that a 3.4 percent annual risk may seem small but is not. That's because the risk of civil war compounds over time so that a 3 percent annual risk translates into a 150 percent risk over a fifty-year period if conditions remain the same. A good analogy is the risk of cancer due to smoking. Early on, a smoker has a low risk of getting lung cancer, but if he or she continues to smoke over a lifetime that risk increases significantly. Source: "Polity5 Annual Time-Series, 1946–2018," Center for Systemic Peace. I thank Monty Marshall for this clear explanation.

198 **they tend to repeat themselves** Barbara F. Walter, "Does Conflict Beget Conflict? Explaining Recurring Civil War," *Journal of Peace Research* 41 (May 2004): 371–88; Walter, "Why Bad Governance Leads to Repeat Civil War."

198 **Experts call it "the conflict trap"** Paul Collier et al., *Breaking the Conflict Trap: Civil War and Development Policy* (Washington, D.C.: World Bank and Oxford University Press, 2003).

199 **Most countries that were able to avoid** Barbara F. Walter, "Conflict Relapse and the Sustainability of Post-Conflict Peace," World Bank, 2011; Walter, "Why Bad Governance Leads to Repeat Civil War."

199 **"a significantly greater risk"** Fearon, "Governance and Civil War Onset."

199   **a wealthy country like the United States** Walter, "Conflict Relapse and the Sustainability of Post-Conflict Peace"; Walter, "Why Bad Governance Leads to Repeat Civil War."

200   **"all good things tend"** Fearon, "Governance and Civil War Onset."

200   **According to the political scientist Pippa Norris** Sean Illing, "A Political Scientist Explains Why the GOP Is a Threat to American Democracy," *Vox,* October 20, 2020.

200   **Canada's election system is run** Elliott Davis, "U.S. Election Integrity Compares Poorly to Other Democracies," *U.S. News & World Report,* October 7, 2020.

200   **An independent and centralized election management** Illing, "Political Scientist Explains Why the GOP Is a Threat."

201   **found that the quality of U.S. elections** Davis, "U.S. Election Integrity Compares Poorly to Other Democracies."

201   **In states that have already adopted** Nathaniel Rakich, "What Happened When 2.2 Million People Were Automatically Registered to Vote," *FiveThirtyEight,* October 10, 2019.

202   **Canada focused on reaffirming voting** "Trudeau Breaks Promise on Reforming Canada's Voting System," BBC, February 1, 2017; "Canada," Freedom House, 2020.

202   **"create a registry of digital"** "Canada," Freedom House.

204   **"too many people are profoundly"** Eric Liu, *You're More Powerful Than You Think: A Citizen's Guide to Making Change Happen* (New York: PublicAffairs, 2017), 8.

204   **A 2016 survey led by** "Americans' Knowledge of the Branches of Government Is Declining," Annenberg Public Policy Center, September 13, 2016.

204   **A group of six former U.S. education secretaries** "America Needs History and Civics Education to Promote Unity," *The Wall Street Journal,* March 1, 2021.

205   **we spend 1,000 times more per student on STEM** It should be noted that if America eventually experiences a civil war, any advances in STEM will grind to a halt. Countries that experience civil war see their GDP per capita dramatically decline, their institutions weaken, and public services such as

health and education break down. Collier, P. (1999), "On the Economic Consequences of Civil War," *Oxford Economic Papers,* 51(1), 168–183. Retrieved August 19, 2021, from http://www .jstor.org/stable/3488597; Hannes Mueller, Julia Tobias, (2016), "The Cost of Violence: Estimating the Economic Impact of Conflict," International Growth Center.

205   **"works only if enough"** Author interview with Eric Liu, April 2021.

205   **all confess that they didn't see** Anton Melnyk is a pseudonym.

205   **"One had no time to think"** Cass R. Sunstein, "It Can Happen Here," *The New York Review,* June 28, 2018.

206   **unlike in other countries** "Labeling Groups Like the Proud Boys 'Domestic Terrorists' Won't Fix Anything," *Vox,* February 19, 2021; "An Old Debate Renewed: Does the U.S. Now Need a Domestic Terrorism Law?," NPR, March 16, 2021.

207   **a threat that is common** Lewis, *How Insurgency Begins*.

207   **observed that "right-wing extremism"** Janet Reitman, "U.S. Law Enforcement Failed to See the Threat of White Nationalism. Now They Don't Know How to Stop It," *The New York Times,* November 3, 2018.

207   **based on a 2008 FBI assessment** Ibid.

207   **"Having personnel within law enforcement"** "White Supremacist Infiltration of Law Enforcement," FBI Intelligence Assessment, October 17, 2016.

207   **A follow-up report, in 2015** "The FBI Has Quietly Investigated White Supremacist Infiltration of Law Enforcement," *The Intercept,* January 31, 2017.

207   **the recruitment of former fighters** Lewis, *How Insurgency Begins*.

208   **The 2009 Department of Homeland Security report** "Rightwing Extremism: Current Economic and Political Climate Fueling Resurgence in Radicalization and Recruitment," Department of Homeland Security, April 7, 2009.

208   **"metastasizing across the country"** "Domestic Terrorism

Threat Is 'Metastasizing' in U.S., F.B.I. Director Says," *The New York Times,* March 2, 2021.

208 **In less than a year** "The Oklahoma City Bombing: 25 Years Later," Federal Bureau of Investigation, April 15, 2020.

209 **various of the new JTTFs** "The Department of Justice's Terrorism Task Forces June 2005," U.S. Department of Justice, June 2005.

209 **the FBI enlisted more than 1,400 investigators** FBI, "Oklahoma City Bombing: 25 Years Later."

209 **put in charge of the investigation** "Merrick Garland Faces Resurgent Peril After Years Fighting Extremism," *The New York Times,* February 20, 2021.

209 **"remedy grievances and fix problems"** David Kilcullen, *The Accidental Guerrilla: Fighting Small Wars in the Midst of a Big One* (New York: Oxford University Press, 2011), 265.

210 **"much more money and energy"** Evan Osnos, "Doomsday Prep for the Super-Rich," *The New Yorker,* November 30, 2017.

211 **Following the Unite the Right rally** "Six More Defendants Settle Lawsuit Brought After 'Unite the Right' Rally," Georgetown Law, May 16, 2018.

212 **Lawsuits have been particularly effective** David Cook, "The Time Has Come for the Story of the Five Women Who Defeated the Klan," *Chattanooga Times Free Press,* February 22, 2020; "Attorney, Victim Share Story of 1980 KKK Shooting on MLK Boulevard," WRCB-TV, February 20, 2020.

212 **a man named Michael Donald** "Donald v. United Klans of America," Southern Poverty Law Center; "Inside the Case That Bankrupted the Klan," CNN, April 11, 2021.

213 **Delivering basic services can help** Carrie O'Neil and Ryan Sheely, "Governance as a Root Cause of Protracted Conflict and Sustainable Peace: Moving from Rhetoric to a New Way of Working," Stockholm International Peace Research Institute, June 20, 2019.

215 **"It's kinda weird that deplatforming"** Matthew Yglesias (@mattyglesias), "It's kinda weird that deplatforming Trump

just like completely worked with no visible downside whatso-ever," Twitter, January 21, 2021.

215 **As Voltaire once said** Gregory S. Gordon, "Atrocity Speech Law: Foundation, Fragmentation, Fruition, Oxford Scholarship Online, May 2017, https://oxford.universitypressscholarship .com/view/10.1093/acprof:oso/9780190612689.001.0001/ac prof-9780190612689-chapter-1.

215 **found that fully 17 percent** "More Than 1 in 3 Americans Believe a 'Deep State' Is Working to Undermine Trump," NPR/Ipsos, December 30, 2020.

216 **Facebook, YouTube, and Twitter cracked down** "Unwel-come on Facebook and Twitter, QAnon Followers Flock to Fringe Sites," NPR, January 31, 2021.

217 **used clandestine social media campaigns** "Trends in On-line Foreign Influence Efforts," Empirical Studies of Conflict Project, July 8, 2019.

217 **seven of the ten most-read online pieces** "7 Out of the 10 Most Viral Articles About Angela Merkel on Facebook Are False," BuzzFeed, July 27, 2017.

217 **Facebook account called Blacktivist** "Fake Black Activist Accounts Linked to Russian Government," CNN, September 28, 2017; "Exclusive: Russian-Linked Group Sold Merchandise Online," CNN, October 6, 2017.

218 **where groups of citizens** William C. Schambra, "Local Groups Are the Key to America's Civic Renewal," Brookings Institution, September 1, 1997.

219 **"We want to put an end to the myth"** Author interview with Jená Cane, April 2021.

219 **One of the programs** "How Citizen University Is Building an Army of Civic Leaders," Shareable, March 18, 2019.

219 **"The great majority of people"** Author interview with Eric Liu, April 2021.

220 **"We don't know if Tennessee"** Quoted by Eric Liu from a conversation he had with Kate Tucker, in a Civic Saturday ser-mon, January 16, 2021.

224 **People learned that having a multiethnic party** Zoltan L. Hajnal, *Changing White Attitudes Toward Black Political Leadership* (Cambridge: Cambridge University Press, 2006).

224 **California is another successful example** "Gross Domestic Product By State, 3rd Quarter 2020," Bureau of Economic Analysis, December 23, 2020.

224 **Since becoming minority-white in 1998** Note that Hawaii has always been a majority non-white state and that New Mexico became majority non-white prior to California. Kathleen Murphy, "Texas Minorities Now the Majority," Pew Charitable Trusts, August 11, 2005.

224 **Unemployment has dropped** U.S. Bureau of Labor Statistics, Unemployment Rate in California, retrieved from FRED, Federal Reserve Bank of St. Louis (Employment dropped from 6 percent in 1998 to 4.2 percent in 2020 before COVID-19; it did jump to around 9 percent during the pandemic).

224 **California's transition met fierce resistance** "Prop. 187 Backers Elated—Challenges Imminent," *Los Angeles Times,* November 9, 1994; "Pete Wilson Looks Back on Proposition 187 and Says, Heck Yeah, He'd Support It All Over Again," *Los Angeles Times,* March 23, 2017.

225 **California still has many challenges** "California Is Making Liberals Squirm," *The New York Times,* February 11, 2021.

INDEX

BARBARA F. WALTER is the Rohr Professor of International Relations at the School of Global Policy and Strategy at the University of California, San Diego. This, her fifth book on civil wars, was named one of the best books of the year by *The Times* (UK), *Financial Times, Esquire,* and *Prospect* magazine. A member of the Council on Foreign Relations, Walter is a contributor to CNN, MSNBC, and *PBS NewsHour,* and has written for *The Washington Post, The Wall Street Journal, Los Angeles Times,* Reuters, and *Foreign Affairs.* She was the recipient of the 2022 Peacemaker of the Year Award, National Conflict Resolution Center.

barbarafwalter.com
Twitter: @bfwalter